D1064410

STUDY II
IN THE COUNCIL OF INDUSTRIAL
STUDIES SERIES

SMITH COLLEGE STUDIES IN HISTORY

Vol. XX, Nos. 1-4

Economic History of a Factory Town

A Study of Chicopee, Massachusetts

by

Vera Shlakman

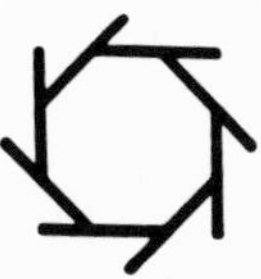

1969

OCTAGON BOOKS

New York

Originally published 1934-1935

Reprinted 1969

by permission of The Trustees of Smith College

OCTAGON BOOKS

A DIVISION OF FARRAR, STRAUS & GIROUX, INC.

19 Union Square West

New York, N. Y. 10003

LIBRARY OF CONGRESS CATALOG CARD NUMBER: 75-86286

Printed in U.S.A. by

TAYLOR PUBLISHING COMPANY

DALLAS, TEXAS

THE COUNCIL OF INDUSTRIAL STUDIES

The Council of Industrial Studies of Smith College is engaged in studying the economic development of the Connecticut Valley region of New England. When the Council was established in 1932 both historical and contemporary projects were envisaged, but major emphasis was to be placed upon locating and utilizing the rich store of primary documentary materials to be found in the region.

Each Council study is planned as a unit complete in itself. It is a feature of our plan, however, that each is also a part of a coördinated series, and it is hoped that eventually out of the series may be built a regional account, the result of the painstaking research that has gone into the separate investigations.

In projecting these coördinated studies the Council seeks at the same time to enrich the research training and opportunities of the graduate students who serve on its staff as research fellows. It also permits research fellows to offer the studies they carry out under Council direction as dissertations for the doctor's degree at the institutions where they have already done their graduate work.

The Council is made up of a committee of five professors from the Departments of Economics and History of the College. Professor Esther Lowenthal of the Economics Department, chairman, Professors Harold U. Faulkner and Merle Curti of the History Department, and Professors William A. Orton and Dorothy W. Douglas of the Economics Department, are members of the Council. The staff comprises a part-time director of research and two full-time research fellows.

The present study, *Economic History of a Factory Town,* by Vera Shlakman is our second study to appear. It has peculiar value for our series, in that in it Miss Shlakman traces the transformation of a rural Connecticut Valley village into a factory town, brought about when large-scale outside capital established textile mills there. Some Valley industrial centers followed this pattern of development, while others trace their original impetus to local business enterprise. The study goes on to treat subsequent economic development in the community, with special emphasis upon labor and the rise of the middle class. Miss Shlakman has given to her study more than two years of careful research and analysis.

The Council's first monograph, *Shutdowns in the Connecticut Valley,* was a contemporary study prepared by the director of research and published in the fall of 1935. The third, *Industrial Development of the Northampton Region,* an account of the rise and decline of manufactures along the Mill River of Hampshire County, by Agnes Hannay, will be published shortly. The fourth and fifth studies, now in progress, treat the rise of early railroads in the Connecticut Valley and the development of the metals industry before 1860. Studies VI and VII will be begun in the fall of 1936.

KATHARINE DU PRE LUMPKIN,
Director of Research, Council of Industrial Studies.

April 14, 1936

ACKNOWLEDGMENTS

In the preparation of this study I have been fortunate in the assistance and counsel that I have received both in the search for data and in the evaluation of their significance. Mr. N. P. Ames Carter, Mrs. J. C. Buckley, Mr. F. D. Howard and Miss Ruth McKinstry, residents of Chicopee, were very helpful. I wish to express my thanks and appreciation to Mrs. F. C. Rickert, of Springfield, who very kindly permitted me to make use of the diary of the late George S. Taylor. Mrs. E. W. Hale, of Chicopee, was very generous in placing at my disposal her remarkable collection of Ames Papers. Dr. Arthur Cole allowed me to make use of the facilities of the Baker Library of the Harvard Graduate School of Business Administration. Professors Esther Lowenthal and Harold U. Faulkner, of Smith College, read the manuscript, and I am grateful to them for their comments. I also wish to thank Professor Carter Goodrich, of Columbia University, who has read the manuscript, for his interest in the project and for his helpful suggestions. I owe a special debt of gratitude to Dr. Katharine Lumpkin, Director of Research of the Council of Industrial Studies. I have always been able to call on her for advice and criticism, and I am deeply appreciative of the aid she has given me.

V. S.

CONTENTS

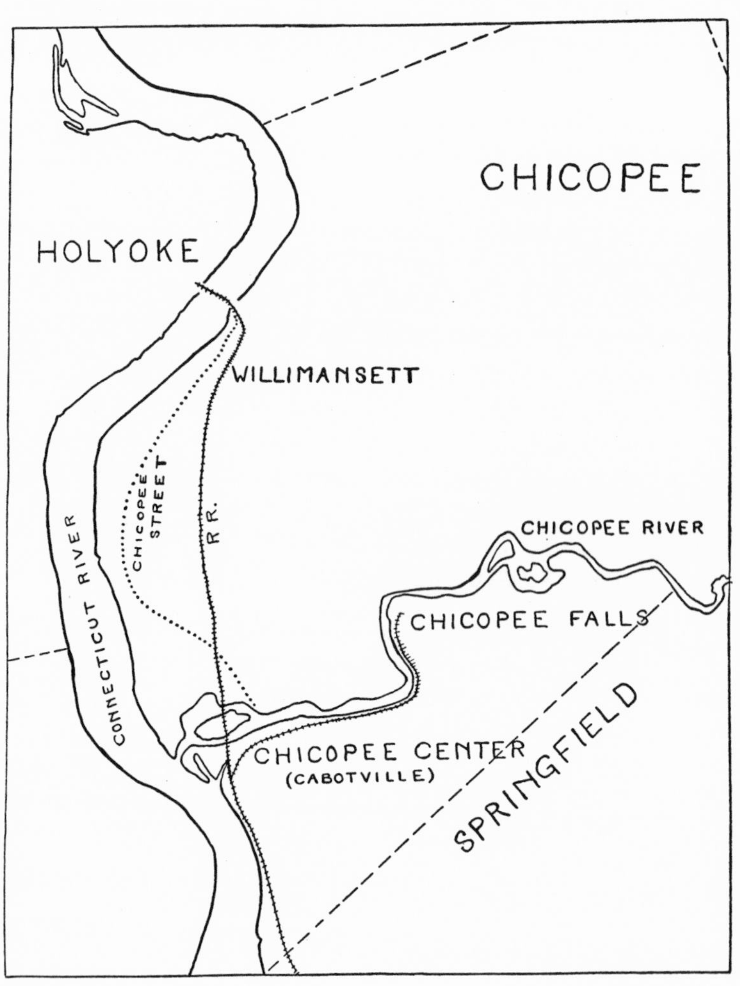
CHICOPEE
HOLYOKE
WILLIMANSETT
CHICOPEE STREET
R.R.
CONNECTICUT RIVER
CHICOPEE RIVER
CHICOPEE FALLS
CHICOPEE CENTER
(CABOTVILLE)
SPRINGFIELD

CHAPTER I

THE COLONIAL COMMUNITY

I

The impact of industrialism, occasioned by the rise of the factory system of manufacture reacted in various ways on the New England village community. Always a significant social unit, it had served in the first instance as a nucleus of settlement. As colonists went out from it to take up new land, it supplied them with important economic and social services, and constituted the distributing center for goods which could not be produced on the farm. Over a period of years the form of the village community, with its meeting-house, its tavern, its corn mills and saw mills, its stores and its home industries, its mode of government, followed a fairly uniform pattern. There were deviations of degree rather than of type, for at a time when the frontier was moving westward, and when settlements between the frontier and the coast were spreading radially, stages of development varied. The scatter of colonists who moved out from the original village, or of newcomers who were too late to occupy land within it, sometimes resulted in the development of a subsidiary village community. A church, a few stores, and perhaps a tavern, were often established at the secondary point of colonization in order to provide more accessible and more convenient services for the settlers. But such an offshoot of an established community frequently relied upon the parent organization for important services and for political life before striking out as an independent town as the result of the further development of its economic and social life to a point which warranted secession.

When the industrial revolution came to New England, and it came rapidly, the village communities were not all affected in the same degree and in the same way, and this for obvious reasons. If, in a particular case, the local circumstances were favorable to the new processes, the economic development of the town was accelerated. If not, it remained permanently, or at least for the time being, a village community, surviving as a cell of a gradually disappearing industrial stage, and its main function remained, as before, to serve as the trading center for an agricultural area.

Chicopee, one of such village communities, was in a formative period when the new industrial processes were being adopted in New England. An offshoot of Springfield, and dependent on that town for much of its social and economic life, its interests were mainly agricultural, although at the end of the colonial period there were traces of industrial activity. The effect of the industrial revolution upon the town of Chicopee may best be understood by first examining the usual pattern of the industrial development of what is considered an "average" town, after its primary establishment as a village community.

In numerous cases the process of industrialization, compared with the rapidity of the whole movement in America, came rather gradually. Given a favorable conjuncture of circumstances—the proximity to raw materials, the existence of water power, the availability of transportation facilities—certain men of substance, thanks to the ownership of liquid capital, or because their occupations were such as to permit the accumulation or transformation of capital, may have been able to establish a factory on a small scale. Unskilled laborers were attracted from the poor farms of the hill country, and these, together with propertiless artisans, mechanics and poor independent producers of the locality, settled beside the new producing unit. With this congregation of new residents at hand, whose occupations were now specialized, retail trade was able to expand. Professional services of all kinds were required, especially the services of bankers and lawyers, those of the latter to an even greater extent than had been needed by the frequent land transactions of the preceding period. This was especially marked if the town happened to be the county seat. As profits and professional earnings were invested and re-invested in the new industrial enterprises and the other economic activities which grew up with them, the middle class thrived. Merchants extended their activities, some of them investing their savings in manufacturing enterprises. Occasionally new merchants and petty producers rose from the ranks of the independent artisans. More often members of this class lost their lower middle class position and were forced into factory employment. Sons of the middle class carried on the business activities of the fathers; daughters married the business associates. The whole movement possessed an inherent driving force which gathered momentum and pushed outward, for a time at least, into an ever-widening sphere of business activity.

While these changes were taking place, the original settlement may have coincided, geographically, with the new industrial community; early Springfield became the heart of modern Springfield. In many cases the roots of the industrial town are to be found in the older village community. Even if the town's manufactures are dependent upon nearby water power, and the center of activity shifts, with the productive units and the working class homes concentrated near the water power, resulting in the emergence of the old community as a residential district for the middle class, or as a mercantile center, there is still a very vital relationship between the two points of settlement—that of ownership. Between workers and employers there remains for some time a social contact which is maintained and furthered by common traditions and church membership. For a number of years at least, the owner of the factory is not far removed from the mechanic, or even the factory operative, in the social scale, or in possession of financial power or independence. But a line of demarcation must inevitably arise, owing to the increasing prosperity of the middle class, a prosperity accompanied by more ambitious social interests, and the fact that the majority of the workers remain in a propertiless condition. With the later influx of Irish, French-Canadian, and Polish workers, as in New England, the widening social and economic cleavage between the classes is further accentuated by differences in language and religion. Business activity and leadership remain in the hands of the native local and near-local middle class. Whether or not the latter will be able to retain this leadership as economic conditions of the community change is uncertain. The time elapsing between the first settlement of the town and the rise and establishment of the modern form may be one century or three.

Many industrial communities in New England and elsewhere have experienced a development along these lines; the process is typical, but not universal. Other forms have been of some importance in America, and are sufficiently well-known to require no more than a passing word. Towns sprang up over night in the West during the days of the gold rush, and in the oil fields. The possibilities for their survival were as speculative as the conditions which brought them into being. Required, as they were, to meet the needs of a sudden agglomeration of persons, their economic foundations were to be found in trade and services. Some survived; others, after hectic careers, disappeared from the scene, forgotten, except for an antiquarian interest in "ghost towns." The modern company town is also typical, the product or creation of quite recent capitalist activity, the rational result of the decision of a board of directors. Houses and stores and churches and schools are laid out with the precision of a factory, without any direct geographical relationship to the other business activities or homes of the owners. The roots of the town are to be found not in genetic, but in "architectural" beginnings; they go no further back than the blue-prints of the engineers. When the community has been constructed and peopled, the assumption of police powers by the absentee landlords lend it all the aspects of a feudal community, but one which happens to be industrialized. However, the company town in its essential outlines, is not an invention of latter day American capitalists. It was first established in Waltham, Massachusetts, in 1813-14, and was quite generally adopted by an important group of New England cotton magnates. This does not mean that the degree of control exercised by the early cotton corporations was comparable to the kind of activity with which we have grown familiar during the past four or five decades. But as an institution, as a type community, the company town existed none the less, and was of great significance, for it tells the story of how the modern industrial processes came to

America,[1] and with it a sociological development of importance, for "industry—for the first time in our history—began to disintegrate the family. Hitherto sailors had been about the only people who left their homes in order to maintain them; now women were withdrawn from the domestic circle to recruit the mobile forces of manufacturing labor. This attacked not only the economic but also the social integrity of the family, and was the first evidence that new methods of production were destined profoundly to modify the constitution of society."[2] Furthermore, it set up a series of important communities in which for many years there was to be a preponderance of female workers.

When we examine the rise and growth of industrial communities in New England, where the industrial revolution comes with the introduction of cotton manufacture, we find that whole new communities were designed and created for the specific purpose of manufacturing textiles. While there may have been, in some cases, a relationship to a pre-existing settlement, that was entirely dependent upon the latter's proximity to the new industrial development. If there did exist some beginnings, not purely agricultural, the new form, imposed from without, eliminated the intervening "gradualist" stage of industrialization. The result was the spontaneous birth of an industrial community. Such were the beginnings of Chicopee, as of Lawrence and Lowell and Manchester—a manufacturing town established by large-scale business enterprise directed from a financial center, Boston. Such a community, it is expected, having an industrial genesis partly divorced from its immediate environment, will experience tendencies in subsequent development peculiar to itself and to other communities similar in origin.

II

The Valley of the Connecticut River represented the first inland frontier of New England. The river, flowing into Long Island Sound, permitted access by water transport into Western Massachusetts and Connecticut. The valley land was fertile, and

[1] Caroline F. Ware, *The Early New England Cotton Manufacture*, 3.
[2] Victor S. Clark, *History of Manufactures in the United States*, I, 529.

good farms could be cleared and worked, with comfortable towns established along the river banks. Local produce could be shipped down the river, and goods from the East received without undue difficulty. As early as 1634 prospecting parties from the coast had explored the valley with a view to settlement.[3] In the spring of 1636 William Pynchon and his associates set out from Roxbury, after sending supplies in a ship owned by Governor Winthrop, and made the journey overland as far as Springfield, where they bought land from the Indians.[4]

For the first two years of its existence this new frontier post was harassed by war with the Pequot Indians, but at the conclusion of hostilities, it was possible to settle down to a quiet life. Until the frontier warfare came to an end, little expansion was possible, and the "town" of Springfield remained primarily a trading post for a few years.[5] As was to be expected, the most important activity of the post at this time was centered in the fur trade, and this was reported to have been ruined by excessive competition by 1645.[6] Pynchon, the leader of the Springfield community, as an adjunct to his trading activities which were extensive, built a warehouse at Enfield Falls for the transshipment of goods moving up and down the Connecticut River; thus he ensured a regular supply of manufactured goods and an outlet for the products of the region.[7] When the fur trade declined it became increasingly necessary to turn to agricultural pursuits. With the assurance of adequate transportation services the little community grew, and families were soon settled at Westfield, Longmeadow, Enfield, in Connecticut, and at what is now called Chicopee.[8]

Just when the first settlement in Chicopee was made is uncertain. There was no cultivation prior to 1645, and there is evidence that two Chapin brothers, who came from Springfield, were permanently settled in the region by 1675.[9] Other settlers were not

[3] A. M. Copeland, *History of Hampden County,* I, 32.
[4] *Ibid.,* 33, 34. [5] *Ibid.,* 40, 41.
[6] W. B. Weeden, *Economic and Social History of New England,* I, 181.
[7] E. M. Bacon, *The Connecticut River and the Valley of the Connecticut,* 304.
[8] A. M. Copeland, *op. cit.,* I, 41.
[9] G. J. Holland, *History of Western Massachusetts,* II, 43; C. S. Palmer, *Annals of Chicopee Street,* 6.

long in joining the Chapins in opening up the North Springfield district. The first settlers occupied land along the banks of the Connecticut River near, and just north of the Chicopee River which flows into the Connecticut above Springfield. This oldest settlement, and the most important for many years to come, was known as Chicopee Street. Other settlers followed the Chicopee River to the east of the Connecticut where two large power sites were situated. It is reported that a saw mill was built by the colonists in 1687, and that 1694 saw the establishment of a corn mill and a blacksmith shop, the latter using bog ore which was found in the vicinity.[10] By 1713 it was considered necessary to make provision for some schooling in the neighborhood, and a grant of ten shillings per annum was made to a farmer's daughter for this purpose. A schoolhouse was built about the year 1721.[11] The new community, in its ordinary life, must have closely resembled almost any other pioneer settlement of the time. There was a difference, however, for due to its proximity to Springfield, Chicopee relied upon that town for much business and social activity; its political life was centered there, as was its organized church life, although occasional religious services were held at home.[12] The new community itself was cemented by strong family ties. Of 49 petitioners to the Massachusetts General Court for incorporation as a separate parish in 1750, 24 bore the name of Chapin.[13] The request for incorporation was granted, and in 1751 work on a church was started.[14] However the settlement remained under the municipal jurisdiction of Springfield until 1848.

The territory in which this little community was situated was still frontier land. Until about the middle of the eighteenth century the region was never wholly free from the fear of Indian attack. As late as 1745-46 Deacon Edward Chapin made frequent reference in his diary to Indian troubles, and to misfortunes which befell his friends on nearby farms. The Chicopee settlers must have taken the offensive at this time for Chapin wrote that "E. Chapin proceeded on his journey in order for a march into the

[10] V. Spence, *The Industrial History of Chicopee*, 7.
[11] Palmer, *op. cit.*, 13.
[12] *Ibid.*, 20.
[13] *Ibid.*, 24.
[14] *Ibid.*, 26.

wilderness to molest ye Indians."[15] Many residents of the neighborhood were drawn into the war, and a rally was held in Springfield to encourage enlistments for the Canada expedition.[16] Even this inland frontier felt its position as part of the British Empire. In meeting these requests for military aid, no doubt fear of France's Indian allies was the important factor insofar as the colonists were concerned. A more ceremonial aspect of the relationship with England is brought to light when Chapin notes "this Day offered as a Day of thanksgiving on account of ye remarkable Victory obtained against the Rebels in North Brittain by ye Duke of Cumberland,"[17] though the victory does not seem nearly as remarkable as the interest of a Western Massachusetts farmer in the final victory of the House of Hanover over the Stuarts.

Throughout the colonial period[18] agriculture remained the dominant economic interest of the community. Bricks were made in the town by 1751.[19] Some time between 1740 and 1770 a grist mill was erected on the Chicopee River at the point where the Ames Manufacturing Company was later to stand. Here rye was ground, not only for local use, but for shipment down the river to distilleries at Warehouse Point, in Connecticut.[20] When the nineteenth century came, the community had a church, a school, a tavern, and a store. The latter, it is interesting to note, was not opened for business until 1800.[21] Not for over 100 years after its first settlement was the community ready to support a retail trader.

With the turn of the century, attempts were made at manufacturing enterprises of various kinds, but on a very small scale. Though there seemed to be very little money in the village, the farms were good, and the farmers were not forced to turn to other economic pursuits because of the pressure of poor land.[22]

[15] *Chapin Diary,* Feb. 15, 1746.
[16] *Ibid.,* June 30, 1745. [17] *Ibid.,* Aug. 14, 1746.
[18] From the point of view of economic development the colonial period ends about 1820, in spite of political independence achieved earlier.
[19] Spence, *op. cit.,* 9.
[20] *Springfield Republican,* Dec. 21, 1890.
[21] Palmer, *op. cit.,* 85.
[22] The prosperity of the region is attested to by the fact that while

Yet even though the farms were prosperous, they do not seem to have produced enough *cash* to find its way into other investment, and the village, for one reason or another, had not, at the end of the colonial period, developed to the point which permitted the emergence of mercantile capital.[23] A saw mill built as late as 1791 was operated as a jointly-owned enterprise by several individuals, and the various owners, for work performed in connection with it, were credited with payment at the rate of three shillings per day.[24] The arrangements were primitive and it is exceedingly doubtful whether it should be called a business enterprise at all. Chicopee men had not invested in the various local internal improvements that were made in the vicinity of Springfield—the bridges, canals, and turnpikes. But in spite of the seeming lack of capital resources and of the absence of various artisans, there were some beginnings of independent non-agricultural activity.

The first real business enterprise was the work of two Springfield men, James Byers and William Smith, who leased some land and water privilege at Chicopee Falls with the intention of starting an iron works. They did build a shop, but the product manufactured was insignificant in value.[25] The property changed hands in 1801, and Benjamin Belcher emerged as the sole owner in 1805. He conducted the business for many years after that.[26] In 1812 we find him advertising for 30,000 bushels of coal to be delivered to his furnace, for which he will "pay in goods at the store of J. & E. Dwight, or debts due at this store" which was located in Springfield.[27] He obviously was operating on a small scale as is evidenced by the business arrangement just described to facilitate payment; part of his own purchases he paid for by placing goods at the merchant's disposal to be sold at retail. The Springfield merchant, in this case, acted as a kind of financial, or "barter"

Chicopee had been a rallying point for a time for the participants in Shays' Rebellion, there is no evidence that residents took part in the movement. See Palmer, *op. cit.*, 41.

[23] See below, Chapter IV. When the merchants came they were not natives.

[24] *Manuscript*, Connecticut Valley Historical Society.

[25] Holland, *op. cit.*, II, 44.

[26] *Ibid.*

[27] *Hampshire Federalist*, Feb. 16, 1812.

agent for the local manufacturer. Even if there was a merchant in Chicopee capable of performing that function, it would still be necessary to have a trading arrangement with a Springfield store because of the importance of that town as a marketing center.

At about this time the Belcher Iron Works took the first and most simple step toward the extension of its activities by trying to expand its sales territory. Such action had naturally to precede the diversification of production. When advertising in the local press that his furnace was in blast, Belcher asked the *Connecticut Courant*, the *Massachusetts Spy*, the *Hampshire Gazette* and the *Franklin Herald* to copy his notice, and to send their bills to the editor of the *Hampden Federalist* for payment.[28] These papers, published in Hartford, Worcester, Northampton and Greenfield covered a much wider territory than was reached by the Springfield press. In 1822-23 Belcher sold a large piece of land and water privilege, most of his property, to the Chicopee Manufacturing Company,[29] the first of the large cotton mills to be established in Chicopee. This sale of property put liquid capital into Belcher's hands, and a real expansion of business became possible. The new cotton mill itself, with its machinery and machine shops would offer an outlet for Belcher's iron castings. Then, in 1825, for the first time, he was able to offer more to his customers than plain castings. "The subscriber wishes to inform the public and his customers that his works are in constant operation, and that he is able to furnish at short notice every description of castings for cotton and woolen machinery. . . . He also has the use of the patterns of the Boston and Springfield Manufacturing Company (the Chicopee Manufacturing Company) which will be furnished his customers for a small consideration."[30] In other words, the coming of a large manufacturing enterprise from the outside helped the local business man to achieve a greater degree of industrial maturity, thanks to an increase in his capital resources, and to an additional outlet for some of his products. Moreover, this came at a time when the market for machine parts was expanding, and

[28] *Hampden Federalist*, Oct. 22, 1812.

[29] L. H. Everts, *History of the Connecticut Valley in Massachusetts*, II, 971. See Chapter II for description of the coming of the cotton mills.

[30] *Springfield Republican*, June 8, 1825.

Belcher was able to take advantage of this, thanks again, in measure, to the use of the large corporation's machine patterns.

Oliver Chapin, who in 1801, had settled on the north side of the Chicopee River at Chicopee Falls, sold the water privilege which he owned to William Bowman and to Benjamin and Lemuel Cox in 1806. They built a small paper mill there and operated it for about 16 years. The organization of this mill was simple. In 1812 one of the proprietors sought to sell his share in the property, and advertised in the papers for a buyer.[31] The property was described as consisting of a mill, a double tenement for the housing of two families, a sizing house, another dwelling, a barn, out-houses, and four and one half acres of arable land. The factory contained one vat, said the notice, but it was possible to install a second at little cost, since the building had been designed to receive two. The other equipment consisted of two iron and one wooden screw presses.[32] The entire property passed into the hands of Springfield men in 1822 or thereabouts, and was finally taken over by David Ames of that town in 1827. He introduced the machine process in the manufacture of paper; up to this time all the work had been done by hand.[33]

In 1801 William, Levi, and Joseph Chapin built a small cotton mill, housing carding machines and two spinning frames. The yarn that they made was given out to women in the vicinity to weave into cloth on hand looms.[34] This mill must have survived at least till after the War of 1812, for in that year the proprietors advertised the sale of cotton yarn, and plain, striped, and checked cloth. They were willing to accept almost any country produce in exchange for their cloth or yarn.[35] The main functions of this mill, then, were to supplement the home production of yarn and cloth. The organization was quite primitive. One Gustavus Pinney, had a small cotton or woolen "factory" in operation at this time. In 1809 he "would inform the public that his carding

[31] It is curious that his partners were not able to buy him out. They probably did not have the money to do so, for there is no reason to suppose that the mill did not afford a good living. Bowman and at least one of the Coxes operated the mill for another ten years.

[32] *Hampden Federalist,* Nov. 19, 1812.

[33] Holland, *op. cit.,* II, 45.

[34] Copeland, *op. cit.,* III, 501.

[35] *Hampshire Federalist,* Jan. 30, 1812.

machine is now in operation at Chicopee."[36] An 1812 notice mentions wool carding[37] and later he undertook the dying of yarn and the dressing of wool for his customers.[38] These two "factories," it should be noted, really performed quite different functions. The first bought cotton, manufactured it into yarn, farmed it out to home workers, and then sold the finished product; the ownership of the cotton was always vested in the hands of the mill proprietor. This simple organization resembled the English form of the early cotton industry, and was a more advanced stage, industrially, than the Pinney mill.[39] The latter seemed to specialize more in taking over the difficult operations from the household producers, dressing, dying, carding, and the probability is that only woolen products were handled here, though some cotton may have been used. The evidence is not very clear on this point. It would seem that Pinney did not own the raw materials which he worked; he was as much employed as he may have been the employer. An old resident of the town gave the following description of what was probably the Chapin mill in 1810.[40] "The machinery of the mill consisted of two cards, one drawing frame and two short spinning frames of very rude construction. The cotton was all put out to be picked by hand. Six or eight hands were employed and those had no regular pay-day, the company giving orders on stores where they pay in cloth or yarn." Another early attempt at a new enterprise occurred in 1805 when an agreement was entered into by several persons to start and operate a tan works, but there is no evidence pointing to its survival beyond this date.[41]

Thus we see, that as the colonial period was drawing to a close, small industrial beginnings were making their appearance. The high point of activity must have been during the War of 1812. At that time there were in operation a paper mill, two textile mills, the iron works, and the various saw and grist mills that were to be found in any community which had the merest suggestion of a

[36] *Ibid.*, July 23, 1809. [37] *Ibid.*, July 23, 1812.

[38] *Hampden Federalist*, May 6, Sept. 3, 1813.

[39] See G. W. Daniels, *The Early English Cotton Industry*, and T. M. Tryon, *Household Manufactures in the United States*, 272, 273.

[40] Connecticut Valley Historical Society, newspaper clipping, *Springfield Republican*, Jan. 1885.

[41] *Manuscript*, Connecticut Valley Historical Society.

stream. The industrial organization of these enterprises was very simple, however, and all evidence points to the fact that in all of them the least important commodity was *money*. The home was still the important producing unit. The great water powers were lying idle. The community was still subservient to Springfield, especially in regard to mercantile services, and this may have been one of the reasons for the slow development of mercantile capital in Chicopee itself. Certainly there is no reason to suppose that the local producers were incapable of realizing the importance of the water power which lay in their backyards. Farming did not yield substantial cash profits such as to clamor for investment in the new industrial enterprises, but it was not poor enough to force the farmers to turn to something else. They did what they could. The textile mills were swept away with the coming of the power loom, and the end of the war protection. We have already considered one of the factors which contributed to the survival of the iron works, namely the coming of a large-scale business enterprise to the town, but just how important a factor that was, we cannot know definitely. It is fruitless to speculate as to what the economic growth of the town might have been if its course of development had not been interrupted by the decision of a board of directors in Boston. It is significant that the only real factory utilizing power driven machinery was the Ames Paper Company which represented Springfield capital, and even in this case, power did not come until 1827. In fact, there is no evidence of the existence of any liquid capital in the town at this time. There was no investment outside the village, and the few local attempts at industrial enterprise within the community were feeble. It does not seem that the local residents could have possessed the power to make the transition to the new industrial form unaided. By 1820, despite the various aspects of town life, the community was still agricultural. We shall see how local enterprise, when it came, was dependent in the first instance on the primary development of the water power by the cotton magnates to whom it was sold. It is exceedingly doubtful whether the local "business men" could have developed it by themselves.

CHAPTER II

ABSENTEE OWNERSHIP

In examining the economic and industrial development of the United States, it is quite true that one finds that "money flowed into manufactures from the dominant industry of each region."[1] But the study of a special region, of a single town, like Chicopee, suggests deviations from this general rule, so as to modify it to the extent of saying that *sooner or later,* in a given locality, the prevailing economic interest which has permitted an accumulation of liquid capital, sponsors new industrial activity. The first generalization was true in Chicopee only after the dominant industry of Eastern Massachusetts had withdrawn capital from its own region and invested it in Western Massachusetts and New Hampshire. It was then that the salaried managers of the newly-founded cotton mills joined forces with the local merchants (whose prosperity was based very largely on the size of the mill payrolls) to make investments in other enterprises in the vicinity.[2] In Chicopee the transformation of the "village" community into an industrial center was effected by outside capital.

The existence of an important natural water power did not mean that automatically and by reason only of that fact, Chicopee was destined to become a manufacturing center. Had the power site been smaller, it is quite likely that manufactures would have come slowly, and that gradually there would have emerged a local business leadership capable of utilizing the resources that were at hand. But at the end of the colonial period the river with its waterfall was flowing through an agricultural community, one that was just beginning to supplement home industry with certain business enterprises. The industrial potentialities of the town were more advanced than its economic organization. Furthermore, the industrial revolution, ready to sweep through New England, was to do more than introduce the factory system by means of the cot-

[1] Clark, *op. cit.*, I, 192.

[2] See below, Chapter IV.

ton manufacture. In certain localities it was to permit the usurpation of functions which had hitherto rested in the hands of the resident business leaders, by an outside group of capitalists. The Chicopee power sites were important enough to attract the attention of outside capitalists *before* the local economic interests were able to avail themselves of these resources. This meant that as in certain other communities, there was no smooth economic progression from stage to stage—artisan or merchant to manufacturer; craftsmanship to mass production; partnership to corporation. This town did not grow into an industrial community; it suddenly found that it *was* one.

The water power site, which in 1820 was beyond the power of local capital to develop was important enough to attract attention from other quarters. In view of the progress of the introduction of large-scale cotton manufacture in New England, it was destined to be developed in a certain way. For this to have happened in the 1820's, there had to be a force as big as the power, and there was. The cotton manufacture of New England in its most important form during the period 1815-1850 was large-scale, it was highly integrated, it was as big as the power it used, financially and technically. It was modern in every sense of the word.

We have already seen that the Boston and Springfield Manufacturing Company purchased the Belcher property and water privilege. This company secured incorporation in 1823 with a capital of $500,000—a large sum of money for those days, and an enormous sum for Chicopee where the new mill was to be built. Work was immediately started on a dam, a canal, and a cotton mill at Chicopee Falls, and houses for the workers. The first mill was completed in 1825, and work started on a second unit in the same year. A third mill was erected in 1826, and a fourth in 1831, at which time the capital was increased to $600,000, and to $700,000 in 1835. In 1828 the Company changed its name to that of the Chicopee Manufacturing Company.[3] To this point the Company had used only part of the water power. There was another site in its possession farther down the river.

[3] Holland, *op. cit.*, II, 45, 46.

This new corporation was more than a cotton manufacturing company. It owned a large tract of land, water power, and the tenements which housed the operatives, so that it was in the real estate business. It was also in the construction business, for it had erected all the buildings, and built the dam and the canal. It operated a machine shop for the construction and repair of cotton machinery, and was prepared to continue all these activities for new mills which were planned for the region. After a time the owners of this hybrid company decided to separate its manufacturing functions from the construction and machine building business, and this was to be a legal as well as a book-keeping schism. These apparently modern business men were planning to incorporate some new companies in Chicopee, and it was simpler and more business-like to treat every thing not connected with the manufacture of cotton and the ownership of the finished tenements as a separate enterprise. In 1831, then, they incorporated the Springfield Canal Company, with a capital of $90,000.[4] As owners of the cotton company, they transferred to themselves, as owners of the canal company, title to the water privilege at the lower site, the construction business and the machine shops.[5] In the future the canal company would accept all orders for the construction of mills, dams, canals, and tenements. The owners of the Chicopee Manufacturing Company and the Springfield Canal Company were practically identical. The following names appeared in the petition for incorporation of the latter company in 1831: James Brewer, Samuel Henshaw, Edmund Dwight, Jonathan Dwight, Jr., Francis Stanton, Israel Thorndike, Harrison Gray Otis, Samuel Eliot, William H. Eliot, George W. Lyman, James K. Mills, Gorham Brooks, George Bliss.[6]

The development of power at the lower privilege (Cabotville) was foreshadowed in 1829 when a new enterprise was brought to Chicopee by Edmund Dwight, (one of the principal stockholders of the Chicopee Manufacturing Company) and was later backed by the Boston group with which he was associated. This was the

[4] A. M. Copeland, *op. cit.*, III, 501. [5] Holland, *op. cit.*, II, 47.
[6] Mass., 1831 *Private and Special Statutes*, C. 10.

introduction of the manufacture of fine metal products, and was to be of great importance in the subsequent development of the town. The story goes that Edmund Dwight once spent some hours with a travelling companion, Nathan Peabody Ames, of Chelmsford. Ames, his father, and his brother, James Tyler, were engaged in the manufacture of edge tools in Chelmsford. Dwight, who was much impressed by the young mechanic, persuaded him to come to Cabotville with his brother and to carry on the business there. They moved to Chicopee in 1829, locating their shop first at the upper privilege in Chicopee Falls, and continued their work of making tools and cutlery, employing nine workers in their first year.[7] It seems that it was already decided to develop the water power at Cabotville, for the organization of the Springfield Canal Company came soon after, and then the other mills which were to be built at the lower privilege. Furthermore, as soon as the canal and dam were well under way at Cabotville, Edmund Dwight and his partner J. K. Mills incorporated the Ames Manufacturing Company, together with N. P. and J. T. Ames, with a capital of $30,000 and the Ames shop moved to Cabotville to the new power development. That was in 1834.[8] The capital of the company was increased to $75,000 in 1841 and again to $200,000 in 1845, when it took over the properties of the Springfield Canal Company.[9] These included the machine shops for the manufacture of cotton machinery. The principal stockholders and the directors of the enlarged and reorganized company were also large stockholders in the cotton companies. By this time there was a little local investment in the company, aside from the Ames' interests.[10]

Following the establishment of the Springfield Canal Company, a group of men petitioned for and received articles of incorporation for the Cabot Manufacturing Company, to be established at the lower water privilege in Chicopee, with an authorized capital of $1,000,000, "for the purpose of manufacturing cotton and woolen goods, iron, and machinery."[11] The petitioners were

[7] Holland, *op. cit.*, II, 48.
[8] Mass., 1834 *Private and Special Statutes,* C. 31.
[9] Holland, *op. cit.*, 48, 49.
[10] *Ames Papers,* Dividend Book.
[11] Mass., 1832 *Private and Special Statutes,* C. 63.

Jonathan Dwight, Harrison Gray Otis, Israel Thorndike, S. A. Eliot, Benjamin Day, Samuel Cabot, Francis Stanton, George W. Lyman, George Bliss. The capital stock of the company was finally set at $500,000, and another company, the Perkins Mills, was incorporated in 1836 with a similar capitalization.[12] The petitioners for this charter as they appeared in the articles of incorporation, were William Appleton, A. Thorndike and Henry Cabot.[13] In 1841 came the Dwight Manufacturing Company, with a capital of $500,000, the incorporators being T. H. Perkins, William Sturgis, Edmund Dwight, and others.[14] The four cotton companies were obviously under the same management. Those established after 1831 bought land and water privileges from the Springfield Canal Company, which also undertook the building of the canals, mills, and tenements.[15] Most of these investors, all of any importance, lived in Boston, and their names are important in the mercantile and industrial history of Massachusetts. Knowing them, it is possible to trace the sources of capital which established Chicopee as an industrial town, and the nature of its ownership.

The Dwights, who in large measure were responsible for bringing Boston money to Chicopee, were members of an old Springfield family which had extensive mercantile and business interests in the region. Edmund Dwight's father, Jonathan, Sr., was said to have been the richest man in Hampden County, and the silk stockings, short breeches, and silver buckles which he is reported to have worn, seem to have made an impression on his contemporaries, and certainly it was fine attire for a Western Massachusetts merchant.[16] As might possibly be suspected from the foregoing, his sympathies were with the Tories at the outbreak of the Revolution, but discreetly so.[17] He was engaged in business with his cousin Josiah,[18] also a prominent man, who had married a Pynchon, was a Common Pleas judge, had money

[12] 21 Hunt's *Merchants' Magazine,* 682 (1849).
[13] Mass., 1836 *Private and Special Statutes,* C. 20.
[14] *Ibid.,* 1841, C. 13.
[15] A. M. Copeland, *op. cit.,* III, 501, 502.
[16] Connecticut Valley Historical Society, Newspaper Clipping.
[17] Mason A. Green, *Springfield; 1636-1886,* 297.
[18] *Springfield Homestead,* Jan. 27, 1927.

invested in an iron foundry, manufactured potash, and engaged in mercantile activity.[19] Jonathan Dwight was primarily a merchant. His Springfield store, at the beginning of the nineteenth century, had expanded into a chain. He sent clerks out into the neighboring towns, setting them up in business, but retaining a substantial interest in the branches. Stores were thus established in Chester Village, Northampton, Enfield, Connecticut, and at South Hadley Canal. There was also a branch in Boston.[20] Together with other Springfield men, he invested in the Locks and Canals on the Connecticut River, an enterprise which was intended to make the Connecticut navigable north of the Chicopee,[21] in the Springfield Bridge in 1803,[22] and in the Springfield and Longmeadow Turnpike in 1804.[23] He was also the treasurer of the First Massachusetts Turnpike, organized in 1797, which like the other ventures, was a small enterprise serving local needs, as the following directions to toll-keepers suggest: "If you give credit to any person for Toll you will do it at your own risque, and not by any means at the risque of your Employers. For your own Sake, we wish that such trusting, if any, be given as rarely as possible."[24] Jonathan Dwight had three sons, James S., Jonathan, Jr., and Edmund. They were associated with their father in his mercantile enterprises, owned some ships which followed the coastal trade between Hartford, Boston, and New York, and were interested in a shipping company which trafficked between Hartford and Springfield.[25] Another source of the family's money was to be found in land dealings. A Samuel Dwight who died in Enfield in 1763 was later characterised by Sylvester Judd, the chronicler of the region, as "a land speculator like the rest of his family."[26] Josiah Dwight was similarly labeled.[27]

Edmund Dwight, who was born in 1780 was educated at Yale and studied law under Fisher Ames in Boston. Securing his ex-

[19] Green, *op. cit.,* 336.
[20] *Ibid.,* 358.
[21] Mass., *Private and Special Statutes,* Feb. 23, 1792.
[22] *Ibid.,* Feb., 22, 1803. [23] *Ibid.,* March 7, 1804.
[24] *First Massachusetts Turnpike,* Directors' Book, April 14, 1810.
[25] Green, *op. cit.,* 258.
[26] *Judd Manuscript,* Northampton, II, 259.
[27] *Ibid.,* 264.

pected inheritance in advance from his father, he travelled in Europe in 1802-04, then married an Eliot in 1809, and associated himself with his father and brothers in their various enterprises in Springfield. He sat in the state legislature for Springfield during the period 1810-1813, and again in 1815. The following year he made a permanent settlement in Boston and entered into a partnership with J. K. Mills, a merchant.[28] The contacts which he had made while in the law office of Fisher Ames and his marriage brought him into what was probably the most important circle of business enterprise in Boston. Here he met the Lowells and Cabots and Lawrences, the Appletons and Lymans, Ignatius Sargent and William Sturgis, H. G. Otis, the Quincys, the Perkins, Jacksons, Eliots, and Thorndikes, and other well-known personalities—names to conjure with.

These men were the merchant princes of Boston. P. T. Jackson, whose father had been a member of the Continental Congress in 1782 and the treasurer of the Commonwealth, started his career as apprentice to a wealthy merchant of Newburyport. He made a voyage to the far East in 1799 as captain's clerk, and made three more voyages by 1808. In these ventures he was in sole charge of the valuable cargoes. He set up as a merchant in Boston, working in the India trade, and made a great deal of money, some of which he invested in the Boston Manufacturing Company, some in a real estate speculation which collapsed in 1837. He then devoted his entire time to his manufacturing interests. Harrison Gray Otis had studied law under Judge John Lowell, and made a great deal of money in his law practice and in real estate dealings. A popular after-dinner speaker, he had been a Federalist, and then a free trade Whig. In the 1820's he invested in the cotton manufacture and was converted to protectionist ideas. T. H. Perkins had worked for the Shattucks, and then was in the West Indies trade with his brother. He was also associated with Elias Hasket Derby of Salem in a voyage to the East Indies. He was soon fully engaged in the China and India trade, and undertook any speculative venture which showed promise of high profit. He also had

[28] *Dictionary of American Biography.*

been a Federalist, and was a member of the Massachusetts General Court for many years, and president of the Boston branch of the United States Bank. Israel Thorndike, who had commanded a privateer in the Revolutionary War was likewise engaged in the India trade, and sat in the legislature. Abbott and Amos Lawrence were importers of English goods, but were among the first to sell New England textiles, disposing of them on a commission basis, and invested heavily in the cotton manufacture. Abbott Lawrence, important in public affairs, was created ambassador to Great Britain in 1850. Nathan Appleton, another merchant, had made considerable sums of money during the War of 1812. In 1815 his firm became sales agent for the Boston Manufacturing Company. He went to Congress in 1830, and had a hand in framing the 1832 tariff.[29]

These were the men who introduced the company town which came to be one of the features of New England industrial life during the period 1820-1850. The establishment of absentee ownership at this early period is a matter of some importance. Manchester and Dover and Nashua in New Hampshire, Chicopee, Lowell, Holyoke, and Lawrence in Massachusetts became industrial centers controlled by boards of directors sitting in Boston. Chicopee, as a community of this type, was later to develop a resident owning class, as we shall see. The other towns experienced similar development. Because this new absentee ownership ruled so completely the industrial life of the new towns and was responsible so largely for contributing to the industrialization of New England, it is worth while to examine the activities of its principal figures in order to see what kind of business enterprise they represented, and its relationship to the industrial communities which it brought into being. For the sake of brevity, these men will be referred to as the Boston associates. The reasons for this appellation will emerge as their story progresses.

We have already mentioned the fact that Edmund Dwight, an important member of the group as far as Chicopee is concerned, was intimately connected with Fisher Ames and his circle. Ames

[29] All biographical data from *Dictionary of American Biography*.

was the voice of the last of the Boston Federalists; he was also the political philosopher of the rising capitalism of New England,[30] and his ideas were those of the cotton Whigs who were the sons of the Federalists. "The essence, and almost the quintessence, of good government," he wrote, "is to protect property and its rights. When these are protected there is scarcely any booty left for oppression to seize; the objects and the motives to usurpation and tyranny are removed. By securing property, life and liberty can scarcely fail of being secured; where property is safe by rules and principles, there is liberty."[31] This was the expression of the political philosopher. The puritan business man of the period said: "My property imposes upon me many duties, which can only be known to my Maker[32]. . . . The duty of an American citizen, at this period of the world, is that of a responsible agent; and he should endeavor to transmit to the next age the institutions of our country ininjured and improved. . . .[33] An idler, who feels that he has no responsibilities, but is contriving to get rid of time without being useful to anyone, whatever his fortune, can find no comfort in staying here. We have not enough such to make up a society. We are literally all working-men; and the attempt to get up a 'Workingmen's party' is a libel upon the whole population, as it implies that there are among us large numbers who are not working-men."[34]

With this very sketchy, but significant indication of their philosophical background we may examine the business interests of the Boston associates. They had been merchants and commission agents, ship owners and commanders, and had been in the China and India trade, had built bridges and turnpikes and canals, had speculated in real estate in and around Boston.[35] When the war and embargo had crippled their most lucrative enterprises, they were ready to try new fields of endeavor. Francis C. Lowell,

[30] See V. L. Parrington, *Main Currents in American Thought,* Vol. II, "The Romantic Revolution in America," 276 et seq.

[31] From *Phocion.* Quoted in Parrington, *op. cit.,* II, 287.

[32] William R. Lawrence, *Extracts from the Diary and Correspondence of the Late Amos Lawrence,* 28.

[33] *Ibid.,* 98.

[34] *Ibid.,* 104.

[35] See Justin Winsor, *Memorial History of Boston,* Vol. IV, passim, and Mass., *Private and Special Statutes,* 1800-1810, passim.

while on a visit to England for his health, had studied the English cotton industry, and the changes which were transforming it, and he was prepared to launch the American industry in its modern form. Several of Lowell's associates, notably the Appletons, subscribed to his Boston Manufacturing Company because they felt that no great harm would result from losing a few thousands for the sake of an old friend![36] To this extent they were willing to help finance the introduction of the power loom. Israel Thorndike, although he had suffered a loss in the old Beverley enterprise in 1787[37] was willing to try again. Not so the Cabots who had also lost their investment in the Beverley failure. They remained aloof until 1828.[38] By 1832 they were lending their name to new mills[39] and the name "Cabot Street" began to appear in the new cotton towns.

Dwight joined this group in Boston in 1816, although he had had contact with it before that. The next year the Boston Manufacturing Company in Waltham paid a 12.5 per cent dividend, continuing with 16 to 21 per cent per annum. By 1822 104.5 per cent had been paid in all.[40] A new field of profitable investment was opening up to those who were prepared to take the risks. There must have been excited talk in Dwight's group in the second half of that second decade of the century. Mercantile spirits rose under the kind of stimulation which later was to make Harrison Gray Otis write, "The rumor of your profits will make people delirious,"[41] as he looked forward delightedly to a 15 per cent dividend from the Taunton Company in 1835.[42] Edmund Dwight who had come to the Boston associates from Springfield had money, he knew of a water site which he could buy on the Chicopee

[36] *Bagnall Papers,* III, 2131.

[37] The Beverley Cotton Manufactory in Massachusetts was one of the first manufacturing corporations to be established in this country. Of the 40 shares of capital stock subscribed, 18 were held by various members of the Cabot family, and 4 by Israel Thorndike. In spite of financial assistance received from the Commonwealth of Massachusetts, the venture was not successful. J. S. Davis, *Essays in the Earlier History of American Corporations,* II, 270-274.

[38] C. Ware, *op. cit.,* 62.

[39] Mass., 1832 *Private and Special Statutes,* C. 63.

[40] C. Ware, *op. cit.,* 66.

[41] S. E. Morison, *Harrison Gray Otis,* II, 294.

[42] C. Ware, *op. cit.,* 143.

River in his home town. Goods could be hauled the short distance to Springfield proper and shipped down the river; raw cotton could be transported in the same way. The result was the incorporation of the Chicopee Manufacturing Company in 1823. But preparations were already being made in 1821, for in that year a Mr. T. Parsons wrote to Francis Bowen telling of a meeting with Dwight who "remarked that a great manufacturing corporation was then going into business there under favorable prospects, and that it might be useful for me to own a few shares. They were in demand and above par in price."[43] Thus this company, while not incorporated until 1823, was planned as early as 1821 at least.

Francis C. Lowell and his friends introduced the modern cotton manufacture in America when they launched the Boston Manufacturing Company in Waltham in 1813.[44] This company constituted the model after which other companies were fashioned. The new enterprise was to utilize the power loom and consolidate all of the various processes of production in one plant.[45] For this it was necessary to recruit labor to operate these mills on a scale hitherto unknown in America, and it was expected that there might be some difficulties in securing an adequate supply. Aside from the fact that labor was not too plentiful, stories of the degradation of labor in Europe, the evil repute of factory work in England, had reached the United States. The puritan tradition might not lend itself to permit daughters to leave their homes in days when travelling facilities, or lack of them, intensified the distance between home and factory. It would be necessary to make factory labor attractive. The newly-recruited female operatives would be housed in supervised boarding-houses owned by the corporations, under the watchful eye of women selected for their uncompromising respectability. The combination of factory work all day, a sober and genteel boarding-house at night, and church on Sunday would erect a sufficiently protective wall around young ladies' morals as to undermine parental anxiety on their behalf. This was the scheme adopted in the communities or-

[43] F. Bowen, "Memoir of Edmund Dwight," 4 *American Journal of Education*, 20 (September, 1857).

[44] C. Ware, *op. cit.*, 60.

[45] *Ibid.*, 60 et seq.

ganized by the Boston associates. It was devised by F. C. Lowell, and was, as Miss Ware suggests, the result of his desire as a Boston business man, to lay the foundations for a profitable enterprise while maintaining a decent social and personal morality.[46]

The scheme had its publicity value. Harriet Martineau, who in England had been one of those who was particularly responsible for the fact that "economic laws were bandied about and nursery textbooks teaching pure Ricardian economics were given to unoffending children,"[47] and Charles Dickens and Michel Chevalier were properly impressed by more than mere subsistence wages, by the smiling countenances in Lowell, and the niceties of factory girls' behaviour. They publicised the system and incidentally the mills. But there is another aspect to this boarding-house system which has often been overlooked. Lowell and his associates were introducing mass production, and the equipment for the latter was concentrated into almost colonial communities. Hundreds of girls were suddenly thrust into a town and had to be housed and fed. Could the pre-industrial village communities perform this function? It seems fair to suppose that in many cases, it was impossible for the village to do this as rapidly as was required by the swiftly developing factories. The tempo of the business enterprise which brought the factory was characteristic of a higher form of economic development than the selected locality had as yet experienced or reached. The building of large plants, the assembly of hundreds and thousands of girls, had to be supplemented, it seems, by the erection of "barracks" to shelter the newly-recruited industrial army. Under these conditions, it is only to be expected that the Boston business men would lay down rules and regulations of conduct such as were expected in the puritan New England society of that time. And it is only logical to suspect, that if the owners had not exercised the supervision over the operatives that they did, much the same atmosphere would have prevailed. Such were the times.[48]

For such a grand scheme a large capital was needed, and for this the keynote was set with the appropriation of $400,000 for the

[46] *Ibid.* 64, 65.
[47] S. Blum, *Labor Economics,* 21.
[48] See below, p. 51 et seq.

first and experimental company, the Boston Manufacturing Company.[49] The financial success of the undertaking was rapid and spectacular. As pointed out above the stockholders had taken out in dividends more than their original investment by 1822. Any doubts as to the profitableness of the new venture were swept away, and plans for further investment proceeded. Lowell was selected as a cotton center at about the same time or a little before the Chicopee development, and the technical procedure was exactly the same. The first Lowell company organized was the Merrimack Manufacturing Company, incorporated in 1822.[50] The Merrimack Company bought out the assets of the "Locks and Canals on the Merrimack," a local undertaking, and in 1825 reorganized it as a separate canal and machine shop company to which it transferred the land and water power not in its own immediate use.[51] For the next twenty years this canal company sold land and furnished power, built machinery and mills and tenements for the various Lowell companies as they were organized under the leadership of the Boston associates, just as the Springfield Canal Company fulfilled a similar function in Chicopee. In 1845, the same year that the Ames Manufacturing Company took over the Springfield Canal Company, the Lowell Machine Shops were organized by Abbott Lawrence, J. A. Lowell and Nathan Appleton to buy the assets of the Merrimack Canal Company.[52] These activities established the modern city of Lowell. Company after company was incorporated, the capitalizations ranging from $500,000 to $1,000,-000. After the Merrimack Company came the Boott Mills, the Tremont Mills, the Lawrence, Appleton, Suffolk, Hamilton, Massachusetts and Prescott Manufacturing companies in Lowell, the Chicopee, Cabot, Perkins and Dwight mills in Chicopee, the Hopewell and Whittenden mills in Taunton, the Lyman mills in Holyoke, the textile mills in Lawrence, the Laconia and York mills in Maine. In New Hampshire the Boston associates controlled the Cocheco Manufacturing Company in Dover, the Salmon Falls and

[49] C. Ware, *op. cit.*, 301.
[50] Charles Cowley, *History of Lowell*, 44.
[51] *Ibid.*, 49.
[52] *Ibid.*, 50; Mass., 1845 *Private and Special Statutes*, C. 10.

Great Falls companies in Somersworth, the Stark, Manchester and Amoskeag mills in Manchester, and others in Nashua. In Manchester the Amoskeag company bought the land, laid out the city, did the construction, and operated the machine shops. It was the parent company.[53] All of these companies, except the Lyman Mills in Holyoke[54] were in operation before 1850. All were patterned after the Waltham model. The Boston associates were the prime movers in the enterprises and constituted the heart of a wider group. The companies were knit together by duplication of stockholders. These men had been able to solve the technical problems of production at an early stage, their capital resources were adequate, their names were important enough, commanded enough prestige and respect to attract smaller investors and slower associates who were soon willing and eager to entrust their savings and the direction thereof to this enterprising group.

The situation, then, during the period 1825-1850 was that a group of men, living in Boston, had initiated and led a movement which brought the factory in concentrated units to selected localities, developed the water power in these places, mobilized a labor force and organized the conditions of life and conduct for that force. From the business point of view, what position did the Boston associates hold in the cotton industry? Table 1 indicates the extent of their interests and the series of interlocking directorates by means of which they controlled the management of the various companies. The table also shows roughly the cotton spindleage under their control. It amounted to some 20 per cent of the 3,600,000 spindles in the United States in 1850.[55] This means that about one fifth of the industry was managed by a fairly small group of men.[56] While this seems to have been a loose arrange-

[53] D. L. Perkins, *Reminiscences of Manchester*, 21.

[54] J. K. Mills, G. W. Lyman, and others of the Boston associates were responsible for the development of the water power at Holyoke. They planned to sell land and power to new companies as they did elsewhere.

[55] M. T. Copeland, *The Cotton Manufacturing Industry of the United States*, 6.

[56] These business relationships were further cemented by marriages. Francis C. Lowell, whose mother was a Cabot, married P. T. Jackson's sister. (*Bagnall Papers*, III, 1893) Lowell's sister married Benjamin Gorham. Another brother-in-law was Warren Dutton. (*Ibid.*, III, 1893) Samuel Cabot and T. G. Cary married daughters of T. H. Perkins. (*Ibid.*,

ment, and partly unconscious, there really was a plan at work. When the plans for Lowell were being made it was not intended that the various mills should compete. The new Lowell enterprises of the 1820's were not intended to encroach on the market of the Boston Manufacturing Company which was making sheetings and shirtings at Waltham. The associates were now turning to calicoes and prints.[57] Similarly the Hamilton Company, incorporated in 1825 was to make dimities, leaving the calico market to the Merrimack Company.[58] Actually, the Hamilton Company did turn to calicoes in 1830, since the market, which was expanding rapidly, permitted this invasion of the Merrimack field on a profitable basis.[59] However to start with, the Hamilton Company had specialized in heavy drilling, canton flannel, jeans, and stripes.[60] Another method of co-operation was by the exchange of mechanical processes. In 1822 the Boston Manufacturing Company granted the use of patents and the technical advice of Paul Moody to the Merrimack Company. In the matter of the marketing of the goods, the J. W. Paige Company acted as selling agents for the Boston, Appleton, Hamilton, and Merrimack companies.[61] J. K. Mills was the treasurer and selling agent for at least three, and probably all four of the Chicopee cotton mills in the thirties and forties.[62] We already know that J. K. Mills and his partner, Edmund Dwight, had invested in these and many other mills. Familiar names in the Paige Company were Nathan Appleton, S. A. Appleton, and Abbott Lawrence.[63] It was only natural that the selling agencies be given to commission houses which were related in one way or another to the Boston group. The selling of the product was at many times one of the most lucrative of the

III, 2254, 5) F. C. Lowell's daughter married John A. Lowell who had been a partner of J. W. Boott. (*Ibid.*, III, 2367) Edmund Dwight married S. Eliot's daughter. George W. Lyman married the daughter of Harrison Gray Otis who had been associated with Kirk Boott's father. (*Ibid.*, IV, 2558) William Amory was the son-in-law of David Sears. (J. W. Meader, *The Merrimack*, 200).

[57] *Bagnall Papers*, III, 2132.

[58] *Ibid.*, III, 2410.

[59] *Ibid.*

[60] *Ibid.*, III, 2234 et seq.

[61] *Ibid.*, III, 2242.

[62] *Company "A"* Journal; *Company "B"* Journal, 1837; *Company "C"* Books, 1840's passim.

[63] *Bagnall Papers*, III, 2334.

TABLE 1. OFFICERS AND PRINCIPAL STOCKHOLDERS OF SPECIFIED COTTON MILLS BEFORE 1850*

Company, Date of Incorporation, and Location	Spindleage in 1849	Officers and Principal Stockholders	Office Held and Date of Tenure When Known	
Amoskeag Co., 1831, Manchester, N. H.	61,400	William Amory	Director	
		N. Appleton	"	23 years
		W. Appleton	"	25 "
		P. T. Jackson	"	
		F. C. Lowell	"	15 "
		J. A. Lowell	"	
		J. K. Mills	"	33 "
		Joseph Tilden	President,	1849
Appleton Co., 1828, Lowell, Mass.	17,920	N. Appleton		
		W. Appleton	Treasurer,	1828
		T. G. Cary	"	1841–59
		E. Francis		
		P. T. Jackson		
		J. A. Lowell		
		John Lowell, Jr.		
		G. W. Lyman	"	1832–41
		T. H. Perkins		
		William Sturgis		
		I. Thorndike, Sr.		
		I. Thorndike, Jr.		
Atlantic Mills, 1846, Lawrence, Mass.		E. Chadwick		
		J. W. Edmunds		
		A. Lawrence		
Boott Mills, 1835, Lowell, Mass.	34,374	N. Appleton		
		K. Boot		
		H. Cabot		
		Warren Dutton	President,	1838
		George Kuhn	"	1851
		Abbott Lawrence		
		J. A. Lowell	Treasurer,	1835
		G. W. Lyman		
		G. W. Pratt		
		J. H. Wolcott		
Boston Manufacturing Co., 1813, Waltham, Mass.	40,000	N. Appleton		
		E. Brooks	President,	1831–44
		U. Cotting		
		Warren Dutton		
		John Gore		
		Benjamin Gorham		
		Charles Jackson		
		P. T. Jackson		
		James Lloyd		
		Francis C. Lowell		
		John A. Lowell	Treasurer,	1827–44
			President,	1844–77
Cabot Manufacturing Co., 1832, Chicopee, Mass.	14,000	N. Appleton	President,	1841–50
		P. C. Brooks	Director,	
		H. Cabot	"	1841–50
		S. Cabot	"	1841–50
		E. Dwight		
		George Kuhn	"	
		G. W. Lyman	"	
		J. K. Mills	"	
		H. G. Otis		
		T. H. Perkins		
		I. Sargent	"	1850
		I. Thorndike		

* Compiled from J. D. Van Slyck, *Representatives of New England Manufacturers,* 44, 342-43, 463, 570; *Bagnall Papers,* III, 1892 et seq., 2252 et seq., IV, 2551 et seq.; New England Mercantile Union, *Business Directory* for 1849, 73, 106; W. T. Davis, *The New England States,* I, 144 et seq., and *A Professional and Industrial History of Suffolk County, Massachusetts,* III, 511; Holland, *op. cit.,* II, 47; J. W. Meader, *The Merrimack River,* 200; C. A. Nelson, *Waltham, Past and Present,* 133; Mass., *Private and Special Statutes,* passim; New Hampshire, *Laws,* 1839 C. CXVI; *Springfield Republican,* Jan. 14, 1837, June 8, 1839, Jan. 16, 1841, Feb. 4, 1843; *Chicopee Telegraph,* Jan. 23, 1850.

TABLE 1 (continued)

Company, Date of Incorporation, and Location	Spindleage in 1849	Officers and Principal Stockholders	Office Held and Date of Tenure When Known	
Chicopee Manufacturing Co., 1823, Chicopee, Mass.	23,000	W. Appleton	Director,	1823–43
		P. C. Brooks, Jr.	"	1841–50
		H. Cabot		
		E. Dwight	"	1823–47
		G. W. Lyman	"	1837–50
		H. G. Otis	"	1837
		I. Sargent	"	1850
Cocheco Manufacturing Co., 1823, Dover, N. H.	43,000	E. T. Andrews		
		W. Appleton	Treasurer	
		George Bond		
		F. Coffin		
		E. Francis	President,	1849
		W. Payne		
Dwight Manufacturing Co., 1841, Chicopee, Mass.	14,000	W. Appleton	Director,	1850
		S. Cabot	"	1850
		E. Dwight		
		W. H. Gardiner	"	1843
		George Kuhn	"	1843
		T. H. Perkins		
		I. Sargent	President,	1843
		William Sturgis	Director,	1841–50
Essex Co., 1845, To Develop Lawrence		N. Appleton		
		J. B. Francis		
		P. T. Jackson		
		Abbott Lawrence		
		S. Lawrence		
		J. A. Lowell		
		G. W. Lyman		
		Theodore Lyman		
		C. S. Storrow		
Great Falls Manufacturing Co., Somersworth, N. H.	64,216	P. T. Jackson	Treasurer and Agent in 1840's	
Hadley Falls Co., 1847, To Develop Holyoke, Mass.		P. T. Jackson		
		G. W. Lyman		
		J. K. Mills		
		I. Sargent		
Hamilton Co., 1825, Lowell, Mass.	36,228	E. Appleton	Treasurer,	1825–33
		N. Appleton		
		W. Appleton		
		S. Batchelder		
		J. W. Boott		
		T. G. Cary	"	1839–54
		E. Chadwick		
		Warren Dutton		
		B. Gorham		
		P. T. Jackson		
		J. A. Lowell		
		G. W. Lyman	"	1833–39
		W. Pratt		
		W. Sturgis		
		I. Thorndike		
Hopewell Co., 1833, Taunton, Mass.		S. Crocker		
		E. Dwight		
		S. A. Eliot		
		J. K. Mills		
		H. G. Otis		
		C. Richmond		
Jackson Co., Nashua, N. H.	12,000	William Amory	Treasurer,	1830's
		David Sears	President,	1849
Laconia Mills, Biddeford, Me.	25,000	S. Batchelder	Director,	1845
		E. Chadwick	President,	1849
Lawrence Manufacturing Co., 1831, Lowell, Mass.	44,000	N. Appleton		
		W. Appleton		
		B. R. Nichols		

Table 1 (continued)

Company, Date of Incorporation, and Location	Spindleage in 1849	Officers and Principal Stockholders	Office Held and Date of Tenure When Known
Lowell Manufacturing Co., 1828, Lowell, Mass.		F. Cabot	
		P. T. Jackson	
		G. W. Lyman.......	Treasurer, 1831
		W. Sturgis	
		I. Thorndike	
Manchester Mills, 1839, Manchester, N. H.	22,000	W. Amory..........	Treasurer, 1839–45
		N. Appleton........	Director, 1848
		O. Dean	
		S. Frothingham.....	Incorporator, 1839
		J. C. Howe	
		I. Livermore	
		F. C. Lowell (II)....	" 1839
		Willard Sayles	
		David Sears........	President, 1847–49
Mass. Cotton Mills, 1839, Lowell, Mass.	45,720	O. Goodwin	
		Abbott Lawrence	
		J. A. Lowell	
Merrimack Manufacturing Co., 1822, Lowell, Mass.	67,965	N. Appleton........	President, 1825–61
		J. W. Boott	
		K. Boott	
		N. Bowditch	
		E. Chadwick........	Treasurer, 1822–54
		W. Dutton.........	President, 1822–25
		B. Gorham	
		P. T. Jackson	
		F. C. Lowell (II)....	Treasurer, 1837
Nashua Manufacturing Co., 1823, Nashua, N. H.	37,450	Same Management as Jackson Co.	
Perkins Mills, 1836, Chicopee, Mass.	14,000	W. Appleton........	Director, 1843
		S. Cabot	
		O. Goodwin........	" 1839
		George Kuhn.......	" 1841–50
		G. W. Lyman.......	" 1841–50
		I. Sargent..........	" 1841–50
		W. Sturgis..........	" 1841–50
Prescott Manufacturing Co., 1844, Lowell, Mass. (Absorbed by Mass. Cotton Mills)		N. Appleton	
		P. T. Jackson	
		W. Sturgis	
Salmon Falls Manufacturing Co., Somersworth, N. H.	16,000	E. Francis..........	President, 1849
Stark Mills, 1838, Manchester, Mass.	42,000	W. Amory	
		N. Appleton........	President, 1839
		W. Appleton	
		S. Henshaw	
		F. C. Lowell (II)	
		G. W. Lyman	
		Willard Sayles	
Suffolk Manufacturing Co., 1830, Lowell, Mass.	14,448	S. Appleton	
		W. Appleton	
		H. Cabot	
		G. W. Lyman	
		Joseph Tilden	
Taunton Manufacturing Co., 1823, Taunton, Mass.		S. Crocker	
		E. Dwight	
		H. G. Otis	
		W. H. Prescott	
		C. Richmond	
		I. Thondike	

TABLE 1 (continued)

Company, Date of Incorporation, and Location	Spindleage in 1849	Officers and Principal Stockholders	Office Held and Date of Tenure When Known
Tremont Mills, 1830, Lowell, Mass.	12,960	W. Appleton George Hallet Abbott Lawrence Amos Lawrence B. R. Nichols W. Pratt David Sears T. B. Wales	
Whittenden Mills, 1835, Taunton, Mass.	6,500	E. Dwight S. A. Eliot C. A. Mills	
York Manufacturing Co., 1831, Saco, Me.	25,000	S. Batchelder E. Dwight A. Lawrence	
TOTAL SPINDLES	733,981		

enterprises connected with the cotton manufacture, and the profits from this were distributed among those friends and business associates who managed the commission houses, not among the whole list of stockholders in the cotton mills.

Another important aspect of this relationship of the cotton companies is to be found in the exchange of cost information. As late as 1853, one of the Chicopee companies had notations of the costs of production of the Pepperell, Prescott, Tremont, Perkins, and Hadley Falls mills, the carding costs of the Lawrence and Appleton Companies, waste data of the Atlantic, Boott and Prescott Mills.[64] Another Chicopee corporation had access to the production figures of one of its neighbors.[65] Thus aside from the duplication of stockholders that bound these companies together, to some extent the behaviour of the managers in their relationship to each other was non-competitive.

Considering the degree of co-operation and community of interest found in these cotton companies, there is no reason to suppose that they bid against each other, or against themselves, as it actually was, in the purchase of raw cotton, nor could very keen price competition between the associated companies in the sale of the finished product be expected under these circumstances.

We have already pointed out that the cotton mills operated by the Boston associates integrated all operations into one unit, and

[64] *Company "C" Papers,* Memorandum Book, 1853.
[65] *Company "B" Papers,* Letter Book, 1855.

that they maintained control over the tenements which housed the operatives. More important, the water power was in their hands too. But this integration was carried a step further. In Chicopee one of the functions of the Springfield Canal Company was to operate a machine shop for the manufacture of cotton machinery, and this was later taken over by the Ames Manufacturing Company, a Boston associate unit. The same happened in Lowell and in Manchester and in Lawrence. It is only natural, then, that we find a Chicopee mill buying turbine wheels from the Ames Company, and other equipment from the Lowell Machine Shops.[66] There were very good reasons for keeping control of the manufacture of cotton machinery. It was a profitable business in and of itself, and to start with, it was probably necessary for the cotton corporations to manufacture their own machinery in the absence of anyone else prepared to do so.

When the cotton companies were first organized, there were no railways in Massachusetts. Boston shipowners were anxious to tap the traffic of the interior, especially after the success of the Erie Canal which was diverting much traffic to the port of New York. It is to be expected that Boston capitalists in general would be interested in railroad development. But the Boston associates were especially interested in building transportation facilities because it was important to establish connections with their busy manufacturing centers in the interior. The first railway of any length in the state was the Boston and Lowell road, incorporated in 1830 by the petition of Kirk Boott, P. T. Jackson, G. W. Lyman and others.[67] It was opened to traffic in 1835. In subsequent years other familiar names which appeared on the board of directors were Joseph Tilden, William Appleton, William Sturgis, and E. Chadwick. The Taunton Branch road was directed at various times by T. B. Wales, J. K. Mills, William Sturgis and G. W. Pratt. Certain members of the group participated in the initiation of the Boston and Worcester and the Western railroads. The latter road, in the promotion of which Edmund Dwight had been

[66] *Ibid.*, 1853.
[67] Mass., 1830 *Private and Special Statutes*, C. 4.

very active, provided the connecting link from Boston to Springfield via Worcester. The Connecticut River road, a project which received the management and investment of some of the associates brought Chicopee and Holyoke into the chain. Both Samuel Batchelder and George H. Kuhn sat on the board of the Boston and Maine road which in 1843 brought railway transportation to Dover and Somersworth in New Hampshire.[68] The result of this activity was that in the late forties the associates, through their directorates shared in the control of some 25 to 30 per cent of the railway mileage in Massachusetts.[69]

When we turn to the financial institutions of the state we find the same story. This group of men, by reason of the directorates which they held, and the prestige and respect which their names commanded, shared largely in the control of about 40 per cent of the Boston banking capital in 1848.[70] As was only natural, the cotton mills banked with those institutions in which the cotton shareholders were financially interested. One of the Chicopee companies transacted business with the Merchants', Columbian, and State Banks, the first two being family institutions.[71] Another dealt with the Merchants' and the Globe Banks.[72] Ignatius Sargent was connected with the latter.

Together with their other financial and industrial interests the associates were of importance in the development of the insurance institutions of the State. Of all the insurance business recorded in Massachusetts in 1846, those companies with which members of this group were closely connected held 77 per cent of the fire and 41 per cent of the marine insurance. The insurance capital represented by this group of companies amounted to about 39 per cent of the Massachusetts total.[73] The natural result of this financial and industrial integration was to place the cotton mills' insurance with those companies in which the cotton owners had invested. When a Chicopee company held insurance in the Manufacturers', the Boston, the Merchants' and the American insurance com-

[68] Mass., *Annual Reports of Railroad Corporations,* 1837-1850, passim.
[69] See Appendix A. [70] *Ibid.*
[71] *Company "A" Papers,* Journal, 1837.
[72] *Company "B" Papers,* Journal, 1843.
[73] See Appendix A.

panies,[74] it is not surprising to find on the directorates of these companies the names of Samuel Appleton, Charles H. Mills, J. A. Lowell, E. Chadwick, and others.[75] Another Chicopee mill borrowed $25,000 from the Massachusetts Hospital Life Insurance Company.[76] Practically every member of the group sat on the board of this institution.

A number of these men participated actively in public life, especially at the beginning of the period. In 1822, the 31 Boston members of the Massachusetts General Court included several members of the group, namely Warren Dutton, Joseph Tilden, T. H. Perkins, Josiah Quincy, P. C. Brooks, F. C. Gray, W. Prescott, and Nathan Appleton.[77] Abbott Lawrence, we have seen, was high in the councils of the Whig party. Daniel Webster was the voice of the associates in the United States Senate, first representing their mercantile interests, and after 1828, as these declined in importance, he spoke for their manufacturing investments. Nathan Appleton, one of the most important of the group, served his term in Congress, and was in close touch with important banking circles.[78] Over a period of years his extensive correspondence included such personages as Nicholas Biddle, Charles Sumner, Daniel Webster, Benjamin Silliman, Millard Filmore, Dorothea Lee Dix, and others of importance.[79]

[74] *Company "B" Papers,* Journal, 1853.
[75] See Appendix A.
[76] *Company "A" Papers,* Journal, 1848.
[77] Winsor, *op. cit.,* III, 297.
[78] *Dictionary of American Biography.*
[79] *Appleton Papers,* Massachusetts Historical Society. It is worth noting that both Webster (who was his friend) and Horace Greeley applied to Appleton, one of the most important personalities of this group, for tariff information. These applications for aid are of sufficient interest to quote at some length. The letters are indicative of Appleton's position as a tariff authority, and the acceptance of his position as such by two influential persons who figured so prominently in public life, and in shaping tariff policy. The letters follow.

N. Y. July 8, 1846.

My dear Sir:

The state of the Tariff Bill at Washington is such, that we shall need the advice of our best informed and most prudent friends, next week and the week after; and I write this, to bespeak your attention, and to express the hope that we may hear from you and your neighbors, as fully as possible. It would be very well, I think, if some intelligent Gentleman from Boston could spend the next ten days at Washington. *Information,* on many subjects will be very much needed.

These men, then—merchants, bankers, legislators, manufacturers, railroad builders—conditioned the character of the business enterprise which was responsible for the establishment of absentee ownership in Chicopee and elsewhere in the first part of the past century. The wide ramifications of their interests, and the scale on which they were conducted indicate the essential difference between the type of enterprise which they represented and the comparatively petty nature of "local" enterprise which was gradually, and on a modest scale, developing manufacturing units in many incipient industrial centers of New England. The latter type of

---

The first practical question is; shall we make any attempt at amendments?

My own impression rather inclines toward two convictions. 1st, that we cannot make any thing of this Bill, at all likely to satisfy the Country, unless we can alter its *ad valorem* principle materially. And I doubt whether we can do this. And consequently, it is doubtful policy to propose amendments. 2. That our best chance of killing the Bill is, to put to the vote, just *as it is.*

I would like to learn what is thought in your circle, on these points.

With whatever chance of successful opposition, I think we ought not to let the occasion pass without attacking the whole principle of the Bill, and exposing the follies of ??? Pray take the trouble *to book me up,* in these respects. Since 1840 I have not been brushed up on Tariff subjects.

etc., etc.,
DANIEL WEBSTER.

August 17, 1844

Respected Sir:

I am but casually in your City, and have not the time to solicit personally of you the information of which I stand in need. I am to debate the tariff question at Newburgh on Friday next, and am greatly in want of information on these points which I hope you may be able, as I am sure you will be willing to supply. The present ??? is being directed against the alleged excessive profits of manufactures under the present tariff and profits of manufacturing generally. I desire to know, therefore,

1st. What have been the *average* profits of manufacturing, say since 1816? What the average dividends of any company doing a fair business, say of the Waltham Mills?

2nd. What have been the *average* profits of the cotton and woolen manufacture since August, 1842, that is, for the two years that the present tariff has been in operation?

3. If profits have been unusually high the past year, is it not probable that they will be lower for the ensuing year?

4. Are the prices of cotton and woolen fabrics generally—plain and fancy—higher now than in 1841-42? And how do they compare generally with those of 1842?

5. Are not prices now falling? And is it not extremely probable that they will go still lower? How are they now with those of February and March last?

etc., etc.,
HORACE GREELEY.

activity, to start with at least, was purely "middle class" in its nature, and in Chicopee was to *follow* the establishment of manufacturing industry. The former represented capitalist enterprise of a surprisingly "modern" kind. Fundamental differences in the constituent elements of the middle class—a broad label—were apparent early, and will emerge strikingly when we come to consider the activities of the Chicopee business men as compared with those of the business men who were in the first instance responsible for the founding of Chicopee as an industrial center.

CHAPTER III

YANKEE LABOR, 1825-1840

Chicopee Falls was the first section of the community to become industrialized. Here was the Belcher foundry which for the first twenty years of the century had been turning out iron castings and some hollow ware. On the north side of the river stood the paper mill, the employees of which were lodged nearby. Then, following the decision of a Boston board of directors, came the Chicopee Manufacturing Company, and suddenly this little community found a mill and tenements springing up on what had been farm land. The company was going to put hundreds of girls to work, and had to have houses for them, for the original settlement here was not sufficiently developed to undertake that responsibility even if the policy of the corporations were such as to delegate it to other hands. The few farmers and the foundrymen of the neighborhood looked upon a kind of industrial activity of which they had never seen the like. A long narrow cotton mill paralleled the newly-built canal. Rows of tenements arose alongside the mill. These were dwellings new to the vicinity. They were not ordinary houses surrounded by decent plots of ground, but long blocks of buildings, edging right up to the street and pressed closely together, looking as though a section of a distant city had been lifted and transplanted bodily to Chicopee Falls. And this transformation went on. No sooner was one mill completed than another was started. Engineers, supervisors, and overseers, representatives of the absent proprietors, were hard at work, directing the duplication, on a smaller scale, of the Lowell project. A curious feature about the enterprise, so far as the natives of the village were concerned, was that the owners of the development were not to be seen, except on occasional visits of inspection. They lived in Boston, but one of them, Edmund Dwight, was a Springfield man, and his family and the Dwight store were well known. The village was now the home of a corporation.

This cotton corporation, and the others which followed it, operating on an extensive scale, could not depend upon local labor supplies, or wait until workers drifted in from the neighboring towns. The mills had to be filled up at once. At the very beginning some of the laborers engaged in the construction work were of local and near-local origin. The *Springfield Republican* carried advertisements calling for men to work on the Chicopee Falls project.[1] However, when the time came to dig the canal for the Cabot Manufacturing Company in 1832-34 a group of Irishmen were imported to do the work.[2] Another group came in 1841 to work on the Dwight Canal.[3] These Irish laborers were said to have been paid 75 cents per day and three "jiggers."[4] The latter seems to have been a measure of some alcoholic beverage, a curious item to find in the wage contract of the puritan cotton companies.

The first female operatives to work in the cotton mills in Chicopee came from Granby, West Springfield, Belchertown, and other nearby communities. Some were the daughters of the mechanics and machinists who were employed in the Springfield Armory.[5] For many years the farms to the north and west were to be tapped for new material, each year the company agents having to go farther afield in their search for girls who were willing to enter the employ of the cotton mills. Before the coming of the railroad, both to Springfield and to those parts of Vermont, New Hampshire and New York whose labor supply was to be tapped, it was customary to send a wagon out into the country to bring in the girls. The labor recruiter who was in charge received from the cotton mills a fixed fee per capita and either operated independently, undertaking to fill the orders of any prospective employer, or devoted all his time to the service of one mill. As in the case of immigration, letters from the pioneers to friends and

[1] *Springfield Republican*, September 28, 1825. Incidentally the cotton corporations never advertised for female operatives. Miss Ware did not find any advertisements calling for operatives for the Lowell mills either. (See C. Ware, *op. cit.*, 213.) This may have been due, in part, to the scruples of mill owners in taking help away from other mills.

[2] *Springfield Republican*, Feb. 24, 1895.

[3] Newspaper Clipping, Chicopee Public Library.

[4] *Springfield Republican*, March 22, 1908.

[5] *Ibid.*, March 31, 1901.

relatives at home must have played their part in attracting some girls to the factory towns, or indirectly, by paving the way for the labor recruiters.

What brought the girls into the cotton mills? Before the era of the cotton factories, women had not been gainfully employed in large numbers. This was really their first experience in industry. Some came to escape dependence upon male relatives, to help their families achieve greater economic freedom by the purchase of land, or to help pay off a mortgage. To some it was to be a period of amassing some savings before marriage. Doubtless many looked on their entrance into the cotton mills as a great adventure. But it does not seem correct to over-emphasize this last factor, and to say that women were not forced into the cotton mills. It depends, of course, on what is meant by the word "force." Certainly there is no evidence to show that a desperate economic situation and dire necessity drove the girls into factory employment as the alternative to starvation. But on the other hand, thousands of girls of that period did not leave their homes and undertake hard and tedious work for long hours, even at fairly good wages, for fun.

When the new industrial army entered Chicopee in the 1820's and 1830's they found that their mode of life was already arranged for them. The laissez-faire of English and Rhode Island mill life was replaced by the paternalism of the "boarding-house system." Waltham had led the way in this regard, and Lowell followed, as did Chicopee and other new mill communities. The corporations, as we have seen, built dwellings to house the labor force. The arrival in Chicopee of large numbers of unmarried men and women, rather than families, meant that it was necessary to provide food as well as lodging. Houses and tenements were leased at low rentals to persons who were prepared to take boarders, and the workers were assigned to live in specified boarding-houses. The corporations fixed the price of board, and deducted the charges incurred from the monthly wage bill, and this was paid over to the boarding-masters. As the Chicopee mills were under the same management as those in Lowell, we may expect to find the same general regulations laid down to govern the conduct of the operatives.

The matrons of the boarding-houses where the girls were obliged to live were under the direct supervision of the cotton corporation, and were required to act as the agents of the latter in enforcing the various rules and regulations which reached out from the factory to the home life of the operatives. The Hamilton Company in Lowell held the boarding-house keepers "answerable for any improper conduct in their houses, and are not to permit their boarders to have company at unseasonable hours. The doors must be closed at ten o'clock in the evening and no person admitted after that time without some reasonable excuse. The Keepers of the boarding-houses must give an account of the number, names and employment of their boarders, when required, and report the names of such as are guilty of any improper conduct, or are not in the regular habit of attending public worship."[6] There is no doubt that similar regulations were enforced in Chicopee. A veteran mill girl who for years had been in the employ of the Chicopee Manufacturing Company mentioned the fact that there was a ten o'clock curfew regulation and that habitual church attendance was obligatory.[7] Now these rules and the eagle eye of the boarding-house keeper may have been required to attract labor supplies to the mill towns in the face of a general labor scarcity, to reassure the parents, to keep the communities decent. But the same condition of labor scarcity was prevalent in the Rhode Island mills, and these enlisted a labor force without recourse to the Waltham system. Mr. Norman Ware very pertinently commented upon this fact[8] to suggest that the Waltham system was as much the product of puritan society as of philanthropic motivation or labor scarcity. Of course the fact that the Boston capitalists did maintain this system as a rational institution was conditioned by their position as members of that society. And here, in Chicopee, as elsewhere, was a cell of that puritan society, where young

[6] J. R. Commons, *A Documentary History of American Industrial Society*, VII, 137.
[7] *Springfield Republican*, March 31, 1901.
[8] See *The Industrial Worker*, 75.

ladies knew that their place after ten o'clock in the evening was at home, where public opinion expected them to be. In no such New England community was it customary for young women to carouse about the streets till all hours of the night, whether there was a watchful and paternalistic cotton corporation there or not. Another regulation enforced in all cotton towns which were the seat of Boston associate corporations stated that "the company will not employ any one who is habitually absent from public worship on the Sabbath, or known to be guilty of immorality."[9] But virtue was the stock in trade of *any* puritan community; none has ever been known to tolerate the lack of it. And since when was it necessary for Boston capitalists to legislate New Englanders into church on the Sabbath in the 1820's and 1830's? This, in its way, would be similar to a regulation ordering confirmed tee-totalers not to drink. We must not, of course, deny the existence of many—often articulate, who felt that they could well dispense with the puritan discipline. When there was either active or passive opposition to the code, we may reasonably suspect its attempted enforcement by a vigorous and vigilant section of the citizenry which insisted on its observance. Certainly, any development toward a relaxation of the conventions tended to be held in check by the boarding-house system and all that it involved. Chevalier, the French traveler, who had been much impressed by this regimentation in Lowell observed that it was surprising to him, and doubtless would excite commotion in France, but that in the New England town, it was accepted as the most natural thing in the world,[10] and to illustrate this point he commented further on the fundamental difference between the New England and the European Sabbath. His tersely summary description of a puritan factory town was shrewd. "Lowell is not amusing, but Lowell is clean and decent, peaceful and sober."[11]

While this ordinary regimentation may not have involved any real hardship for these stated reasons, yet the corporation agent,

[9] Commons, *op. cit.,* VII, 136.
[10] *Lettres sur L'Amérique du Nord,* I, 233, 234.
[11] M. Chevalier, *op. cit.,* I, 235. "Lowell n'est pas amusant, mais Lowell est propre et décent, paisable et sage."

as a power in the community, was able to decide what amusements were to be available, what lectures were to be offered to the operatives. A Chicopee mill hand remembered that a company agent forced a candy peddler to discontinue his monthly visits, because he did not like his operatives to spend their money in this frivolous way.[12] Possibly it was due to his desire to discourage the development of the habit of luxury expenditures on the part of the operatives.

The price of board in the company houses, as set by the corporations was $1.25 per week for women, and $1.50 for men,[13] the difference, it is thought, being due more to the men's higher wages and ability to pay more than to the extra cost of feeding them. At times, during high cost of living periods, the companies supplemented this charge by a payment of 12½ cents per capita to the boarding-house keepers.[14] If the basic charge for board was raised when food prices went up, it would have been immediately felt as a wage cut, and the companies preferred to pay a premium on board rather than upset the stability of earnings, the latter being regarded by the operatives as the difference between their total wages and the price of board. The charge for board included the washing of clothes for the operatives, but it has been impossible to find out how extensive this service was.[15]

All in all, there is little evidence bearing on life in the Chicopee boarding-houses. "The chief problem," said one who knew the life, "was overcrowding. The low rent of the tenements brought with it the expressed necessity of keeping boarders, besides the family. Six girls often slept in one room, in three double beds. The population in the tenements, apparently, rivaled the best Polish record of today.[16] They ate together at long tables and were fed plain and hearty food. Among the appurtenances of the back yard of the Chicopee tenements was a conventional line of pig pens, operated by each boarding-house in the interests of economy. Near these were the wells. When the ground became properly

[12] *Springfield Republican,* May 8, 1897.
[13] *Ibid.,* May 8, 1901. [14] *Ibid.* [15] *Ibid.*
[16] These reminiscences were written by an old mill hand in 1901, when Polish workers constituted a large proportion of the mill population.

saturated during the early forties there was an epidemic of typhoid fever that was a record breaker. This resulted in the securing a water supply from the hill above the town, and gradually the pig pens were abolished."[17]

In view of the widespread acceptance of the idea that the factory operatives of the period enjoyed much "social life," attended numerous lectures, and were interested in self-improvement circles, the complete lack of evidence bearing on the conditions of factory girls' life in Chicopee, except what is quoted above, is of some significance. No doubt it tells the whole story. For most girls, after the daily round of working, eating, and sleeping, there was little time left for other things.

When the mills were first opened in Chicopee it was reported that the work was not very hard and that discipline was fairly lax. Operatives, it was said, were able to snatch a little time from loom or spindle for reading or knitting, although this was against the regulations, and the materials for such diversion had to be smuggled into the mills.[18] However another witness reported that general mill discipline was strict.[19] But it is possible that the latter report referred to a somewhat later period as there is evidence elsewhere pointing to the lack of intensity of work when cotton mills first went into operation.[20]

The factories operated by the Boston associates stipulated that all persons entering their employ contract to work for one year, and failure to comply with this regulation was penalized by the refusal of the company to grant a "regular discharge" without which it was difficult to secure employment in another mill on account of the operation of the blacklist.[21] The latter institution was rigorously upheld by the large cotton corporations, especially in times of labor conflict.[22]

The hours of labor were long. Work started at five o'clock in the morning and lasted through until half past seven in the eve-

[17] *Springfield Republican,* May 8, 1901.
[18] *Ibid.,* March 31, 1901. [19] *Ibid.,* May 8, 1897.
[20] C. Ware, *op. cit.,* 255. [21] *Ibid.,* 267.
[22] U. S. 61st Cong. 2nd Sess., *Senate Doc.* 645, "Report on the Condition of Woman and Child Wage-Earners in the United States," Vol. IX, "History of Women in Industry in the United States," 94-96.

ning with two half hour breaks for breakfast and dinner, making the actual working time 13½ hours per day.[23] A Massachusetts legislative investigation reported a 12½ hour day in Chicopee in 1825.[24] The former report may refer to the thirties when it was observed that the hours of work tended to be a little longer than in the previous decade.[25] During the summer months the mills relied upon natural light, and the work day was longer than during the period of artificial lighting which began on September 20th. Artificial lighting was expensive, and not good enough to permit facile work. The lamps continued in use through the winter and were removed on March 20th. Balls were held on these two occasions, according to a local newspaper report,[26] but it seems much more probable that the celebrations were confined to March 20th when the lamps were "blown out" as was the case in other factory towns, when the operatives "decorate their large hanging lamps with flowers, and form garlands of almost every ingenious description in honor of 'blow out' evening."[27] From most reports there was little cause for rejoicing when artificial lighting went into effect, for it ushered in the season of longer hours of work than usual under trying conditions. On at least one occasion it precipitated a strike in Nashua, New Hampshire.[28]

The evidence as to the earnings of female factory workers is conflicting. One observer reported a range of $3 to $5.40 per week.[29] These figures are too high. The upper range was beyond the reach of even the most skilful and fastest workers. Other mills in Massachusetts were paying $2.50 to $3 per week.[30] Another report sets the wages for the most skilled operatives at $8 to $10 per month, with average wages ranging from $3.50 to $6.[31] This estimate is too low, for the upper limit of the average would

[23] *Springfield Republican,* May 8, 1897.

[24] U. S. 61st Cong. 2nd Sess., *op. cit.,* Vol. IX, 62.

[25] *Ibid.,* 63.

[26] *Springfield Republican,* May 8, 1897.

[27] From the *Voice of Industry,* March 26, 1847. Quoted in U. S. 61st Cong. 2nd Sess., *op. cit.,* Vol. IX, 66.

[28] *Ibid.*

[29] *Springfield Republican,* May 8, 1897.

[30] U. S. 22nd Cong. 1st Sess., *House Exec. Doc.* 308, (1832) "Documents Relative to the Manufactures in the United States," I, 171.

[31] *Springfield Republican,* March 31, 1901.

hardly more than cover the cost for four weeks board. It must be a computation of the margin left after the payment of $1.25 per week for board. Thus if $5 is added to the month's earnings we find an average weekly wage ranging from $2.10 to $2.75, with a few of the most skilled operatives getting as much as $3.25 to $3.75 per week. These estimates are much more reasonable than the first, and practically correspond to those reported by the Chicopee Manufacturing Company to the government in 1832, when the average wages of women and girls were said to be 46 cents per day, or $2.75 per week.[32] This was a fairly high wage if it is considered that board and lodgings accounted for only about half of the total earnings. However, there is no evidence as to the regularity of employment.

The employment of large numbers of young children was never a feature of mill life in the corporations operated by the Boston associates, as it was of the Rhode Island "family" mills.[33] It has not been possible to ascertain much about the employment of children in the Chicopee mills. It was reported that when the mills were first established, there were some as young as eight years, but that this was unusual. However, there were quite a few ranging from ten to twelve years of age.[34] In 1832 the Chicopee Manufacturing Company reported 141 boys employed who were under the age of sixteen, but girls were grouped with women.[35] The average daily wage for the boys under sixteen years of age was 42 cents as compared with 46 cents for the women,[36] and for this reason it seems likely that the majority of them were not much younger than fifteen or sixteen.

Information concerning the employment and remuneration of male workers in early mill days is inadequate. In 1832 the Chicopee Manufacturing Company was reported as employing 103 men at an average weekly wage of $5.40.[37] But we do not know in

[32] U. S. 22nd Cong. 1st Sess., *op. cit.*, I, 285.

[33] Miss Ware points out that in 1832 children constituted 21 per cent of the cotton mill population in Massachusetts, the stronghold of the boarding-house mills, as compared with 41 per cent in Rhode Island, where mills of the family type were established. C. Ware, *op. cit.*, 210.

[34] *Springfield Republican*, May 8, 1897.

[35] U. S. 22nd Cong. 1st Sess., *op. cit.*, I, 285.

[36] *Ibid.* [37] *Ibid.*

what capacity they were employed. Doubtless, some were wood and metal workers; others may have been overseers or assistant overseers of the textile departments. Another report, relying upon hearsay evidence, set the average earnings of male mill workers at $3 per week.[38] This sum may possibly have been received in addition to an allowance of $1.50 for board. Still another report said that men in the mills earned a gross weekly wage of $6 to $7.50.[39] There is a little more exact information available about the earnings of metal workers. One man in the Ames shops contracted to work "for twenty dollars a month of 25 days and board myself" in 1831.[40] In 1835 a bronze molder received $2.50 per day, and his helper 83 cents.[41] Other metal workers in the shops received $1 to $1.50 per day in the period 1831-1835.[42] The Willimansett Card Manufacturing Company employed a few men probably mechanics, at $26 per month.[43] Thus on the whole, the skilled male workers of the community were earning good wages at the time, but again, we do not know whether they secured regular employment throughout the year.

While the family mills made a practice of paying wages quarterly or semi-annually, it was customary for the boarding-house mills to pay wages monthly in cash.[44] However, it is interesting to note that until 1836 the Chicopee Manufacturing Company paid wages only twice a year, and in consequence pay day became a gala event, and took its place with the only three holidays celebrated annually, Thanksgiving Day, Fast Day, and the Fourth of July. Purchases, made in the company store, were charged against wages.[45] In its early years the Ames Manufacturing Company also paid wages at infrequent intervals.[46]

The company store owned by the Chicopee Manufacturing Company does not seem to have been in operation for more than

[38] G. H. T. Babbitt, *Chicopee Falls, Past and Present,* 5.
[39] *Springfield Republican,* May 8, 1897.
[40] *Ames Papers,* Receipt Book, 1831.
[41] *Ibid.,* Memorandum: "Cost of Making Webster."
[42] *Ibid.,* Receipt Books, 1831-35.
[43] U. S. 22nd Cong., 1st Sess., *op. cit.,* I, 285.
[44] C. Ware, *op. cit.,* 226, 247.
[45] *Springfield Republican,* May 8, 1897; *Taylor Diary,* passim.
[46] *Ames Papers,* Receipt Books, 1831-33.

about ten years, and possibly not nearly as long as that. When large numbers of men and women flocked to the little agricultural village in the middle of the 1820's to build the canals and factories, and to operate the latter, they received wages in cash, and there was no store near at hand which could meet their needs. The local farmers had produced most of their food and clothing themselves, but when necessary could drive into town, into Springfield, that is, in order to buy groceries and dry goods. But the factory workers and the new boarding-house masters had to have an arrangement that was more convenient, and to meet this need the cotton company opened a store in 1824,[47] and advertised in the county papers for produce, calling for wood, butter, cheese, cider, flannel, socks, and anything else that anyone had for sale.[48] There were not enough farmers in the immediate vicinity to supply all the produce needed. In 1825 David Bryant, who had come from Springfield, was operating a general store[49] which factory operatives patronized, and competitors were soon to follow. The mill employees were never forced by regulation or by scrip payments to make their purchases in the company store. It was a convenience for the workers until such time as outside enterprise invaded the mercantile field. The Chicopee Manufacturing Company also operated a tavern until 1834.[50] Further down the river, at Cabotville, the cotton companies established themselves, we have seen, in the period 1834-1841. Here seven mills in all were erected, and block after block of tenements. But the Cabot, Perkins and Dwight corporations do not seem to have operated stores, further evidence that the company store was not intended to be a permanent institution. In Cabotville, because the mill development came a decade later than in Chicopee Falls, mercantile interests had the time to take advantage of the "boom," and were then capable of supplying local needs without assistance from the mills.

From 1820 to 1845 the great bulk of the factory workers in Massachusetts were Yankee girls, who for the most part had re-

[47] Babbitt, *op. cit.*, 6.
[48] *Springfield Republican*, Nov. 10, 1824.
[49] C. W. Chapin, *Sketches of the Old Inhabitants of Old Springfield*, 85.
[50] Babbitt, *op. cit.*, 6.

ceived a very fair schooling before coming to the mills, and those who came to Chicopee were no exception to this rule. The congregation of a large number of such persons, so many of whom had experienced a tradition of respect for study and mental activity, stimulated a movement for reading and discussion with a view to "self-improvement." Girls who had lived on isolated farms suddenly made a great many new contacts, met new personalities, lived a group life (outside the family) for the first time. Concern with the new life which they had taken up presented new movements and ideas to them. Reading and study were in great favor, insofar as the physical exigencies of the factory system permitted it. Thus an operative wrote

> It so happens that I was born in New Hampshire, where my mother still resides, with a large family of young children, dependent on her for support, and hard does she have to struggle to gain a livelihood for herself and offspring; and but for the charity of several kind friends and neighbors, she would have to put them out before they knew the first rudiments taught in our common schools. Sensible that she had a weight upon her heavy to be borne, to lighten the load, I left home and came to Cabotville. When I came here I could not read, except by spelling out the words like a child of very few years. I had not commenced learning to write, and all the learning I now have has been gained without instruction, having obtained it alone, and that too, after I had labored in the mill twelve hours a day on the average through the year.[51]

There were such girls who were able to study after work. The wide publicizing of the *Lowell Offering* in the forties tended to build up the idea that factory work was not irksome, that the social life of the mill town was delightful, that study and discussion and literary activity were possible, and that if all of this was no longer obtainable in the forties, at least it was part of the life of the thirties to which the *Lowell Offering* looked back with nostalgic longing. In this way developed the idea of the idyllic period in American labor history. And yet a Chicopee report stated that there was little social life in the thirties, owing to the long hours of labor.[52] By the time the supper hour was over it was soon

[51] *Olive Leaf and Factory Girls' Repository,* Chicopee, Sept. 16, 1843.
[52] *Springfield Republican,* May 8, 1897.

time to go to bed so as to be sufficiently rested in order to get up at 4:30 or 5 o'clock the next morning. As stated above, there were only three holidays during the year. The New England Sabbath was too stern an institution to permit much relaxation or literary activity on that day. The lack of privacy occasioned by the overcrowding in the tenements could not give the average worker much opportunity for study even if she had the physical energy or the time for it. No doubt there were some who were able to read and study and form literary circles and write for publication as the contributors to the *Lowell Offering* and the Chicopee factory girls' paper did.[53] All it proved was that there were a few girls, like the writer of the letter above, who were able to undertake these extra activities. But it is stretching the evidence too far to make such activity a characteristic part of the factory life of the period.

A reading of the local press in the thirties throws little light on factory conditions. If they were as good as was later to be claimed, it is difficult to explain the unrest of the decade.[54] Chicopee grumbled, as did Lowell and Dover, New Hampshire. The mill operatives after all, were staid Yankee "young ladies" who had always conducted themselves with the utmost propriety. But the "young ladies" so far forgot themselves in Lowell in 1834 as to protest a wage cut by striking and marching around the town.[55] In Dover a workers' committee announced that "we think our wages already low enough, when the peculiar circumstances of our situation are considered; that we are many of us far from our homes, parents and friends, and that it is only by strict economy and untiring industry that any of us have been able to lay up anything."[56] They were also bitter in the knowledge that they were losing status as compared with other classes in the community. "We view this attempt to reduce our wages as part of a

[53] See below, pp. 107, 108, 119, 120.

[54] General unrest throughout the East had already been apparent in the late twenties. Workers were dissatisfied with the lack of leisure, the employment of children, the absence of free public schools. They felt that these conditions prevented the worker from meeting the requirements of good citizenship, and that political equality was not accompanied "by equality before the conditions of life." At least 173 strikes occurred in the United States from 1833 to 1837. J. R. Commons, *History of Labor in the United States,* I, 169 et seq., 177, 381.

[55] *The Man,* Feb. 20, 1834.

[56] *Ibid.,* March 8, 1834.

general plan of the proprietors of the different manufacturing establishments to reduce the Females in their employ to that state of dependence on them in which they openly, as they do now secretly, abuse and insult them by calling them their 'slaves'."[57] A labor paper asked, "Why is it that we who uphold those who rank highest among the sons of men should be degraded below those who are dependent upon us for their very existence?"[58] Eight hundred of the Dover operatives went on strike.[59] Apropos of their reference to slaves there was printed at this time a poem telling of the death of a factory operative from overwork. The concluding verse follows:

That night a chariot passed her,
While on the ground she lay;
The daughters of her master
An evening visit pay—
Their tender hearts were sighing
As negroes' woes were told;
While the white slave was dying
Who gained their father's gold.[60]

The workers of the North had recognized the analogy between their position and that of the chattel slave long before Senator Jare Clemens bluntly told the North to look to its own affairs.[61] It is interesting to note that this analogy was being drawn in the thirties, before the abolition movement was well launched, and certainly before it had time to draw fire from the South. It was also before the factory controversy of the forties.

Chicopee must have felt the same unrest, though there is no

[57] *Ibid.*

[58] *Working Man's Advocate,* April 10, 1830.

[59] *The Man,* March 11, 1834. [60] *Ibid.,* May 17, 1834.

[61] The word "slave" was much bandied about in the thirties and forties. All admitted that the negroes of the South were slaves. The slaveholders referred to the white slaves of the North, and in this were joined by many northern labor leaders. This characterization was denied by the factory owners, such as John A. Lowell, for instance, who urged protection for the American cotton industry lest the free workers of the North be reduced to the position of the "white slaves of England, France and Germany." (From *Appleton Papers,* J. A. Lowell to N. Appleton, Jan. 7, 1833) Similarly, a Chicopee paper, rising to defend the "character" of factory operatives, when in 1850 the South was goaded into speaking of the white slavery of the North in the United States Senate, by some strange transmutation of thought shifted the defence to end by referring to the "slaves of the British looms." See below, p. 136.

reflection of it in the local press. But in 1836 the dissatisfaction was sufficiently well developed to provoke a strike, the first in Western Massachusetts. The conflict was precipitated when the corporations increased the price of board without a corresponding increase in wages. The result was equivalent to a wage cut, and was so regarded by the operatives. A record of the incident found its way into the labor press. "The same species of injustice (advance in the price of board without an increase of wages) which caused the turn-out at Lowell recently, seems to be prevalent at this time in the factory villages nearly all over New England. It has been introduced among the help at Cabotville, Massachusetts, and the effect has been the same as at Lowell. The girls belonging to the factories have left the mills 'en masse,' and express a determination not to go back till a different and more liberal system is agreed upon."[62] As no further information about this strike appeared, it was very likely more in the nature of a demonstration than an attempt at a prolonged strike. It is possible that the increase in the price of board was not solely responsible for starting the strike. In the years after the opening of the mills, work was gradually getting harder. The working day tended to be longer than it had been, discipline was tightening up, the machinery was running faster. The process of intensification of work had already set in, and the board increase in 1836—actually a wage cut—no doubt touched off rising feelings of resentment and disgruntledness.

It required some spirit for Yankee "young ladies" to brave public opinion in order to develop strike tactics at this early period. A few years later the typical reaction was to be voiced by a merchant in Chicopee when, although he was not out of sympathy with the aims of some striking operatives, yet deprecated the methods used.[63] It was felt that young women should not march about the streets making a spectacle of themselves. And yet, in spite of this disapproval of the community, they were prepared to do this in order to protect their standards, whether it was conventional or not. One of the reasons for the designation of the conditions

[62] Reprint from *Norwich Mechanics' Advocate* in the *National Laborer,* Oct. 29, 1836.

[63] See below, p. 122.

in the cotton mills during the thirties as an "industrial idyll"[64] after it was quite generally conceded that the forties were no longer the "good old days," was that it was thought that any time factory conditions were undesirable or work became slack with a consequent reduction of earnings, the girls could go back to the farm.[65] Perhaps some could. Yet in the period 1834-36 in Dover, Lowell and Chicopee, there were groups of women who saw the solution to an attack on their standards in a fight to maintain these rather than in escape from the factory towns. It meant that for significant numbers, escape was impossible.

[64] E. C. Kirkland, *History of American Economic Life,* 348.
[65] *Ibid.,* 237.

CHAPTER IV

THE RISE OF THE MIDDLE CLASS, 1825-1860

The organization of the community established by the cotton corporations in the twenties and thirties was comparatively simple. To start with, there was practically no resident propertied class. It is true, of course, that there were some farmers and others living in the neighborhood who owned property, but these held no important place in the set of relationships and the methods of production which determined the character of the industrial community. The majority of the workers were female operatives who did not expect to remain a permanent part of the factory population. At any given time many of them, for one reason or another, may not have been able to withdraw from factory employment, but on the whole the tendency was for the working group to change. There was constant movement from within. These early mill operatives were not natives of Chicopee. They lived in company-regulated boarding-houses, as did the unmarried male wage-earners of the community. Obviously, for the greater part of the factory population there was no family life. Their mode of living was completely uniform, barrack-like, and as such conditions were substantially the same for most members of the community. The entire working population, recruited from the New England countryside, was a homogeneous group in the early days. Most of the workers were employed in the cotton mills. By 1832 the Chicopee Manufacturing Company had in its employ 781 persons.[1] The Cabot, Perkins and Dwight mills which went into operation from 1834 to 1841 were to employ another 1600 workers. In addition to these were the skilled mechanics employed by the Ames Manufacturing Company, the metal workers of the Belcher Foundry, and the paper mill hands on the north side of the river at Chicopee Falls.

There were not many members of the working population who were not operatives or mechanics. Aside from the cotton textile

[1] U. S. 22nd Cong., 1st Sess., *op. cit.*, I, 285.

overseers the existence of the mills did not directly entail the presence of middle class elements. While the cotton mills were highly integrated undertakings from the business point of view, their organization, insofar as Chicopee was concerned, was in certain respects as simple as the community life of the early years. There was a division between the pecuniary and industrial activities of the enterprises. Cotton was manufactured in Chicopee under the direction of a resident agent, assisted by departmental overseers and a small office staff. But the financial affairs of the companies were conducted in Boston, and those persons employed to administer these lived in Boston, and not in Chicopee, as would have been the case if the ownership had been vested in local hands. Furthermore, as a result of this situation, all the important banking was transacted in Boston, with a corresponding loss of business to the banking interests of Chicopee, which would have to be satisfied with small affairs. When the cotton was manufactured the resident agent had no hand in the selling of it, and so was not required to employ a staff for that purpose. The product was sold through the offices of a Boston commission agent. Thus the organization of the cotton corporations was such as to minimize the number of salaried workers who would naturally take their place in every day life with the resident property owners.

The same simplicity extended to the conduct of town business. The manufacturing villages (Chicopee Falls and Cabotville) were still under the municipal jurisdiction of Springfield, and political life was centered there. But considering the fact that most of the Chicopee residents were newcomers and propertiless, they could have little interest in municipal affairs as long as that condition continued. Home rule was to come only with the rise of a vigorous propertied class which directly felt its stake in town government.

It is obvious that the merchant and petty manufacturing class was as conspicuous by its absence immediately after the establishment of the industrial community, as it was before. However, the coming of the mills provided the necessary stimulus for its development. The process of building the large factories and housing facilities for so many newly-arrived workers in a short time meant that the town enjoyed a boom.

We have seen how the Chicopee Manufacturing Company was obliged to open a store in 1824 in order to supply trading facilities for its working force. The next year David M. Bryant, who had been operating a dry goods store in Springfield, moved his business to Chicopee Falls.[2] T. W. Carter came from Brimfield, Massachusetts, in the same year and went to work in Bryant's store, becoming a partner in 1830.[3] S. A. Shackford arrived in 1834 from New Market, New Hampshire, and opened a general store.[4] Wells Southworth, who had been a merchant in Pelham, opened a store in Chicopee Falls in 1828.[5] Jerome Wells, who had clerked in South Hadley Falls and worked for a silversmith in Springfield went into business in Cabotville in 1835.[6] The Bullens brothers, who came from Dedham, opened a store in Cabotville some time between 1833 and 1835.[7] Others came steadily during the period 1825-1845. The infiltration of mercantile investment in the first ten years of this period was a little slower than during the second decade. Some acceleration was to be expected as the boom gained momentum. Another reason may, perhaps, be found in the fact that it was during the second decade that the Ames Company, an enterprise employing skilled metal workers, enjoyed considerable expansion. Skilled metal workers were able to spend more on goods that would yield a profit then could the factory operatives, and doubtless this permitted some trade growth. The system of semi-annual wage payment in the mills from 1825 to 1836 may possibly have retarded the opening of many stores. As long as this situation lasted, the merchant had to extend credit to his customers for six month periods. Under the new conditions of payment the merchant's capital requirements were not as great as had hitherto been the case, and this would automatically extend the field to smaller mercantile investment, and correspondingly enable more persons to make such investments.

Lawyers were not long in following the new property owners

[2] C. W. Chapin, *op. cit.*, 85.
[3] *Ibid.*, 135.
[4] *Ibid.*, 349.
[5] *Ibid.*
[6] *Ibid.*, 403.
[7] *Ibid.*, 89.

to the boom area. Land was being bought, houses built, deeds and contracts had to be drawn up, and a place was made for the legal profession in Chicopee. With the rapid increase of population it was soon possible for the community to support physicians and dentists, in spite of a story circulated to the effect that "the people are hale, hearty and cheerful. A physician who attempted to make a living among them was, compelled to change his quarters."[8]

An hotel was probably opened quite early. By 1852 there were five in operation.[9] Livery stables, barbers, hairdressers, dressmakers, tailors, carriage and cabinet makers followed—in other words, the establishment of trade was accompanied by a development of the professional and personal services such as would be required by the new middle class and such of the workers as could afford them.

The establishment of banking facilities came in 1845 with the incorporation of the Cabot Bank.[10] The first directorate consisted of John Chase, engineer of the Springfield Canal Company, T. W. Carter, who started out as a merchant and later was appointed agent of the Chicopee Manufacturing Company, Jerome Wells, a merchant, R. E. Bemis, agent of the Cabot Manufacturing Company, N. P. Ames, of the Ames Manufacturing Company, John Wells, a lawyer, and Homer Foot, a Springfield merchant.[11] A savings bank came in 1854, with Jerome Wells as the first president.[12] These two banks were situated in Cabotville. A savings bank was not established in Chicopee Falls until 1875.[13] The opening of the banks was the result of the needs of the merchants and small manufacturers. The cotton corporations did not need them, for their important financial work was transacted in Boston, and for petty services and payroll accomodation the Springfield banks were near enough.

The constituent elements of the new middle class were made up of four groups of economic interests. These were the mer-

[8] *Nile's Weekly Register*, Vol. 40, p. 307 (1831).
[9] G. Adams, *The Massachusetts Register*, 1852, p. 120.
[10] A. M. Copeland, *op. cit.*, III, 506. [11] Everts, *op. cit.*, II, 976.
[12] A. M. Copeland, *op. cit.*, III, 507. [13] *Ibid.*

chants, (including independent purveyors of services of various kinds) the cotton agents and overseers, the professional men, and the small manufacturers. At the outset the merchants were the backbone of the middle class by reason of their enterprise and their assumption of the leadership and direction of the new community.

One is much tempted to include the highly skilled mechanics in the ranks of the middle class. It is true that they worked for wages, but their earnings were sufficiently above those of the other wage-earning groups to enable them to identify their position with that of the business and professional men who were not a wealthy group at that time. Furthermore, their position in society and their importance to the church organizations permitted this identity of interest. This was due to the continuation of social attitudes developed during the simpler colonial and the beginning of the factory periods. For these reasons, and because of the psychological attitude which has placed office workers in the same position when actually they are wage-earners, the mechanics, for a time, occupied a place on the fringe of the middle class. It is also a moot point as to whether the boarding-house keepers should be placed in the middle class grouping. While they were financing their own enterprises and seemed to be working independently, the prices which they could charge were fixed by the corporations, and their very existence was dependent on the continued good-will of the mills. This placed them in a subsidiary position, and when one considers the conflict with the mills into which they were presently to be drawn,[14] their position resembles more that of wage-earners than of independent members of the middle class. But as they did have some measure of economic independence, they also take a border-line position.

The development and the nature of small industry during this period was dependent upon a number of factors. We have already seen that for one reason or another the industrial attempts at the end of the colonial period had proved abortive. But now there was a larger population capable of absorbing certain consumption goods made in the village, and the rapid growth of the town at-

[14] See below, p. 125 et seq.

tracted artisans who were prepared to make some efforts at manufacture, even as the merchants were attracted by the boom. Another favorable factor at this point was the need of the cotton mills for certain small products which could be supplied by local producers. Moreover the cotton waste of the mills could be used by small industry. Under these circumstances the ingenuity of the manufacturer was of obvious importance. A limiting factor was the extent of the market. So long as the transportation facilities of a region remained comparatively primitive the extent of its market for manufactured goods depended upon the ratio of their cost of transportation to their bulk and value, and this, in relationship to competing producers at different points.[15] Cotton goods, for example, which had to use a combination of team, river and rail transport, until the railway came to Chicopee in 1845, could, by reason of large-scale manufacturing advantages, reach a national market in spite of the high costs of transportation. Hardware and tools and the general run of products of the Ames and Massachusetts Arms companies[16] were able to command an extensive market because of the high value of the commodities in relation to the cost of moving them. Furthermore, the fact that some of their products were not produced under purely competitive conditions, but under patent protection, automatically extended their market even if the cost of moving the goods was high.

Under such conditions the development of local enterprise tended to follow a pattern. The existence of the cotton mills opened a home market for certain products. Cards, bobbins, reeds and loom harness were needed. The first to enter this field was the Willimansett Card Manufacturing Company, established in 1829 for the manufacture of cards and small hardware. The product was sold in the vicinity, and the sales amounted to $40,000 in 1832. The company was small, only 17 men and a few women and girls being employed.[17] The owner of the enterprise was Stephen Bemis, who at the age of fourteen left Harvard,

[15] As a matter of fact, the development of railway facilities did not so much change this situation as it tended to level the differences.

[16] See below, pp. 78, 79, 85.

[17] U. S. 22nd Cong. 1st Sess., *op. cit.*, I, 284, 285.

Massachusetts, and came to Chicopee Street to be a clerk in the store owned by Joseph Pease. He later bought the store and operated it in partnership with Chester Chapin, and then with Sylvester Chapin.[18] He finally withdrew his capital from trade and started the card factory, adding the manufacture of hardware almost immediately.[19] The Chicopee cotton mills must have been his main customers, but occasional advertisements of his cards for woolen and cotton machinery which appeared in the *Springfield Republican* in 1833 indicate that perhaps he had some sale to small mills in Western Massachusetts. An 1837 advertisement for 8 or 10 men experienced in the manufacture of hardware suggests that he was preparing to expand that branch of his business.[20] This seems to have been the case, for in 1840 he moved his plant to Springfield, starting the Bemis and Call Hardware Company.[21]

A bobbin shop supplying local needs came into existence some time before 1848. The owner was Benning Leavitt who came from Northampton, New Hampshire.[22] J. Alden was operating a shop for the manufacture of cane, steel and brass reeds for cotton and woolen weaving in 1839.[23] In 1852 he was also making loom harness, but just when he started to manufacture this product is uncertain.[24] There was a second loom harness shop in operation at this time. In 1846 two men were using waste from the mills to make cotton batting.[25] Aside from the Willimansett Manufacturing Company, there is no evidence which throws any light on the size of these shops. The absence of any newspaper comment concerning their activities suggests that they were very small and of no great account. All these shops, with the exception of the card and hardware company, perhaps, were directly dependent upon the existence of the cotton mills which either created a market for them, or furnished the necessary raw materials. Expansion in the ordinary way of business was precluded. Every other cotton center had its own independent undertakings.

[18] C. W. Chapin, *op. cit.*, 85.
[19] *Springfield Republican*, Nov. 3, 1830.
[20] *Ibid.*, April 10, 1836. [21] C. W. Chapin, *op. cit.*, 85. [22] *Ibid.*, 245.
[23] *Springfield Republican*, Aug. 10, 1839.
[24] Adams, *op. cit.*, 120.
[25] *Chicopee Telegraph*, April 11, 1846.

A second group of shops were those which manufactured consumption goods for local use, and were for the most part the kind of industries that almost any community of equal size would have. These represented the efforts of artisans to use their small savings in order to capitalize their skill in an effort to achieve economic independence. In 1838 a millinery shop advertised for 3 or 4 apprentices, and so must have been trying to make hats for the store trade in addition to those for direct retail sale.[26] H. Hutchins, who owned a millinery store, advertised for 12 straw sewers in 1846,[27] and announced his readiness to undertake the pressing and bleaching of bonnets.[28] Whether the straw sewers worked in the proprietor's premises or at home was not indicated, but as the bulk of straw products at that time was manufactured by home work, no doubt the latter arrangement was adopted.[29] In 1837 A. Nettleton advertised the sale of 100 sets of window blinds which he had manufactured,[30] and three years later E. Barnard announced the opening of a new sash and blind "factory."[31] There was a brush making shop in 1852;[32] in 1855 it had a capital of only $800 and was making brushes to the annual value of $3500. Four people were said to be employed in this enterprise.[33] A broom shop made $10,000 worth of brooms in 1855, and employed 6 men.[34] In the middle fifties there were also two saddle and harness shops which gave employment to 3 men and sold $1500 worth of goods per annum.[35] Three tinsmiths sold their products to value of $1500.[36] It would seem possible that the activities of the latter included general repair work. In 1857 C. M. Kendall took advantage of a current style to go into "the manufacture of elastic steel hoops for the ladies,"[37] but nothing else is known of his activities.

[26] *Springfield Republican*, Sept. 15, 1838.
[27] Adams, *op. cit.*, 119; *Chicopee Telegraph*, March 11, 1846.
[28] *Chicopee Telegraph*, April 1, 1846.
[29] U. S. 61st Cong. 2nd Sess., *op. cit.*, IX, 157, 158.
[30] *Springfield Republican*, Aug. 12, 1837.
[31] *Ibid.*, April 18, 1840. [32] Adams, *op. cit.*, 116.
[33] Mass., Sec'y of the Commonwealth, *Statistical Information Relating to Certain Branches of Industry in Massachusetts*, 1855, p. 215.
[34] *Ibid.*, 216. [35] *Ibid.*, 215. [36] *Ibid.*, 216.
[37] *Springfield Republican*, April 4, 1857.

All of these attempts to manufacture consumption goods were small-scale. None of them developed into anything indicative of promise. There were similar attempts elsewhere, and unless one of these producers was able to slash the costs of manufacture, or had special advantages from the point of view of raw materials, his market of necessity was limited to his own town and the nearby countryside, and he might lose that too if someone invented a process which permitted cheaper manufacture. Until that happened he was fairly secure. But with the development of adequate railway facilities competition was bound to become increasingly serious for the small local producer who enjoyed no special advantages.

A somewhat larger and apparently more vigorous enterprise than those indicated above was a boot and shoe factory organized quite early in the century in the Chicopee Street section by Otis Skeele. He was succeeded by A. G. Parker, who moved the shop to Cabotville in 1853.[38] About 30 men were employed in the shop as early as 1830, it was reported, and the market for the shoes was quite extensive, goods being shipped down the Connecticut River to Hartford and New York.[39] In 1855 the Chicopee Boot and Shoe Company was incorporated. Whether this was an entirely new venture or a reorganization of Parker's company with the investment of new capital is uncertain. An official Massachusetts report noted only one boot and shoe company in 1855, but it is possible that the second company was organized after the report was made. This one company employed 30 men and 8 women in 1855, and the annual value of the product was $17,000.[40] The Chicopee Boot and Shoe Company was incorporated with a capital of $8,000 subscribed by 25 to 30 stockholders.[41] Among the people who invested in it were John Wells, the lawyer, N. Cutler, a merchant who sold ready-made shoes among other things, G. H. Chapman, the brush-maker, T. A.

[38] A. M. Copeland, *op. cit.*, III, 497.
[39] V. Spence, *The Industrial History of Chicopee,* 4.
[40] Mass., Sec'y of the Commonwealth, *op. cit.,* 1855, p. 216.
[41] *Chicopee Weekly Journal,* May 12, 1855.

Denison, W. E. Wintworth, I. Bullens, J. A. Denison, all merchants, and J. T. Ames, of the Ames Manufacturing Company.[42]

Another enterprise of a somewhat similar nature was a woolen mill which employed 25 men and women in 1855.[43] This mill was located in Willimansett. After Bemis moved his card and hardware factory to Springfield, he probably sold or rented the plant to some woolen manufacturers. How long the enterprise lasted and what power was used is unknown. In 1855 cassimere was produced, and in 1865 satinet.[44] There was no expansion of employment during those years, nor is there any evidence available which might throw any light on the ownership of the mill.

There were a few miscellaneous enterprises at one time or another during the period. In 1837 J. Benson and T. B. Russell announced the opening of a shop for the manufacture of "turning engines and lathes, together with various kinds of tools and machinery."[45] The venture could not have lasted long, for no further word was heard of the partners. The papers of 1854 and 1855 carried occasional references to the boiler works of J. D. Ashton.[46] According to a State report of the latter year Ashton employed 9 men and turned out goods to the value of $30,000, but as there was only a capital of $2,000 reported, there seems to be some error.[47] The shop went out of existence some time before 1865. In 1856 a small factory which manufactured paring machines gave employment to about 10 hands, but lack of further information concerning it suggests that it too was short-lived.[48] Another shop which manufactured molasses gates and faucets lasted for a few years toward the end of the period.[49]

Friction matches were made on Chicopee Street during the thirties. Alonzo Phillips, a Connecticut man, had produced some

[42] Names of investors from *Springfield Republican,* May 14, 1855; Stock Certificate of Chicopee Boot and Shoe Company in *Ames Papers.* Occupations compiled from Adams, *op. cit.,* 115 et seq.
[43] Mass., Sec'y of the Commonwealth, *op. cit.,* 1855, p. 215
[44] Mass., Sec'y of the Commonwealth, *op. cit.,* 1855, p. 215; 1865, p. 246.
[45] *Springfield Republican,* June 24, 1837.
[46] *Ibid.,* April 3, 1854; *Chicopee Weekly Journal,* June 30, 1855.
[47] Mass., Sec'y of the Commonwealth, *op. cit.,* 1855, p. 215.
[48] *Springfield Republican,* Aug. 18, 1856.
[49] *Ibid.,* March 2, 1857; July 25, 1859.

friction matches near Norwich, but had no capital with which to start manufacture. Somewhere he met Daniel Chapin of Chicopee Street, and Chapin, probably the son of a farmer, was willing to finance the manufacture of matches. Phillips came to Chicopee, and with his newly-found partner started to make his matches in a very small shop in 1834. Their first sales were made in the immediate vicinity, but as their business grew they sent two wagons out into the countryside to take orders and to make deliveries. Phillips made the sulphur mixture himself, and 8 or 10 girls were employed to pack the matches, which were made up in sections on a thin wooden card in much the same way that cardboard matches are put up today. The wood was taken from the nearby woods and cut up in a local saw-mill. The actual work of making the matches was done by hand.[50]

In 1837 Phillips announced that he had obtained a patent for his matches, and that they were manufactured by Chapin and Phillips of Chicopee and by L. C. Allin and Company of Springfield.[51] It is possible that the latter was only an authorized dealer, for there is no evidence which points to the manufacture of the matches outside of the original shop on Chicopee Street. It is said that the profits that were earned were not reinvested in the business, but were squandered, so that the little company never achieved the sound basis necessary to expansion. Both Chapin and Phillips died prematurely, and it was reported that the business was carried on by the Abbey family for about 10 years. One Silas Abbey had been employed by the original proprietors.[52] This may have been so, but there is a complete lack of newspaper comment about this continuation of the business, and as the match factory was a matter of great local pride, it is doubtful if the shop remained in production far into the forties. There is not enough information available about this industrial episode to throw any light on the reasons for its final disappearance. Had it been situated in Cabotville or in Chicopee Falls, some of the local mer-

[50] Newspaper Clipping, Chicopee Public Library; *Springfield Republican,* June 13, 1897.
[51] *Springfield Republican,* Jan. 21, 1837.
[52] *Ibid.,* June 13, 1897.

chants might have become interested in the enterprise. As it was it left the scene quietly without leaving much mark in the records of the day.

It will have been noted that none of this industrial activity had any roots in the pre-industrial period. The personalities concerned were newcomers for the most part. The same was true of the merchants. However, there was one enterprise of long standing which developed with the town—the Belcher Iron Works. These had been started in 1786; in 1801 Benjamin Belcher was one of the proprietors, and he had gained sole control of the business in 1805. He had manufactured iron castings, it will be recalled, receiving some trade from the cotton companies. When he died in 1833 his three sons, Benjamin B., John W. and Bildad B. carried on the business until 1846 when John W. became the sole proprietor.[53] The Belcher brothers had no doubt worked in the shop with their father, and were craftsmen. In 1846, when John W. took over the company, he started to manufacture agricultural implements.[54] At this time John R. Whittemore, who had been employed in a plow company in Worcester, came to work for Belcher, and became a member of the firm in 1851.[55] George L. Squier, a local lawyer, was a member of the firm from 1852 till 1857.[56] It is possible that the coming of the railroad to Chicopee Falls in 1846 permitted this specialization in the manufacture of agricultural implements by opening up a wider market. The business expanded quite steadily, and after some recession in 1853[57] the plant was enlarged, and the company made plows, cultivators, harrows, corn shellers, hay cutters, and other farm tools, and was selling them in various parts of the country. Plows seem to have been the principal product, however, and during the season in 1857, six to seven hundred were turned out monthly.[58] In 1860 some exports were being made to South America.[59]

[53] A. M. Copeland, *op. cit.*, III, 498. [54] *Ibid.*

[55] *Springfield Republican*, Jan. 18, 1891.

[56] A. M. Copeland, *op. cit.*, III, 498. The name of the company was changed several times during the period, being known as Belcher and Company, Whittemore, Squier and Company, and Whittemore, Belcher and Company. [57] *Taylor Diary*, March 2. 1854.

[58] *Springfield Republican*, May 5, 1856; April 4, 1857.

[59] *Ibid.*, May 17, 1860.

After the original Belcher company was dissolved and John W. had organized what came to be known as the Whittemore, Belcher Company, his brother, Bildad B., started another factory. Together with Bailey West, who had been employed by the Ames Company, and George Dunlap, he rented space from the Massachusetts Arms Company, and started to manufacture feed cutters.[60] West and Dunlap withdrew from the firm in 1854-55,[61] and at about this time Belcher added a subsidiary product to his shop's output—curtain fixtures.[62] Belcher found himself in difficulties in the panic of 1857, but his creditors permitted a settlement, and in the subsequent depression, when the demand for feed cutters fell off, the curtain fixture business helped to keep the shop in operation.[63] As business picked up he was able to concentrate on the manufacture of feed cutters again, and he sold the curtain fixture business and machinery to a Boston firm.[64] The sale of this branch of the business and the fact that Belcher had been obliged to sell his house in 1856 in order to get money to put more capital into the business point to the fact that he had been operating with a very small capital from the beginning.[65]

These two Belcher companies were the only enterprises which grew up with the town from early days. The sale of Belcher land to the Chicopee Manufacturing Company released some money for investment in the iron works. Some professional money went into the Whittemore, Belcher Company, as in the case of the Squier investment, and Whittemore's stake represented an investment of savings and the reinvestment of profits. Some profits must have been plowed back into both companies before they were withdrawn. Real growth came with the national railway development of the fifties and the rapid opening of the West.

To this point we have seen that local industry in its various aspects was not so much an investment of savings as a method of making a living for various artisans and craftsmen who possessed small capital resources. Except for Squier's investment in the

[60] *Taylor Diary,* March 2, 1853.
[61] *Ibid.,* March 2, 1856; A. M. Copeland, *op. cit.,* III, 498.
[62] *Taylor Diary,* March 2, 1857.
[63] *Ibid.,* Nov. 29, 1857, March 2, 1858.
[64] *Ibid.,* Oct. 29, 1859.
[65] *Ibid.,* Aug. 13, 1856.

Whittemore, Belcher Company, and one or two other unimportant exceptions, it was almost universally true that all the men who were interested in manufacturing establishments worked in them, and had no other means of livelihood.

At an early period an attempt was made to establish an "investment" industry. Certain men were willing to buy shares in a local incorporated company, and delegate the management thereof to one or more of their members. The first of these was the Chicopee Falls Company, organized in 1836, with an authorized capital of $25,000, for the purpose of manufacturing hardware and firearms.[66] In 1839 the capital authorization was raised to $100,000.[67] The president of the company was T. W. Carter who at the time was agent of the Chicopee Manufacturing Company. Others interested were David M. Bryant, first merchant in Chicopee Falls and Carter's erstwhile partner, John Chase, manager of the Springfield Canal Company, T. W. Buckland, and Benjamin Belcher.[68] N. P. Ames, of the Ames Manufacturing Company, was also an investor.[69] Thus the capital was drawn from mercantile and metal manufacturing profits and from managerial earnings. There is no information available as to the progress of the company, or how much money was actually invested. At the beginning of 1841 the company was forced out of business, advertising the sale of all its property—land, power site, machine shops, tools, guns, saws, and a few tenements.[70] The company was reported to have been in difficulties the previous year, its misfortunes being ascribed in part to inefficiency and bad management.[71] The entire property was bought up by the Ames Manufacturing Company.[72]

In 1849 some of these men were ready to try another investment, and they were more successful in their second attempt. The Chicopee Falls shops which had been sold to Ames in 1841 were re-purchased, and men were put to work making pistols under the

[66] Mass., 1836 *Private and Special Statutes,* C. 163.
[67] *Ibid.,* 1839, C. 37.
[68] *Ibid.,* 1836, C. 163; *Springfield Republican,* March 16, 1839.
[69] *Ames Papers,* Memorandum of Meeting of the Chicopee Falls Company.
[70] *Springfield Republican,* Feb. 20, 1841.
[71] *Ames Papers,* Letters, J. K. Mills to N. P. Ames, July 31, 1840.
[72] Holland, *op. cit.,* II, 48.

direction of T. W. Carter.[73] In a few months the company secured incorporation as the Massachusetts Arms Company, with an authorized capital of $70,000, for the manufacture of firearms, sewing machines and other machinery.[74] In addition to Carter, J. T. Ames, John Chase, T. Warner, Chester W. Chapin and R. A. Chapman invested in the company.[75] Warner was a Springfield man, and an experienced millwright. He worked in the Springfield Armory, and was a master armorer by 1842. He managed the Whitneyville Firearms Works for a time and then came to Chicopee Falls to start work with the newly organized Massachusetts Arms Company.[76] Another gun maker who came to Chicopee in 1849 to work in the new company was J. Stevens who had manufactured Colt's gun in Hartford. A gun of his invention was to be made by the new arms company.[77]

The company was soon employing 60 to 70 men and was doing very well indeed when Colt sued for patent infringement.[78] Colt won his case, and it was rumored that this affair had proved to be very costly for the company, and that $25,000 had to be paid to Colt in order to settle the case.[79] As was to be expected, production fell off and a number of men found themselves out of work, but the purchase of the rights to manufacture the Maynard rifle permitted their reëmployment in a short time.[80]

[73] *Taylor Diary,* Sept. 28, Nov. 6, 1849.

[74] Holland, *op. cit.,* II, 44.

[75] Mass., 1850 *Private and Special Statutes,* C. 53. Chester W. Chapin was to become one of the most important business men of the Connecticut Valley. It will be recalled that for a time he had operated a country store on Chicopee Street. He was later engaged in local ox team transport in Springfield and in the operation of stage coach lines. He transferred his investments to Connecticut River steamship lines with the coming of steam river transport. When this, in turn, gave way to railway transportation, he shifted his investments to the New England roads. After serving as president of the Connecticut River railroad he became president of the Boston and Albany road. *(Dictionary of American Biography)* R. A. Chapman was a Springfield lawyer, one of whose clients was John Brown. This association between Chapman and Brown no doubt explains the latter's relations with the Massachusetts Arms Company as described below. (Green, *op. cit.,* 506.)

[76] C. W. Chapin, *op. cit.,* 380.

[77] *Springfield Republican,* Jan. 22, 1907.

[78] *Taylor Diary,* July 16, 1850; July 7, 1851.

[79] *Ibid.,* Jan. 26, 1853; Everts, *op. cit.,* II, 972.

[80] *Ibid.,* Aug. 9, Oct. 13, Nov. 4, 1851.

The winter of 1852-53 was dull for the Arms Company.[81] The next year however, they were kept quite busy making sewing machines, and their prospects were bright,[82] as well they might be, for very soon they were selling rifles to the United States government and to Great Britain, and curiously enough, were receiving orders for gun-making machinery from Colt.[83] They did not seem to suffer any setback in the panic of 1857, for just a few months later they were employing 100 men.[84] There was some loss sustained in 1859, but the next year this was more than made up, for the company earned a great deal of money.[85]

A number of factors contributed to the success of a gun factory at this time. The investors had been able to secure skilled direction and mechanical ingenuity in the persons of Warner and Stevens. By 1849 T. W. Carter, who managed the enterprise, had had a great deal of experience in plant management behind him, for he had been the agent of the Chicopee Manufacturing Company, and had probably learned much in his attempts to make the Chicopee Falls Company a success. J. T. Ames who was interested in the company, was managing a very successful firm, and had contacts with Washington which may have been of some service to the Massachusetts Arms Company. His advice must have been very valuable. The existence of the Springfield Armory nearby meant that there was a nucleus of skilled labor available. An expanding frontier and unsettled conditions in the South made a good market for firearms.

This latter situation, for instance, led to the sale of guns to John Brown who had lived in Springfield for a time; he may have been personally acquainted with T. W. Carter. We have already pointed out that Chapman, his Springfield attorney, was a stockholder in the Arms Company. In 1850 Brown had an account in the Cabot Bank in Chicopee.[86] In 1855 the company sent a shipment of arms to Brown which elicited the following reply:

[81] *Ibid.,* Jan. 6, 1853.
[82] *Ibid.,* Jan. 23, March 2, 1854. [83] *Ibid.,* March 2, 1856.
[84] *Springfield Republican,* June 13, 1858.
[85] *Taylor Diary,* Jan. 29, 1860, March 2, 1861.
[86] C. G. Burnham, "The City of Chicopee," *New England Magazine,* Vol. 18, New Series, 365. (May, 1898).

Osawatomie, Kansas Territory,
20th February 1856

T. W. Carter Esq. Agt
Chicopee Falls
Mass
Dear Sir

Your kind favor of the 5th Jany was received a few days since, mentioning receipt of Draft and offering a further supply of arms. I would again immediately take the responsibility of ordering another lot, but I am not at this moment prepared to say how I would *dare* to have them directed. The other lot I came on with myself, bringing with them other Arms contributed by the Friends of Freedom in Mass. and other parts. I cannot just now name anyone who is coming on, suitable to take charge of them. Gen. Pomeroy went East lately, but I do not know where a letter would find him. I now think I shall immediately make a *further and more earnest* appeal to the lovers of Freedom in New England for the means of procuring Arms and Ammunition for the maintenance of that cause in Kansas, as I think the crisis *has not yet come.* I firmly believe that the Administration intends to drive the people here to an abject submission, or to fight the Government troops (now in the territory ostensibly to remove intruders from certain Indian lands). Bow in submission to the vilest tyranny or be guilty of what *will be called treason,* will I believe be the next and only alternative for the Free State men of Kansas. O God must this thing be? Must the people here shoot down the poor soldier with whom they have no quarrel? Can you not through your extensive acquaintance aid me in this work, if you can be satisfied that I am *trustworthy.* I am well known by many at Springfield. I very much want a lot of the Carbines as soon as I can see any *way clear* to pay for them, and to get them through safe. Please write me the lowest terms at wholesale for just such Carbines as you furnish the government. I may write you further within a few days.

Very Respectfully Your Friend
JOHN BROWN.[87]

Carter, the managing director of the company, offered to supply Brown with 200 guns at a reduction of 50 per cent because, he wrote, he wished to help "in your project of protecting the free state settlers of Kansas and securing their rights to the institutions of *free America.*" Possibly Carter felt uneasy about these shipments, for he added that he hoped "that there may be no occasion

[87] John Brown to T. W. Carter. This letter is in the possession of Mr. N. P. Ames Carter of Chicopee Falls.

for their services in securing rights which ought to be guaranteed by the principles of justice and equality . . . we have no fear that they will be put to service in your hands for other purposes."[88]

Another enterprise, one which in many respects was as important as the cotton corporations, for it gave, in its time, employment to large numbers of skilled male workers, was the Ames Manufacturing Company. Strictly speaking, it was not a "local" company, for the majority control was vested in the hands of the Boston associates. But the company was actively managed for many years by the Ames brothers, Nathan Peabody and James Tyler, and they were residents of the community and owned fairly large blocks of the stock. There were also a few shares held by other residents of the town. The Ames brothers were clever mechanics and were given a free hand by the Boson associates who financed their mechanical ability.

When they first came to Chicopee Falls in 1829 they started to manufacture cutlery and hardware in a small shop which gave employment to only 9 workers.[89] For the next few years they did a great variety of work, making mechanical repairs for the cotton and paper mills, building shafts and fixing bolts, making knives for the rag machines of the paper mill. In 1830 they were manufacturing knives and small tools which were sold through local merchants. Thus a miscellaneous lot was "left with Mr. Dwight at 10 per cent commission or 13 per cent cash in advance."[90] In the next two or three years the business expanded rapidly, a great deal of merchandise going to Hartford and New York by direct consignment, as well as to nearer towns, and some as far as Philadelphia. The goods were either ordered and paid for immediately, or taken by the merchant to be sold on a commission basis. In 1832 the company was making spindles for the Chicopee Manufacturing Company, and doing odd jobs for the Willimansett Card Company.[91] In that year the bulk of the product, valued at $10,000, consisted of chisels, axes and hatchets, hammers, adzes, paper knives, drawing knives, and a variety of

[88] O. G. Villard, *John Brown,* 289. [89] Holland, *op. cit.,* II, 48.
[90] *Ames Papers,* Account Book, 1830.
[91] *Ibid.,* 1830-32.

small miscellaneous tools.[92] Some American iron was used at this time, but most of the raw material consisted of Russian and Swedish iron.[93]

We already know that Edmund Dwight was responsible for bringing the Ames brothers to Chicopee, and that he and his partner, J. K. Mills were planning to expand the business. But to this point the products of the company, while varied, were comparatively simple, and the books which record the transactions are really no more than small business account books. However in 1831 and 1833 we find that this small company was selling swords to the United States government,[94] which was quite an advance for a firm which not long since had sold a butcher knife for 50 cents, and accepted some apples in payment.[95] Before long the company was able to use the following testimonial:

Ordnance Office,
Washington, Sept. 25, 1835

The bearer of this, Mr. Nathan P. Ames of Springfield, Mass., has been extensively engaged in the manufacture of swords and sabres for the United States, for several years past, and has given entire satisfaction to this Department in all his engagements with it.

The work that he has finished and delivered for the Government has been very superior in quality and workmanship, and as far as is within the knowledge of this Department he is equal, if not superior as a Cutler to anyone known in this country.

Signed by Colonel of Ordnance.[96]

There is no doubt that the Ames Company was making a fine product, but it is very possible that contacts in Washington were first made with the assistance of J. K. Mills and his Boston friends. Some of the correspondence which appears below tends to confirm this idea.

If they had not already done so before, Mills and Dwight invested money in the enterprise in 1834, incorporating the company with a capital of $30,000. The plant, now employing 35 men, was moved to Cabotville.[97] In 1836 the government contracts

[92] U. S. 22nd Cong. 1st Sess., *op. cit.*, I, 288, 289.

[93] *Ibid.*

[94] *Ames Papers*, Letter, 1833; J. L. Bishop, *History of American Manufactures*, II, 687.

[95] *Ames Papers*, Account Book, 1829.

[96] *Ames Papers*.

[97] Holland, *op. cit.*, II, 48.

were important enough for N. P. Ames to go to Washington to solicit business in person, and while there he succeeded in getting an order for a number of swords for naval officers.[98] In 1840 he was sent to England and France on a government mission to study foreign methods of ordnance manufacture. It was as a recognized munitions expert that he was sent abroad.[99]

While N. P. Ames was in Europe his brother was left in full charge of the business at home. The government orders which were very profitable were falling off, and J. K. Mills' letters to N. P. Ames at this point throw some light on the reasons for the decline.

> Business is at a low ebb, but we think will generally improve, partly from real causes, such as bountiful crops and habits of economy with people, and partly from imaginary ones such as a change in the administration which we are confidently looking for. We should look upon the latter, in truth, as a *real* blessing, for it would inspire many with confidence who are now broken down, and it is not improbable that it would lead to a change of measures which would give more stability and security to property and business. But we have very little confidence in any party. The leading men in both go for the loaves and fishes and by far the larger part of both are either fools or knaves. . . . Your brother has lately been at Washington, but without much success. The truth is, the government are so poor, that any expenditure which can be avoided must be put off. We have no expectation that much work will be found for the shop, but we have the most entire confidence in your brother's good judgment in managing the business, so that if we should not have a profitable year we shall at least continue to pay our expenses.[100]

It was at this time that Mills wrote that it would be possible to buy up the Chicopee Falls Company, as it was on the verge of bankruptcy.[101] Apparently it was the government business which yielded most of the profits at this time, and with government orders lacking, Mills asked Ames to look about for "any kind of goods in England which can be manufactured at a large and certain profit."[102] It seems that it was because of Mills' desire for "large and certain" profits that he was looking forward to a change in

[98] *Ames Papers,* Letters, N. P. Ames to J. K. Mills, Jan. 5, 28, 1836.
[99] *Dictionary of American Biography.*
[100] *Ames Papers,* Letters, J. K. Mills to N. P. Ames, July 31, 1840.
[101] *Ibid.* [102] *Ibid.*

administration despite, or perhaps because of, his cynical attitude. He was soon writing that "it is fully certain . . . that we have nothing to expect from the kindness and friendship of the officers of the Ordnance department."[103] However, it was not long before Mills reported that prospects for business were improving. "There will be a change in the administration, and no doubt an entire change in the policy of the War department. We think it probable that large contracts will be offered, and it may be important for you to be here . . . Colonel . . . writes your brother that we may soon expect to hear from that department and that if no swords should be ordered immediately it is probable that a few cannon will be wanted. So that there is good prospect for work for a few weeks."[104] It was felt that a government contract would make possible the purchase of the Chicopee Falls Company's shop where it was planned to manufacture new products.

Whether the profits permitted it or not, the Ames Company bought up the property of the defunct Chicopee Falls Company in 1841, expanding its capital to $75,000 in order to do so.[105] The business outlook was probably quite good. In 1839 electro-plating and gilding had been introduced;[106] the next year a large bell was cast for a Hartford church and another for the New York City Hall.[107] In 1845 there were 130 men employed in the manufacture of swords and cutlery, machinery, firearms, cannon, and in various bronze and brass castings. The total value of the product was $132,000.[108]

In 1845 the capital of the company was increased to $200,000, and the property and plant of the Springfield Canal Company were taken over.[109] It must have been at about this time that the Boston associates joined Mills and Dwight in the project. No doubt more cash was put into the company, but as the Springfield Canal Company was already owned by the Boston associates, the greater

[103] *Ibid.,* J. K. Mills to N. P. Ames, Jan. 12, 1841.
[104] *Ibid.,* J. K. Mills to N. P. Ames, Oct. 31, 1841.
[105] Holland, *op. cit.,* II, 48.
[106] *Ames Papers,* Miscellaneous Papers, 1864.
[107] *Ibid.,* Letters, N. P. Ames to J. K. Mills, Feb. 27, 1840; C. W. Chapin, *op. cit.,* 25.
[108] *Ames Papers,* Memo. of Statistics, 1845.
[109] Holland, *op. cit.,* II, 48.

part of the transaction must have consisted of the exchange of one stock certificate for another. Two years later the stock was held in the following proportions:[110]

	shares		*shares*
J. K. Mills and Co.	70	John Bryant	10
N. P. Ames	56	J. P. Cushing	10
Edmund Dwight	40	W. H. Gardiner	10
J. T. Ames	28	S. Hooper	10
I. Sargent	26	Theodore Lyman	10
T. H. Perkins	20	G. W. Lyman	10
Samuel Cabot	12	Harriette Mills	10
Henry Cabot	12	W. Sturgis	10
William Appleton	10	H. Timmins	10

In addition to these a few shares were held by T. W. Carter, Sylvester Adams, agent of the Dwight Manufacturing Company, Robert Bemis, agent of the Cabot Manufacturing Company, John Chase, and two or three others. The board of directors in 1850 consisted of William Sturgis, William Appleton, Samuel Cabot, Ignatius Sargent, and probably J. T. Ames.[111]

The expansion and reorganization of the company in 1845 could not have been better timed. The Mexican War was not long in coming, and the shops were kept busy making swords and firearms and cannon for the army. At the close of the war followed a rather astonishing example of industrial "integration." With the drop in demand for service swords, the company turned to the manufacture of presentation swords for the heroes of the war, and in two years sold about $25,000 worth of fine swords, ranging in value from $30 to over $1000 a piece.[112]

By 1848 there were in all 300 men employed in the Ames shops. Of these, 220 were employed in the machine shops, especially in the manufacture of cotton machinery and water wheels, while the rest of the men operated the foundry and produced weapons, mostly for the United States government.[113] In 1849 the Chicopee Falls plant was sold to the Massachusetts Arms Company, as we know,

[110] *Ames Papers,* Dividend Book, 1847.
[111] *Chicopee Telegraph,* Jan. 23, 1850.
[112] *Ames Papers,* Memo. of Mexican War Presentation Swords.
[113] *Ibid.,* Statement signed by J. T. Ames, Oct. 6, 1848.

and production was confined to the Cabotville shops. The next year the capital was raised to $250,000.[114]

In 1851 J. K. Mills was again dissatisfied with the company's prospects. He wrote to J. T. Ames, the active manager of the shops after the death of his brother, that

> In looking over your accounts for the last year and considering the gloomy prospect before us, the questions occur which it may be well to examine and determine now. We can go on making machinery as we did the last year at a probable loss.
>
> We may find work of another description for the shops which would require a small outlay for (?) and which promises a profit.
>
> We can close the shops for making machinery and confine ourselves to the business of making cannon, swords, and iron castings.
>
> The first two would require all the present capital. The second would permit of a reduction of one fifth, and enable you to pay your stockholders dividends of ten per cent on the balance.
>
> My own opinion is that the expenses of your machinery shops should be reduced to the lowest point by dismissing as many of the overlookers and principal men as you can part with and still retain sufficient force to make the slight alterations, additions, and experiments, which the new work of plating and other things which may follow, may require.
>
> If after having failed in an experiment with such new things as promise the best results we should find ourselves with no better prospect than the present in regard to cotton machinery, it will be time enough to reduce the capital and confine your operations principally to work for the Government.[115]

It would seem that the manufacture of industrial machinery did not yield profits such as were obtained from government arms contracts. Dividends had fallen to 10 per cent in 1851.[116]

In 1853 the company added the manufacture of bronze statuary to its products.[117] In addition to this, it was making cotton and woolen machinery, tools, turbine water wheels, iron and bronze castings, swords and belts, plated ware, belting and engine hose, shafting, pulleys, and general factory equipment.[118] Its gun stocking machinery was sold all over Europe.[119]

[114] *Chicopee Telegraph,* Jan. 23, 1850.
[115] *Ames Papers,* Letters, J. K. Mills to J. T. Ames, Feb. 27, 1851.
[116] See Table 2.
[117] L. L. Johnson, *Chicopee Illustrated,* 66.
[118] Mass., Sec'y of the Commonwealth, *op. cit.,* 1855, p. 217.
[119] J. W. Roe, *English and American Tool Builders,* 229.

Table 2. Dividends Paid By the Ames Manufacturing Company, 1847-1875.*

Dividend Number	Date	Per Cent Paid	Dividend Number	Date	Per Cent Paid
1	January, 1847	20	16	December, 1862	20
2	February, 1848	20	17	June, 1863	12
3	February, 1849	25	18	November, 1863	12
4	February, 1850	20	19	February, 1864	20
5	January, 1851	10	20	January, 1865	25
6	February, 1852	10	21	January, 1866	25
7	January, 1853	10	22	September, 1866	10
8	January, 1854	6	23	January, 1867	25
9	January, 1855	5	24	January, 1868	8
10	January, 1856	8	25	January, 1869	6
	1857	0		1870	0
	1858	0	26	April, 1871	5
11	January, 1859	8		1872	0
12	December, 1859	8		1873	0
13	January, 1861	10	27	June, 1874	5
14	December, 1861	12	28	January, 1875	5
15	June, 1862	12			

* *Ames Paper,* Dividend Book, 1847-1875.

Profits were moderate during the middle fifties, but the directors tended to pay out in dividends as much of the operating profits as possible. James Tyler Ames, as the manager of the business, felt the need of building up some kind of reserve, of cutting down the outstanding indebtedness as much as possible, before paying dividends. If dividends were paid up to the hilt, it was up to him, as the director of the production side of the company, to produce more profits in order to keep the company in a fair operating condition. The tendency to pay out all the operating profit was, to some extent, a means of applying pressure on him to produce more profits. This conflict between the technical and pecuniary aspects of a modern business undertaking is well illustrated by Ames' letters in 1855 to J. K. Mills. He wrote three letters in as many days, saying, "No one *wants* or *needs* a dividend more than the writer, but I shall prefer a *small* one if any, until we are a little clearer from a few large accounts," and "I hope no dividend will be made until at least one of the large (mining?) accounts are arranged." Still again, he expressed the hope that "although we have 10 per cent of profits on hand . . . the directors will not divide more than 6 per cent."[120] But his plea was disregarded by the directors who paid out 8 per cent.[121]

Toward the close of the period the Ames Company was indirectly responsible for starting a new enterprise. This was the Gaylord Manufacturing Company, a factory started in a small way by Emerson Gaylord. He was a South Hadley man who had been apprenticed to a harness maker for a short time, and then had learnt how to make gaiter boots. In 1841 he came to Chicopee to work in the Ames shops, and started by making harness and then sword scabbards and general military accoutrements. In 1843 he arranged to work for Ames under contract, furnishing the leather goods which Ames needed.[122] This arrangement was no doubt more profitable to him than working as head of a department, and in 1856 he bought the department from Ames, and started out entirely on his own, with about a dozen workers.[123] He now added the manufacture of leather hose and machine belting.[124] He worked on government orders for military goods from the start, and in 1861 contracted to make mail bags for the Post Office.[125]

We may now stop to consider the interrelationships of the various elements of the industrial community. So far as the greater part of the working population was concerned, the cotton mills constituted the heart of economic life. The very existence of some of the small manufactures was dependent on the continued and steady operation of the cotton mills. This is obvious, of course, for those producers and their employees who manufactured mill supplies. Other petty producers were dependent on sustained consumer demand which was largely conditioned by the level of mill employment and earnings. In the same way, the merchants were at the mercy of the corporations, for any change in wages had immediate repercussions on retail trade. On the other hand, when the arms companies worked at capacity, the larger earnings of the metal workers swelled mercantile profits. In the case of the Ames Company the connection with the cotton mills is plain.

[120] *Ames Paper,* Letters, J. T. Ames to J. K. Mills, Dec. 25, Dec. 27, 1855.

[121] See Table 2.

[122] Everts, *op. cit.,* II, 982.

[123] *Springfield Republican,* Aug. 25, 1856; W. T. Davis, *The New England States,* I, 425.

[124] Everts, *op. cit.,* II, 982.

[125] *Ibid.*

The capital requirements of the Massachusetts Arms Company were met by the combined efforts of local merchants and important salaried employees of the mills. A stimulus to general economic activity in the forties may be ascribed to the fact that capital was imported by the Ames and Dwight companies, and that individuals owning some capital were attracted to the town. There was also railway building in the neighborhood.

Trade was reported excellent in 1843 and 1844.[126] As a matter of fact cotton mill wages fell off somewhat in this period, but the general development, and the bustle of building up a community contributed to local business prosperity. In 1845 it was said that "there is a spurt of improvement in town unequalled in this part of the State. They are building some elegant blocks for stores on Main Street and the old stores are having new fronts put into them. . . . I never saw so much building going on in town as at present. It looks like a city."[127] The next year, 1846, was likewise encouraging to the merchants, for the Chicopee Manufacturing Company was increasing its labor force and the Ames shops were growing rapidly, employing more men than ever before.[128] But the combination of high food prices and low board rates presented a discouraging outlook for the winter of 1847-48. "The prospects for business are not very flattering for the coming winter," wrote a merchant, "for provisions are very high and board is low."[129] His fears were substantiated, for while trade was quite brisk in the spring of 1848, there followed a period of poor business from 1849 to 1851.[130]

There were ups and downs during the fifties, but on the whole times were not very good.[131] There occurred a fall in population from 1850 to 1860, a factor which alone was capable of affecting established retail trade adversely. The decrease of population in Chicopee during the fifties[132] is not easy to explain. It is natural to expect some recession after a boom. When the rapid development of the thirties and forties came to an end, certain people who per-

[126] *Taylor Diary,* passim, 1843, 1844.
[127] *Ibid.,* June 10, 1845.
[128] *Ibid.,* Oct. 10, 1846.
[129] *Ibid.,* Nov. 18, 1847.
[130] *Ibid.,* May 6, 1848; 1849-51, passim.
[131] *Ibid.,* March 2, 1855.
[132] See Table 3.

haps could not adjust themselves to conditions in the community, left. But it is hard to believe that this would account for a 12.4 per cent decrease from 1850 to 1860. There was some westward

TABLE 3. POPULATION OF CHICOPEE, 1850-1870*

Year	Male	Female	Total
1850	....	....	8291
1855	3257	4319	7576
1860	3174	4087	7261
1865	....	....	7577
1870	....	....	9607

* U. S., *Seventh, Eighth, Ninth Census;* Mass., *Census of 1855, 1865.*

migration from 1855 to 1857,[133] but in view of the absence of any impression made on contemporary observers it could not have assumed the proportions of a movement. Part of the decrease in population may, perhaps, be ascribed to the downward pressure on wages and the intensification of work in the cotton mills during the period.

Thus the business dislocation of 1857-58, resulting in short time employment and extensive wage reductions in the industrial establishments was felt by the merchants very keenly. In 1860 George Taylor wrote that it was becoming increasingly difficult to make a living from retail trade.[134] We do not know for certain whether this difficulty was shared by all the members of the mercantile group. Probably it was, for Taylor was a capable and extremely successful business man. Furthermore, judging from the fact that in the years following 1860 fewer merchants seemed to achieve higher economic and social levels than was noticeable among those who had established themselves from 1835 to 1850 or thereabouts, it is probable that actual and potential mercantile profits were smaller than before. This condition should be kept in mind as we come to consider the subsequent fortunes of the middle class. The expansion of the latter was largely dependent on opportunities for successful investment in retail trade. Already at this comparatively early stage it was apparent that such opportunities were limited.

[133] *Springfield Republican,* May 21, 1855; May 20, 1857.
[134] *Taylor Diary,* July 8, 1860.

During this period of the development of local enterprise, there is little to say about the activities of the cotton mills. It may be noted, however, that in 1852 the Cabot and Perkins companies merged and in 1856 consolidated with the Dwight Manufacturing company.[135] This eliminated a few of the supervisory employees, but not enough to make any mark. The oldest mills installed some new machinery, and made fairly extensive repairs in the fifties.[136] But in addition to their manufacturing operations the corporations did help to finance some "public" works, one of which, at least, was beyond the capital resources of the local business men. In 1849 the cotton mills and the Ames Company organized a gas light company which was primarily intended to illuminate the factories, and the mills invested in the Connecticut River Railway, a north-south road which brought rail connections to Chicopee, and in the Cabot and West Springfield Bridge,[137] spanning the Connecticut River.

Chicopee did not escape a touch of gold fever when the California discoveries became known, but the infection was very slight, and the Yankee merchants responded in characteristic fashion. A meeting was held "to get up a company for California to dig gold."[138] Stock was sold, and the company adventurer, a Mr. Meloney, made arrangements to secure passage for California. The stockholders, recognizing that the life of a forty-niner would be hazardous, insured Meloney's life for $2000.[139] Another company which was sending a Mr. Hough decided to join forces with the first company, and Hough and Meloney set out for California within a few days of the organization of the companies.[140] In the end, Taylor wrote that "the California Company that sent Hough and Meloney out have never received anything from them but letters, although Hough owns one quarter of a vessel which he has sent home,"[141] and the sale of this prevented the investment from

[135] A. M. Copeland, *op. cit.*, III, 503.

[136] *Taylor Diary,* March 2, 1854; *Company "B" Papers,* Journal, 1854.

[137] A. M. Copeland, *op. cit.*, III, 505; *Company "A" Journal,* 1845; *Company "B" Semi-annual Statements,* 1852.

[138] *Taylor Diary,* Dec. 20, 1848.

[139] *Ibid.,* Jan. 1-11, 1849.

[140] *Ibid.,* Jan. 19-29, 1849.

[141] *Ibid.,* March 2, 1851.

being a total loss.[142] Hough returned from California at the end of 1851 and spent a day in Taylor's store where "the eager listeners to his recital is amusing to see—especially those who have the fever."[143] Hough's enthusiasm sent a few men off to the gold fields that winter.[144]

The middle class in this period was purely Yankee. Of all the names of merchants and professionals, small manufacturers and independent artisans, which appeared in a business directory of 1852, only three were unmistakably Irish, although there was a considerable Irish population in the town at the time.[145] In 1848 when Chicopee separated from Springfield and incorporated as an independent town, of a long list of officers elected, no more than one or two were Irish. Even the constables were all Yankees. The town was governed by a combination of the middle class and the farmers of the community; the latter were a small group. A few skilled workers were appointed to minor posts.[146]

As mercantile and industrial life in the new community settled down, Chicopee did not neglect to enjoy itself. While, as in the thirties, the church constituted the most important centre for social activity, amusement in the later period became secularized to a considerable extent. This does not mean that the functions of the church were usurped, but that a new field of social amusement and activity was opened up. As a matter of fact church activities constituted the most important element of social life in the period, supplying even excitement at fairly regular intervals during revival periods. A religious revival ushered in the "fabulous forties." "There is the greatest religious excitement here that has ever been known," wrote J. T. Ames to his brother, who was abroad at the time, "the streets are crowded every evening and day when there is a meeting."[147] Such activity could not be sustained for very long, but there were periodic revivals throughout the period.[148]

But secular recreation was likewise of importance. It was a period of lectures and talk and argument. Increased newspaper

[142] *Ibid.*, Aug. 29, 1851.
[143] *Ibid.*, Dec. 24, 1851.
[144] *Ibid.*, Jan.-Feb. 1852.
[145] Adams, *op. cit.*, 115 et seq.
[146] See Table 4.
[147] *Ames Papers*, Letters. J. T. Ames to N. P. Ames, Feb. 25, 1841.
[148] *Taylor Diary*, passim.

TABLE 4. OCCUPATIONS OF SELECTMEN, 1848-1858, AND OF ALL OTHER TOWN OFFICERS FOR THE YEAR 1848*

Year	Office	Office Holder	Occupation
1848......	Selectmen...........	S. Adams.........	Agent, Dwight Manufacturing Co.
		E. Blake..........	Agent, Chicopee Manufacturing Co.
		A. G. Parker......	Shoe Manufacturer
		H. Rowley........	Farmer
		A. W. Stockwell...	Lawyer
1850......		Bildad Belcher....	Plow Manufacturer
		G. S. Chapin.....	Farmer
		N. Cutler.........	Merchant
		L. E. Ladd.......	Baker
		John Wells.......	Lawyer
1852......		A. B. Abbey......	Carpenter—Merchant
		J. Herrick........	
		C. R. Ladd.......	Lawyer
		M. Pease.........	Probably a Farmer
		G. S. Taylor......	Merchant—Manufacturer
1854......		T. W. Carter.....	Manufacturer
		Austin Chapin....	Probably a Farmer
		N. Cutler........	Merchant
		B. Leavitt........	Bobbin Manufacturer
		J. H. Smith.......	
1856......		O. Chapman......	Cotton Mill Paymaster
		J. A. Denison.....	Merchant
		A. Hubbard......	Merchant
		D. Randall.......	
1858......		G. S. Chapin......	Farmer
		O. Chapman......	Cotton Mill Paymaster
		J. H. Churchill....	
		T. A. Denison.....	Merchant
		J. E. Marsh......	
1848......	Assessors............	S. Adams.........	Agent, Dwight Manufacturing Co.
		A. Bullens........	Merchant
		H. Rowley........	Farmer
	School Committee....	E. B. Clarke......	Clergyman
		R. Kellen.........	Clergyman
		J. G. Warren.....	Clergyman
	Overseers of the Poor.	C. Albro.........	Merchant
		A. Hubbard......	Merchant
		P. Stedman.......	Farmer
	Surveyors of Highways..............	S. P. Brown......	
		Sidney Chapin....	Farmer
		J. B. McCune.....	Boarding-house Keeper
	Constables...........	J. C. Bartlett.....	Manuf.**
		W. L. Bemis......	Tax Collector
		S. Churchill.......	Painter
		A. Doolittle......	Druggist
		S. M. Fairbank...	Machinist
		A. Hubbard......	Merchant
		W. R. Kentfield...	Mason
		G. Mosman.......	Machinist
		Luther Pierce.....	Manuf.
		A. Warriner......	Farmer
		W. Wheeler.......	Bar Keeper
		B. F. Willard.....	Mason
	Board of Health......	C. Albro.........	Merchant
		A. Hubbard......	Merchant
		D. K. Pearson....	Physician
		P. Stedman.......	Farmer
		J. R. Wilbur......	Physician

* Compiled from Everts, *op. cit.*, II, 964; A. M. Copeland, *op. cit.*, III, 489, 490; Adams, *op. cit.*, 115 et seq.; Springfield *Directories*, 1848-1858.

** The abbreviation "Manuf." probably refers to employment in one of the large manufacturing corporations.

TABLE 4 (continued)

Year	Office	Office Holder	Occupation
	Committee of School Boundaries	E. Renney	Overseer
		P. Stedman	Farmer
		John Wells	Lawyer
	Tithing Men	W. Blake	Carpenter
		L. H. Brigham	Overseer
		D. M. Butterfield	Farmer
		A. H. Childs	Brick Maker
		C. P. Collins	Overseer
		H. Colton	Shoemaker
		L. Dickinson	Tailor
		D. Dunham	
		B. H. Ellis	Physician
		Patrick Gorman	Merchant
		J. Kervin	
		L. E. Ladd	Baker
		W. McDermott	Boarding-house Keeper
		J. Osgood	Overseer
		N. Robinson	
		J. L. Sikes	
		L. C. Skeele	Farmer
		C. A. Southworth	Machinist
		C. Spaulding	Machinist
		L. Streeter	Boarding-house Keeper
		R. White	Shoemaker

and magazine circulation stimulated the movement. Political problems and quarrels had very obvious contact with the ordinary life of most of the people. Protection and the high cost of the necessaries of life affected factory worker and merchant and boarding-house keeper. Corporations, the question of the disposal of the public lands and other problems of the moment all affected the community in one way or another. The slavery fight, if not a direct problem, was at least a highly dramatic controversy.

A Lyceum was organized about the year 1843, and its members arranged numerous lectures throughout the forties.[149] In 1848 it was holding weekly debating meetings which were well attended.[150] In 1846 a literary club, the Cabot Institute, was formed, and it started to collect a library which it presented to the town in 1853.[151] At about the same time a few young men started a debating club,[152] and three years later a second Lyceum was organized. Taylor, who took part in these activities, wrote that "during the last year we have had two village Lyceums, one in the Hall and Huzzy's Lyceum in the Baptist Vestry. Both have been well sustained. The Lyceum in the vestry was got up in opposition to the Hall Lyceum and has been devoted to debate entirely, while the

[149] *Taylor Diary,* 1843-7 passim.

[150] *Ibid.,* 1848, passim.

[151] A. M. Copeland, *op. cit.,* III, 511.

[152] *Taylor Diary,* Dec. 17, 1847.

other with the exception of one evening has been confined to lectures."[153] These meetings were held in Chicopee Falls. The Cabot Institute in Cabotville was functioning at the same time. The usual run of lectures and debates fell off somewhat during 1852-53, but soon picked up again.[154] There was a mechanics' association in Cabotville in the fifties, but there is no evidence as to when it was organized, or as to what its activities were.[155] It is most probable that it was more of a debating society than anything else. Certainly there is no evidence that it was a "labor" organization. If we can come to any conclusion from the following letter from a worker addressed to J. T. Ames, Chicopee must have been a pleasant place in which to live, at least for the skilled worker and members of the middle class, in the early forties.

> I take the liberty to send you these lines for the purpose of learning the prospect for business the coming spring in your establishment. I know of a Gentleman that will buy my situation here, and I think if I can have employment with you again I would return to Cabotville in the spring. This living in Springfield is not what it is cracked up to be. I can make some money here, but what is the use of living where we cannot enjoy ourselves. I consider it a poor bargain when I sacrifice my own happiness and that of my family for money, but for that matter I had rather lose money in Cabotville than make it here. Yes, Sir, I had rather be hung in Cabotville than die a natural death here in Springfield.[156]

At the end of the forties more variety crept into the formal entertainments. Many people attended a Shakespearean reading in 1849, and the next year a musical ensemble gave a recital in Cabot Hall which had recently been built.[157] A few days later there was a lecture scheduled in the Hall, and after that a ventriloquist.[158] It was not long before road companies brought some theater to Chicopee, and in 1854 the inevitable "Uncle Tom's Cabin" was presented, and within a few weeks another company appeared in an equally popular vehicle—"The Drunkard."[159]

The social ferment of the forties and fifties is reflected in

[153] *Ibid.*, Mar. 2, 1851. [154] *Ibid.*, passim, 1852-54.
[155] Chicopee *Town Report*, 1859, Tax list.
[156] *Ames Papers*, Letters, worker to N. P. Ames, Feb. 2, 1841.
[157] *Taylor Diary*, May 29, 1849; *Chicopee Telegraph*, Jan. 9, 1850.
[158] *Chicopee Telegraph*, Jan. 23, 1850.
[159] *Springfield Republican*, Feb. 28; May 23, 1854.

Chicopee in these activities. The whole story is significantly summarized in the names of three nationally known figures who lectured in Chicopee in the fifties—Horace Greeley, Ralph Waldo Emerson, and P. T. Barnum; the latter lectured on "Humbug."[160]

The "blowing out" balls of early mill days continued in this period.[161] Parties, song festivals, concerts and dances were sponsored by the Ladies' Sewing Circle and the various church organizations.[162] In 1858 a few people organized the Chicopee Musical institute, and gave a concert a few months after.[163] Fire companies, started early in the forties, were, aside from their obvious function, social institutions, and corresponded in certain respects to the later athletic clubs.[164] Baseball clubs began to be organized at the end of the period.[165]

Temperance work took up a great deal of the time of the Chicopee zealots, a group which probably included almost every Yankee of substance and respectability. This activity began with the influx of the Irish workers and the development of a permanent factory population. In 1849 Taylor remarked that the "Irish have got to a strange pass here; almost half of them sell liquor."[166] By 1853 there were complaints about rowdyism in the streets, the offenders not being confined to the Irish alone.[167] At about the same time a vigilante committee of city officers and citizens raided an hotel which had been suspected of being a brothel. Local politics were soon dividing on the prohibition issue.[168]

The Yankees, at this time, were experiencing their first contact with a foreign working class group whose standard of living was lower than that which had been prevailing in the community. Taylor referred frequently to over-crowding in the Irish tenements, poor ventilation, and the fact that cholera outbreaks were usually confined to the Irish section, to the intemperance, and to the fact that there was a "rum shop in every fourth house."[168a] The Irish

[160] *Chicopee Telegraph,* Dec. 11, 1850; *Taylor Diary,* Dec. 5, Feb. 9, 1858.
[161] *Taylor Diary,* March 18, 1845; March 20, 1851.
[162] *Ibid.,* 1843-45, passim; *Springfield Republican,* Oct. 9, 1854.
[163] *Chicopee Musical Institute Records; Springfield Republican,* Feb. 1, 1859.
[164] *Taylor Diary,* 1843-51, passim.
[165] *Springfield Republican,* April 4, Aug. 24, 1859.
[166] *Taylor Diary,* March 4, 1849.
[167] *Ibid.,* May-July, 1853.
[168] *Ibid.,* March 28-April 1, 1854.
[168a] *Taylor Diary,* Aug. 6, 1854, 1849; 1855, passim.

themselves, were known as the paddies, and their district was called Ireland, or the patch, or the huddle. Other differences contributed to break down any social contact that the Yankees might have had with the working population. The Irish were Catholics, and they celebrated Christmas, and the Yankees did not.[169] Irish funerals were noisy, as compared with a sober Yankee burial and impressed Taylor to record, "A child belonging to an Irishman . . . died this noon. The paddies all congregated that afternoon and such a howling I never before heard."[170] More important, Sunday, for the Irish workers was a day of amusement, and this, more than anything else, offended Yankee sensibilities. Taylor wrote that "the Sabbath has been in the huddle nothing but a holiday for a long time. I think that under God we may do something for them."[171] The missionary work took the form of a Sunday school for the children, but in the face of the parish priest's opposition, nothing came of it.[172]

The appearance of a local press contributed to Chicopee's coming of age. In 1840 T. D. Blossom started publication of the *Cabotville Chronicle and Chicopee Falls Advertiser.* It had a somewhat stormy career, and struggled on somehow until 1850, being published under the titles of the *Mechanics' Offering* and the *Chicopee Mirror.* In 1843 Blossom started a paper in imitation of the *Lowell Offering,* calling it the *Olive Leaf and Factory Girls' Repository.* Many of the contributors were mill girls. Another paper, the *Chicopee Telegraph,* was published from 1846 to 1853, and after that the *Chicopee Weekly Journal* till about 1862.[173] This was the last attempt to maintain a local press for many years to come. The editors were transients, and did not take root in the town. In his farewell editorial, the editor of the *Chicopee Telegraph* warned the community that "if citizens of Chicopee wish to be entirely lost sight of, and to become a mere *suburban* village, let them permit their village paper, the organ of local information and local opinions, to undergo the quiet, noiseless, and easy process of starvation."[174] This was a warning and a prophecy.

[169] *Ibid.,* Dec. 25, 1848. [170] *Ibid.,* July 22, 1846. [171] *Ibid.,* Sept. 4, 1853.
[172] *Ibid.,* 1853, passim. [173] A. M. Copeland, *op. cit.,* III, 513.
[174] *Chicopee Telegraph,* May 11, 1853.

CHAPTER V

WAGES AND LABOR UNREST, 1840-1850

I

The story of the working class in Chicopee from 1840 to 1850 is the story of change and conflict. The downward pressure of wage rates, the speed-up of machinery and its attendant intensification of work was not accepted passively by the factory operatives. This decade was part of a period of far reaching change in other respects. Men, who had hitherto been employed only in a supervisory capacity in the mills or for heavy work in the yards, or in the machine shops, began to enter mill employment in increasing numbers and worked side by side with women in the weaving rooms. Yankee operatives began to be replaced by Irish workers, just as at the end of the fifties there were signs of the coming displacement of the Irish by the French-Canadians. This period saw the beginning of a permanent factory population, and with it the disintegration of the old boarding-house system.

The course of events in Chicopee was not peculiar to it, but was part of what was happening in other cotton centers. An examination of Chicopee's experiences in these years contributes to an understanding of the labor situation in New England as a whole, and throws some light on the movement of wage rates and earnings and the forces making for their adjustment. In the same way the experiences and reactions of labor in Chicopee emerge more clearly and assume significance when examined in the light of the general labor movement.

In this period factory operatives were seldom free from the fear and pressure of reductions in wages and the speed-up of machinery. As was to be expected, as the cotton industry grew to maturity, as the managers gained experience in the efficient operation of their plants and grew more familiar with the capacity of the machinery, the speed of operation increased. In consequence there was a greater productivity per worker which permitted a downward revision of piece rates. This process resulted in frequent wage adjustments which of necessity constituted a source of irritation to the workers.

The situation was further complicated by rapidly changing economic conditions, not only in the decade under immediate consideration, but also in the fifties. It was a period of speculative boom and depression, prices soared and collapsed and rose again. It was a period of frenzied railroad construction, of war, of gold discovery. In this period too, occurred the Irish famine and the migration to America, creating disturbances in the labor market. Under such conditions the cost of living and the rate of industrial profits[1] were subjected to frequent and violent fluctuations. After the panic of 1837 with its numerous bank failures and collapse of the cotton market depression set in. "Hard times" continued for several years, for not until 1843 were there any signs of a real revival. The next year prices of manufactured commodities rose. While 1845 and 1846 were prosperous years on the whole, there were slight setbacks in business activity. In 1847 increasing prosperity was checked by a panic which was followed by a mild depression with revival in 1848. Then came a few years of good business which continued until 1853 when the downward phase of the cycle set in. Recovery came in the latter part of 1855 and was followed by a speculative boom which ended disastrously in the autumn of 1857. Severe depression followed with some revival in 1859.[2] Under such circumstances frequent wage adjustments are to be expected. Every dip in the dividend rate must have inevitably been followed by a demand for retrenchment; thus "hard times" weighed heavily on labor.

In addition to the prevalence of depression periods, from 1840 to 1860 there were two factors relating to the cotton textile industry which tended to influence corporations to make frequent readjustments of wage rates and speed-up machine operation in order to lower the unit costs of manufacture. The first was the condition of increasing competition in a new industry. The sec-

[1] See Table 5.
[2] W. Thorp and W. C. Mitchell, *Business Annals,* 122 et seq.

TABLE 5. ANNUAL DIVIDENDS OF SELECTED COTTON MILLS IN NEW ENGLAND, 1836-1861*

Year	Chicopee Mfg. Co.	Perkins Mills	Dwight Mfg. Co.	Merrimack Mfg. Co.	Amoskeag Mfg. Co.	Tremont Mills
1836.........	10%	..%	..%	15%	8%	11%
1837.........	5	..	..	0	4	26 (20s)
1838.........	5	5	..	40 (37s**)	3	5
1839.........	5	5	..	11	9	11
1840.........	0	5	..	9	0	7
1841.........	3	6	..	12	6	8
1842.........	0	0	3	8	4	2
1843.........	0	9	11	16	7	6
1844.........	7	20	18	20	9	16
1845.........	12	20	20	20	15	18
1846.........	6	13	16	16	35 (25s)	16
1847.........	6	9	9	9	30 (25s)	7
1848.........	0	6	6	7	3	2
1849.........	3	5	8	29 (25s)	23 (20s)	3
1850.........	5	0	7	8	6	3
1851.........	0	3	2	8	4	0
1852.........	0	6	6	10	7	3
1853.........	4	4	4	10	8	8
1854.........	0	3	5	11	8	8
1855.........	0	4	3	10	6	3
1856.........	0	..	3	10	4	6
1857.........	0	..	5	8	3	8
1858.........	0	..	0	9	3	0
1859.........	0	..	3	10	8	6
1860.........	8.3	..	7	10	9	7
1861.........	..	..	6	6	9	7

* Compiled from J. G. Martin, *Seventy-Three Years' History of the Boston Stock Market,* 66 et seq.
** Stock dividend.

ond factor was related to business practice in connection with the accumulation of reserves.

The first flush of high profits in the industry attracted new investment, and the consequent fall in the price of cotton goods lowered the margin of profit per yard of product, stimulating further the expansion of volume to maintain aggregate profits. If competition was strong enough to force prices below the point which would hold profits at their previous level in spite of a larger volume of production, we may expect some pressure on wages to maintain those profits. However, one must be careful not to overemphasize this factor, and it is easy to do so because of the seemingly obvious expansion of the capacity of the cotton textile industry during the period.[3]

[3] There were 2,300,000 cotton spindles in the United States in 1840, 3,600,000 in 1850, and 5,200,000 in 1860. M. T. Copeland, *op. cit.,* 6.

The evidence pointing to severe competition in the cotton industry is varied. There is, first of all, the fall in prices during the period 1820 to 1860. The sharpest drop, using the figures of the Boston Manufacturing Company,[4] came between 1823 and 1830. But this drop cannot be ascribed in entirety to an increasingly competitive situation, for it must be borne in mind that we are dealing with a new industry which as it gained experience and as it expanded its production could cut its unit costs without necessarily involving a lower profit. After 1830 the downward trend of prices is marked, but is by no means indicative of cut-throat competition. If the price of cotton cloth did not soar as high as the wholesale price index, neither did it fall so low.

It is true that while there was a rate of development in the industry of 150 per cent from 1840 to 1860 as compared with a population increase of 84 per cent, that does not necessarily mean, as has been assumed, that there was an excess of productive capacity as compared with the market expansion.[5] It is necessary to take account of the elasticity of the demand for cotton goods in the domestic market, and the export market must be taken into consideration.[6] It is also significant, that while from 1850 to 1860 cotton spindleage and the value of the product increased roughly 46 and 76 per cent respectively, the number of firms showed only a 1.5 per cent increase.[7] This again, is not indicative of competition so severe as to force the owners to maintain rapidly dwindling cotton profits at the expense of labor, as has been suggested.[8] This situation does suggest, however, that if expansion came from within the industry by the reinvestment of cotton manufacturing profits or by the investment of new capital by the established proprietors, the prospects for the maintenance of profits must have seemed good.

Nor is the trend of prices of cotton products from 1840 to 1860 very suggestive of an intensely competitive situation. The

[4] C. Ware, *op. cit.*, 111. [5] *Ibid.*, 109 et seq.

[6] The average annual value of cotton goods exported was $7,310,000 from 1851 to 1860 as compared with $3,960,000 in the preceding decade. M. T. Copeland, *op. cit.*, 15.

[7] C. Ware, *op. cit.*, 115. [8] *Ibid.*, 113.

TABLE 6. PRICES OF SELECTED COTTON PRODUCTS, SEMI-ANNUALLY, 1840-1861*

Date	Amoskeag Tickings	Pepperell Drillings	Amoskeag Denim	Bleached Shirtings, N. Y.	Print Cloth, Metacomet	Atlantic Sheeting, Brown
	Cents	Cents	Cents	Cents	Cents	Cents
January, 1840	17.5	....	....	....	....	....
July	16.	....	....	....	....	....
January, 1841	17.	....	....	....	....	....
July	17.	....	....	....	....	....
January, 1842	16.	....	....	....	....	....
July	14.5	....	12.5	....	....	....
January, 1843	14.	....	12.5	....	....	....
July	13.	....	12.5	....	....	....
January, 1844	15.5	....	12.	....	....	....
July	16.5	....	14.5	....	....	....
January, 1845	15.5	....	13.	....	....	....
July	15.5	....	13.	....	....	....
January, 1846	16.	....	13.	....	....	....
July	16.	....	14.	....	....	....
January, 1847	16.	7.52	14.	13.63	5.5	7.29
July	16.5	7.99	14.5	14.1	5.75	7.75
January, 1848	16.	6.997	12.5	13.63	5.25	7.05
July	15.	6.58	12.	13.16	4.63	6.58
January, 1849	15.	6.11	12.	13.16	4.13	5.99
July	15.	5.99	12.5	13.16	4.13	6.11
January, 1850	15.	7.285	13.	14.1	5.13	7.05
July	15.5	7.52	12.5	14.1	5.13	7.29
January, 1851	15.5	8.225	13.	14.1	5.	7.75
July	14.5	7.167	12.	13.63	4.38	6.11
January, 1852	14.5	6.345	12.	13.63	4.5	6.22
July	15.	7.05	12.	13.63	4.75	6.70
January, 1853	16.	7.285	11.5	13.63	6.	7.17
July	16.	7.52	11.	13.63	6.	7.52
January, 1854	16.	7.285	10.5	14.1	6.25	7.52
July	16.	7.52	11.	14.1	5.38	7.52
January, 1855	15.	7.285	12.5	14.1	4.75	7.29
July	16.	7.285	12.5	14.1	5.13	7.05
January, 1856	16.	7.52	13.	14.1	4.75	7.05
July	16.	7.52	14.	14.1	5.13	7.29
January, 1857	17.5	8.225	16.	14.1	5.63	8.
July	18.	8.46	16.	14.1	5.75	8.46
January, 1858	18.	8.46	16.	14.1	4.75	8.
July	17.5	8.225	14.5	14.1	5.25	7.81
January, 1859	16.5	8.225	14.5	14.1	5.25	7.75
July	17.	8.225	14.5	14.57	5.5	8.23
January, 1860	17.	8.46	14.5	14.57	5.38	8.
July	17.	8.46	15.	14.57	5.38	8.23
January, 1861	16.25	....	15.	....	....	8.23
July	16.75	....	15.	....	....	8.46

* Compiled from U. S. 52nd Cong. 2nd Sess., *Senate Report* No. 1394. "Aldrich Report on Wholesale Prices, Wages and Transportation," Part II, 135 et seq. (1893).

prices of a few products are presented in Table 6. In a market pervaded by extremely active competition one would expect to find a considerable degree of collapse following the panic of 1857. Such was not the case. As a matter of fact some of the prices displayed a stability not at all suggestive of competitive price. It should not be forgotten, furthermore, that approximately 20 per cent of the industry was more or less under the same management, and price competition within that margin could not have been very intense.

The evidence pointing to a rapidly increasing rate of competition seems to be unsatisfactory. An expanding productive capacity and fall in price alone do not mean increasing competition. But the fact remains that cotton dividends did fall from an average of 11.4 per cent till the end of 1836 to 9.7 per cent for the next decade, and to 5.8 per cent in the period 1847 to 1859.[9] However, an annual *average* profit of 5.8 per cent over a period of years including the panic of 1857-58 does not imply cut-throat competition. But the dividend rate should not be confused with the rate of profit. At any given time the two may coincide, but not of necessity. In this connection the records of some of the Chicopee companies present an additional explanation to account for the fall in the rate of dividends.

In the five years preceding 1837 the Chicopee Manufacturing Company averaged an annual return of 10 per cent as compared with 3.6 per cent for the next five years.[10] The Cabot Manufacturing Company which averaged 9.7 per cent from 1836 through 1839 saw its dividends sink to 5, 7, and 2 per cent in the next three years.[11] There was a brief high profit interlude in the forties, when from 1843 through 1846 the Cabot Company paid an annual average dividend of 16.7 per cent. In the same time the Perkins Mills paid 15.7 per cent and the Dwight Company 16.2 per cent. After that final burst of high profits, the result, in part, of a reduction of labor costs, the companies settled down to 4 and 5 per cent per annum.[12] It is possible that the lower returns of the later period were to some extent occasioned by a change in business policy. It is possible that dividends of the early years were kept at a level which precluded the continued maintenance of capital equipment in the most efficient condition possible.

Figures 1 to 3 show the spread between the estimated operating profits and the amount of cash paid out in dividends for three Chicopee companies. In the early years of a company's operation almost all of the operating profit was distributed among the stockholders. It will be observed that beginning with the late forties

[9] *Ibid.*
[10] Martin, *op. cit.*, 66.
[11] *Ibid.*
[12] *Ibid.*

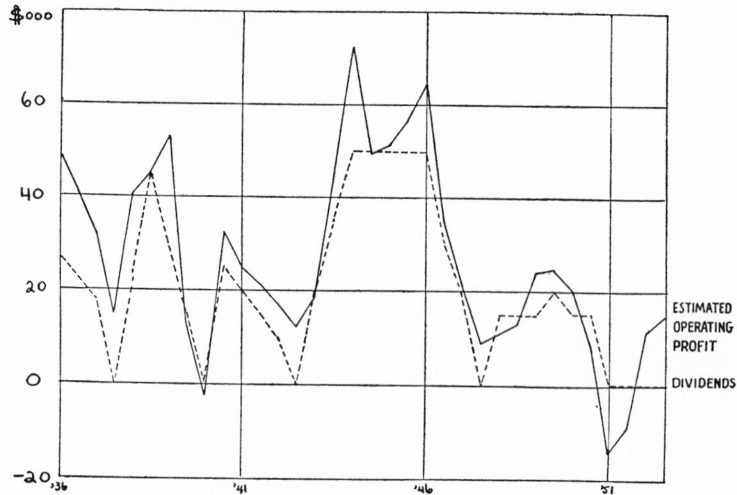

Figure 1. ESTIMATED OPERATING PROFIT AND CASH DIVIDENDS PAID, MAY AND NOVEMBER, 1836-1852. COMPANY "A."

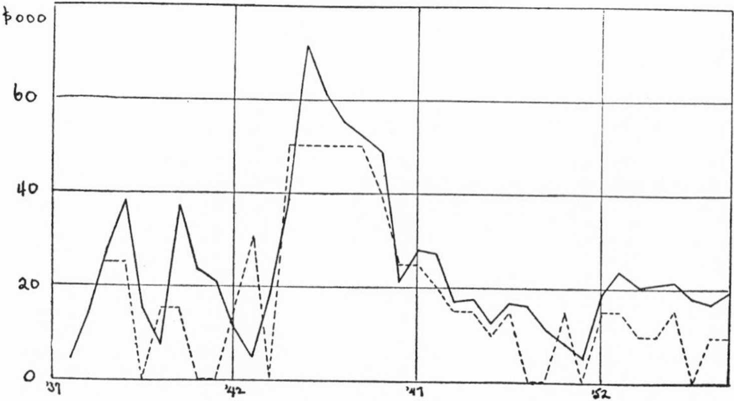

Figure 2. ESTIMATED OPERATING PROFIT AND CASH DIVIDENDS PAID, APRIL AND OCTOBER, 1837-1856. COMPANY "B." THE PRODUCTIVE CAPACITY OF THIS COMPANY WAS DOUBLED IN 1852, THEREFORE THE ORIGINAL FIGURES FROM 1852-1856 HAVE BEEN CORRECTED TO MAKE ALLOWANCE FOR THIS.

the spread grows wider. After this the companies begin to leave more of the operating profits available for reserves and new equipment. This change in policy accounts for part of the drop in the dividend rate. The difference is even more strikingly illustrated in Table 7.

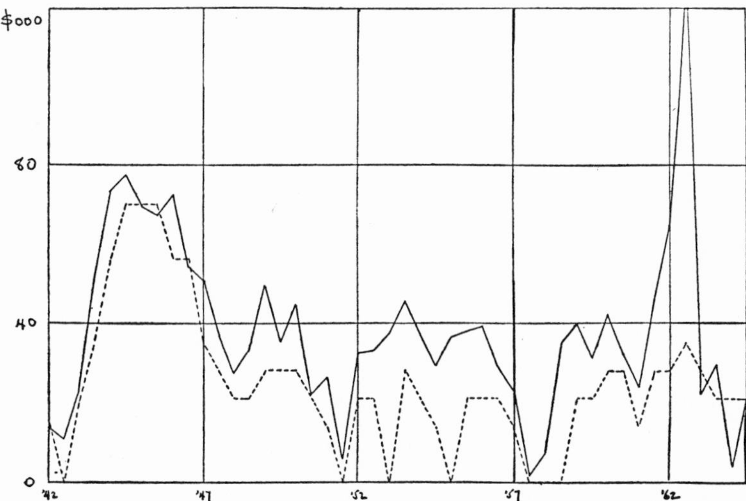

Figure 3. ESTIMATED OPERATING PROFIT AND CASH DIVIDENDS PAID, SEMI-ANNUALLY, 1842-1864. COMPANY "C." THE PRODUCTIVE CAPACITY OF THIS COMPANY WAS INCREASED IN 1856, THEREFORE THE ORIGINAL FIGURES FROM 1856-1864 HAVE BEEN CORRECTED TO MAKE ALLOWANCE FOR THIS.

The companies could not pursue indefinitely a policy of paying out nearly all the earnings of operation. A time came when new machinery was needed, when equipment had to be replaced, extensive repairs had to be made. In other words, the time came when part of the operating profits had to be plowed back into the companies in order to keep them in good operating condition. One Chicopee company made extensive alterations and installed new machinery in 1863.[13] Another was also buying new equipment,—

TABLE 7. TOTAL CASH DIVIDENDS PAID EXPRESSED AS PERCENTAGE OF TOTAL ESTIMATED OPERATING PROFITS, 1836-1860*

Period	Company "A"	Company "B"	Company "C"
1836-1840..................	64.3%	....%	....%
1841-1845..................	81.3	82.4	87.0
1846-1850..................	83.9	75.9	75.3
1851-1855..................	....	58.9	43.3
1856-1860..................	....	....	54.6

* Compiled from Journals and Semi-Annual Statements of *Companies "A," "B," and "C."*

[13] *Taylor Diary,* March 2, 1854.

machines and water wheels.[14] At about this time the agent of the latter company complained very frequently about his equipment which was giving him constant trouble, and about the need for a reservoir to keep up the water supply, the lack of which often prevented capacity production.[15]

Under such circumstances, there was a constant and sometimes intense incentive to cut costs whenever and wherever possible. Whenever costs rose relative to those of another producing unit, the board of directors was not long in calling this fact to the attention of the resident agent whose business it was to earn a profit for his employers. Whenever a business crisis demanded the conservation of liquid capital the agent was called upon to institute further internal economies, since there was little cash reserve accumulated from high profit years. The agent, then, had to exercise increasing vigilance over labor costs, almost the only factor over which he had direct control. Thus on the one hand he had to adjust wage rates to counteract the tendency toward increasing relative costs on account of a previous period of high profits, and on the other hand, when larger sums of money were finally set aside from the operating revenue for new equipment, an action which resulted in the immediate reduction of cash dividends, there was likely to emerge almost automatic pressure to cut costs still further so as to raise the dividend rate once more.

In view of the frequent business fluctuations of the period the question of reserves was of special importance. When the companies were paying out in dividends such a large percentage of their operating profits, there was no possibility of accumulating a cash surplus of any magnitude, and if money became tight, as it so frequently did, it was immediately necessary to reduce wages or to curtail production so as to conserve the operating capital.[16] Furthermore, the accumulation of reserves would have tended to

[14] *Company "B" Papers*, Letter Book, 1853.
[15] *Ibid.*, 1854, 1855.
[16] Compare, in this connection, the letters in relation to the dividend rate, which J. T. Ames sent to J. K. Mills, (above, p. 87) and the reference to shortage of working capital from which the Ames Company suffered after the Civil War. (Below, pp. 163, 164.) It should be remembered that the cotton mills and the Ames Company were controlled by the same group of men.

spread the dividends so as to minimize the disparity between the average rates of return in the earlier and later periods.[17]

This change in business policy and the technical factors involved seem to be of equal, if not of greater importance, than the competitive situation in exacting a higher productivity from the workers. The process was a continuous one, bearing down with increasing severity at critical periods. Wages which had already been cut from 1835 to 1840 were further reduced in the next five years.[18]

II

These technical factors then, superimposed upon frequent periods of "hard times" and repeated in all the cotton centers of New England, could not fail but be productive of lower wage rates, harder work, and the continuance of the same long working day. The situation was not accepted passively by labor. Not only was its protest a personal one, but it became part of the general humanitarian movement of the forties. The workers in Chicopee experienced these conditions, and their reactions can best be interpreted in the light of the general labor movement and the factory controversy.

A vigorous labor press came into being in the forties, and its activities were strengthened, in many instances, by the editorial support extended by sympathetic editors and publicists. The factory system especially came under attack, and was not without its defenders. The boarding-house system as instituted in Lowell and Chicopee had received wide publicity, and a somewhat rosy picture of the system had been painted by Harriet Martineau, Chevalier, and other European visitors. The picture was continued by the *Lowell Offering.* The articles in this newspaper, which started publication in 1840, and was to receive the praise of Charles Dickens, were written by Lowell factory girls. It had a wide circula-

[17] The fact that part of the increasing spread between estimated operating profit and cash dividends may have been due to a change in accounting methods should not be disregarded. However, the payment of such large sums of money relative to the operating profits might easily have tended to handicap the ability of the mill agent to undertake many minor repairs which would have contributed to the operating efficiency of the productive unit.

[18] C. Ware, *op. cit.,* 273.

tion, and seemed to spread the idea that factory workers were bursting with literary activity and discussion, and that therefore any system productive of such activity must, in the nature of things, be good, making allowance for minor imperfections. Directly or indirectly, the *Lowell Offering* was in considerable measure responsible for the dissemination of this idea. It was not intended at first that labor problems would find any place in the columns of this paper; controversial subjects were to be avoided. "With wages and board, etc., we have nothing to do. These depend on circumstances over which we have no control."[19] But as the cotton corporations and the factory system came under attack the editors ended by defending the corporations.[20] The *Offering* was bitterly attacked by the genuine labor press of the period, and was labelled as a tool of the Lowell corporations.[21] "The factory owners," said one labor editor, "unfortunately, for reasons best known to themselves, patronized the publication, and the operatives *did not;* the consequence of which was that it must remain silent, at least, respecting the rights and interests of the operatives wherever they conflicted with those of the employers, or it must be suspended for want of support."[22]

The labor press had to attack the *Lowell Offering,* for not only was the latter opposing labor's plea for shorter hours and better working conditions by refusing to admit that conditions were bad enough to stir up rebellion and agitation, but as a widely publicized paper, *written by operatives,* it continued the tradition of the benevolent mill system, and thus constituted a powerful propagandist weapon in the hands of that system's apologists. Actually, the acceptance of the publication as the voice of factory operatives was ludicrous. For its life span corresponded to a period in which labor was most articulate in denouncing what the *Offering* stood for, when labor was demanding better working conditions, when factory labor was forming associations, holding conventions, and petitioning the Massachusetts legislature for relief.

[19] *Lowell Offering,* Vol. 3, p. 48. Quoted in N. Ware, *op. cit.,* 90.
[20] *Ibid.*
[21] *Ibid.,* 90 et seq.
[22] *Working Man's Advocate,* Jan. 17, 1846.

The part of the laboring population which made itself heard in the turbulent forties no longer trusted in a community of interest between itself and capital, and did not believe in the hopeful conviction of the successor to the *Offering,* that the corporations would "in their own good time . . . introduce the ten-hour system; and will not this be a noble deed?—a noble deed?"[23] as though this philanthropy were already accomplished. There was also evident at this time a general revulsion of feeling against the flattering attitude toward labor which had been adopted by the *Offering,* by foreign observers, by employers, and, it must be admitted, by the operatives themselves. This flattery took the form of wide advertisement of the "gentility" of factory workers, of frequent reference to their "honorable employment," to their "flower pots" and their "smiling faces," to their intellect as displayed in the *Lowell Offering.* And at no time was labor more flattered than when it wanted something. The *Working Man's Advocate* protested the "silly" insistence of the word "lady" as applied to factory workers, "because the latter term has come to be so much abused of late."[24] A pamphlet of the period attacked the "prosy lucubrations, the labored arguments, which circulate from time to time in a miserable cabbage press, to prove that labor is not disgraceful, that it is honorable, indeed! Honorable!"[25] At this time a paper gave high praise to a labor speaker for his break with these methods. "What we particularly liked in this address of Mr. Walsh, was his abstinence from that flattery of the laboring classes so common to the lips of those who profess to espouse their cause. He shamed, rather than flattered his auditors, declaring their neglect to use their power as stupid and culpable in the extreme."[26]

The abolition movement lent fire to the labor movement. Obviously both were part of the general humanitarian spirit of the age, but the preoccupation with slavery and the neglect of conditions at home on the part of the abolitionists must frequently have made factory labor and its champions painfully aware of this

[23] *New England Offering,* Vol. I, p. 1. Quoted in N. Ware, *op. cit.,* 92.
[24] *Working Man's Advocate,* Aug. 17, 1844.
[25] *The Condition of Labor.* A pamphlet published anonymously in 1847.
[26] Reprint from *Baltimore Visitor* in the *Working Man's Advocate,* March 22, 1845.

social myopia. More directly, when the South defended itself, as it was bound to do, it was well able to see and point out what the abolitionists overlooked—labor conditions in the North. They referred to the white slaves of the North, and many labor leaders concurred in the use of this epithet. As a matter of fact, they had used it themselves in the thirties.[27]

> It is a startling fact, that even in this land of ours, this free republic, this glorious country, "where liberty dwells," our *corporation slaves* receive a *less* compensation, and are required to work a *greater* number of hours, than in *some* parts of that detested dynasty, that hated anarchy, old despotic England.[28]

This feeling of degradation, experienced by the workers is well expressed in the following passage which was elicited by the publication of a story to the effect that Lowell operatives had been able to save large sums of money. These savings, claimed the labor press, were actually a pittance, unless compared with foreign labor conditions.

> The question ought to be, Is labor with us where it ought to be? Is it rich in pocket? Is it educated and refined? Is it honored in the social scale? No. For the same reason that it is considered marvellous that a few young women of the entire mass of the country are able to save a little money from constant toil, so is it wonderful that a fraction of a fraction of them can give evidences of an education—that they have time and talent to write for a magazine. The wonder ought to be the other way.[29]

There was more than talk in the period. Wages were lower, work harder, hours long. There was little hope of raising wages, for these, it was believed, were inexorably fixed by forces beyond the power of mortal man to tamper with. If work was harder, it was due to the demands of the machine. But the working day could be cut, and toward this end the labor movement directed itself. A general petition from Fall River reached the legislature in 1842.[30] Lowell sent in a 1600 name petition in 1843,[31] and the

[27] See above, p. 61.
[28] Reprint from *Factory Girls' Garland,* Exeter, N. H. in *Working Man's Advocate,* Oct. 5, 1844.
[29] *Working Man's Advocate,* Aug. 10, 1844.
[30] Mass., *House Doc.* No. 4, 1842.
[31] N. Ware, *op. cit.,* 133.

next year asked again that manufacturing corporations not be permitted to maintain operation for more than ten hours daily.[32]

The situation gave impetus to labor organization. Labor associations were formed, and the New England Workingmen's Convention met in Boston in 1844.[33] The next year it met at Lowell, and was joined by the newly formed Female Labor Reform Association of that city.[34] In 1846 these two organizations adopted the name of the Labor Reform League of New England.[35] However, its attention was distracted from the problems at hand when, in 1847, at its Boston convention, working class leadership was relinquished to a group of philanthropic intellectuals, and the convention declared for Free Soil and anti-slavery.[36] The associationists were also present at the convention, and their spokesman made a very able attack on the factory system and the reformist movement.[37]

This attack crystallizes much of the sentiment and many of the ideas current at that time, ideas which were influencing the labor movement. The evils of society, claimed the associationist, lie in its constitution, and the status quo is merely an outgrowth of precedent institutions, and not a gift of God, as the theologians claimed. He stressed the point that "capital and labor are in direct antagonism. Or rather that labor is passive, while capital makes its own terms with it. I do not say that it does this consciously, intentionally; I say that it does it inevitably." Is not, he asked, the dependence of labor upon capital "the same thing in principle, only differing in degree, with Southern Slavery?"[38] He likewise warned the convention which was to declare that "American slavery must be uprooted *before* the elevation sought by the laboring classes can be affected"[39] that the abolition of slavery would not help the workers. The absence of chattel slavery in Europe, he said, does not make the position of labor there any better than it is in America . "It is not slavery at the South which oppresses you, grinds you down with its iron heel, but slavery at the North. It

[32] Mass., *House Doc.* No. 3, 1844, p. 48.
[33] N. Ware, *op. cit.*, 205.
[34] *Ibid.*, 207.
[35] *Ibid.*, 219.
[36] *Ibid.*, 220.
[37] *The Condition of Labor.*
[38] *Ibid.*
[39] *Voice of Industry*, Feb. 19, 1847.

is not chattel slavery, but wage slavery."[40] And while the reduction of the hours of labor is essential to the welfare of labor, that alone will not alter the fundamental relationship between capital and labor, an immoral relationship, whereby men grow rich by the "unremunerated toil" of workers. "It is not a mere shortening of the hours of labor that is to bring you redemption. The Southern slave frequently completes his task before the sun reaches the meridian. Is he therefore less a slave"?[41]

With ideas such as these in the air, with petitions coming into the legislature, the latter was moved to act in 1845, and a committee was appointed to investigate the situation. Operatives testified that the working day was too long, that there was no time in which to "cultivate their minds," and that their "intellectual, moral and religious habits would also be benefited" by a shorter working day.[42] It was also testified that girls who wished to attend lectures were permitted to leave their work before closing time, but obviously such a practice would be penalized by a loss of wages.[43] Other witnesses said that a shorter working day would cut wages, and was therefore undesirable, and an ex-overseer "gave it as his opinion that the girls in the mills enjoy the best health, for the reason that they rise early, go to bed early, and have three meals regular."[44] The evidence gleaned was sufficient to confound the generally accepted idea that a great many of the operatives could devote themselves to intellectual pursuits in their "spare time."[45] But the committee found comfort in the plants on the window sills, to them "convincing evidence of the elevated moral tone and refined taste of the operatives."[46]

The committee decided unanimously that no corrective legislation was needed.[47] The operatives had asked that the corporations be restrained from running the mills more than ten hours per day. To this the investigators replied that if it was harmful

[40] *The Condition of Labor.* [41] *Ibid.*
[42] Mass., *House Doc.* No. 50, 1845, pp. 2, 4, 5.
[43] *Ibid.,* 5. [44] *Ibid.,* 7.
[45] This idea which has persisted for so long has consistently disregarded the fact that such activity, except in rare cases, was physically impossible.
[46] Mass., *House Doc.* No. 50, 1845, p. 8.
[47] *Ibid.,* 15.

to work more than ten hours a day for a corporation, it was harmful to work more than ten hours a day for any employer, therefore no remedial legislation could be recommended, as the petition referred specifically to corporations.[48] A reduction of the working day would cut wages, and the committee knew better than to meddle with wages; if they did, they would soon be sent about their business.[49] In spite of the fact that labor was asking the legislature for relief, the committee felt that "labor is intelligent enough to make its own bargains and look for its own interests without any interference from us."[50] The committee acknowledged the existence of many abuses in the factory system, and looked for their eradication to a "progressive improvement in art and science, in a higher appreciation of man's destiny, in a less love for money, and a more ardent love for social happiness and intellectual superiority," but not to a ten hour law.[51]

By 1850, when another legislative committee was reporting adversely on a ten hour law, the agitation of the decade was productive of a minority report which urged its adoption. This report recognized the impossibility of any noteworthy utilization of what leisure time there was. "Where, then, is their time and opportunity for moral and mental culture? Where is the time for them to acquire information, and thus keep reasonable pace in general improvement, with the ordinary ranks of life? It is clear, they do not have it. Their daily span of twenty-four hours is all appropriated in regular and stated portions, to working, eating and sleeping, and no allowance is, or can be made for the wants of the mind, without infringing upon time set apart for one of these three purposes."[52] This report also claimed that wages would not fall with a reduction of the working day, but on the contrary would rise, because a shorter working day would place more workers on payrolls and thus reduce the reserve army of unemployed. A shorter working day would also be of service in the regularization of employment and production, and thus benefit the employer as

[48] *Ibid.*
[49] *Ibid.*, 15, 16.
[50] *Ibid.*, 16.
[51] *Ibid.*, 17.
[52] Mass., *House Doc.* 1850, No. 153, p. 9.

well as the worker.[53] These arguments, however, were presented in the minority report.

III

Chicopee shared in the unstable business conditions, in the general developments which produced labor controversy and unrest, resentment and dissatisfaction, prevalent in New England in the 1840's. We turn now from an examination of the situation in its general outlines to its expression in a single manufacturing town. A consideration of cotton textile earnings constitutes the logical basis for an examination of labor developments in the two decades preceding the Civil War. The observations on wage trends used in this and in the following chapter are based on figures which have been compiled from the payrolls of one of the Chicopee cotton companies.[54]

While the data are derived from the original sources, it is necessary to exercise discretion in their use. It has been impossible, for instance, to distinguish between the earnings of adult beginners and young girls. Lower wages which seemingly might be due to the youth, and therefore lower productive capacities of the recipients, might equally well be the earnings of adult beginners. No attempt has been made, then, to weed out arbitrarily certain items which might be the earnings of young girls. As this company never employed children in large numbers, and as at least half of the children employed were boys, the error involved by the inclusion of female children's earnings is not serious. But the wages of adult beginners and of young girls tend to lower the average earnings, and for this reason the results presented probably cannot be used as a reliable measure of the level of wages earned by the

[53] *Ibid.*, 22, 30.

[54] The cotton companies owned several buildings, each of which was a complete productive unit called a mill. The sample chosen consists of the complete payroll of one or two mills. The number of items varies from 175 to about 375 with very few exceptions, and then the sample never falls below 125 items. The sample, in any case, being a complete payroll for a productive unit contains all manufacturing operations in their natural proportions, although it is possible that at certain times, this would not be the case. Wages were paid once a month, for four or five week periods, as the case might be. In order to avoid discrepancies on this account, each month's median wage has been divided by four or five, in order to derive a weekly wage representative of the earnings in any given month.

average female adult. It is quite possible that in some of the productive units which specialized in fine work, earnings were higher than are indicated here. In any case, the data are used to show the movement of wages over a period of time, and for this purpose their value is unimpaired by the foregoing qualifications. There is no reason to doubt their representativeness.[55]

In the examination of the piece rates only one mill has been used, and it is assumed that movements were the same for all the mills in the community. This is reasonable, for we know from other sources that when one mill made a general wage adjustment, all the mills in the town did so. While it has been possible to construct a curve of wage rates for only a short period, it is a significant one. With the passage of time the increasing variety of products does not permit the assumption that a given rate was paid for exactly the same commodity at different times.

The years 1841 to 1845 were marked by business deflation. In this period wage cutting was sharp and frequent. The average weekly median wage for the second half of 1841 was $2.71 for all female operatives, with a slight upward swing during the next six months. But the second half of 1842 showed a drop of some 18

TABLE 8. AVERAGE OF WEEKLY MEDIAN AND UPPER QUARTILE EARNINGS AND INDEX NUMBERS OF ALL FEMALE OPERATIVES BY SIX MONTH PERIODS, JULY, 1841-DECEMBER, 1845. (JULY-DEC., 1841 = 100)

Date	Average of Median	Index	Average of Upper Q.	Index
1841 — 2nd Half	$2.71	100.	$3.46	100.
1842 — 1st "	2.81	103.6	3.48	100.5
1842 — 2nd "	2.23	82.2	2.84	82.
1843 — 1st "	2.50	92.2	3.18	91.9
1843 — 2nd "	2.34	86.3	2.97	85.8
1844 — 1st "	2.54	93.7	3.23	93.3
1844 — 2nd "	2.41	88.9	2.99	86.4
1845 — 1st "	2.38	87.8	2.93	84.6
1845 — 2nd "	2.28	84.1	2.96	85.5

per cent from the 1841 level, and in spite of some pickup in the next six months, the average median earnings were 16 per cent

[55] A second sample, that is, the payroll of second mill, was taken periodically as a check. In spite of occasional discrepancies, the similarity between the two medians derived was satisfactory.

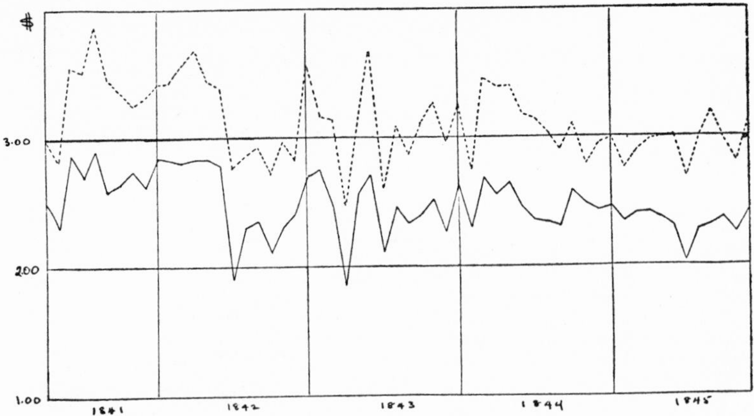

Figure 4. WEEKLY UPPER QUARTILE AND MEDIAN EARNINGS OF FEMALE OPERATIVES, BY MONTHS. APRIL, 1841-DECEMBER, 1845.

lower in the last half of 1845 than they had been at a similar time in 1841.[56]

These figures relate to actual earnings, and therefore vary according as most of the operatives did a full month's work or not. Table 9 is a computation of what the average weekly earnings would have been had the operatives worked full time.[57] It will be noticed that the weavers did not lose nearly as much ground as the other workers. Here we see that while there was an unmistakable decline, earnings started to improve somewhat in 1844-45, so that part of the sharp drop of the first years was very likely due to the curtailment of production occasioned by poor business conditions.

However, it is obvious that this condition does not account for all of the decline. It is necessary, then, to examine wage rates for

[56] These earnings may be compared with the average weekly wage rates paid in Massachusetts, compiled from United States Bureau of Labor Statistics, *Bulletin* No. 499. "History of Wages in the United States from Colonial Times to 1928." pp. 382, 386, 390.

AVERAGE WEEKLY WAGE RATES OF FEMALE WEAVERS, SPINNERS AND SPEEDER TENDERS IN MASSACHUSETTS, 1842-1848.

Year	*Weavers*	*Spinners*	*Speeder Tenders*
1842	$3.66	$2.76	$2.94
1843	3.60	2.70	2.70
1844	2.40	2.58	2.64
1845	2.58	2.64	2.58
1846	2.70	2.58	2.76
1847	2.76	2.64	2.88
1848	2.70	3.06	3.00

[57] This is obviously a very rough measure, and is of little value in measuring the wage level, but useful to illustrate the influence of rate adjustments.

TABLE 9. ESTIMATED AVERAGE FULL TIME WEEKLY EARNINGS OF WEAVERS AND OF ALL OTHER FEMALE OPERATIVES, WITH INDEX NUMBERS, FOR SIX MONTH PERIODS. JULY 1841-DECEMBER 1845.
(JULY-DEC. 1841 = 100)

DATE	WEAVERS		ALL OTHERS	
	Average Weekly Full Time Wages	Index	Average Weekly Full Time Wages	Index
1841 — 2nd Half.......	$3.66	100.	$3.40	100.
1842 — 1st "	3.84	104.9	3.32	97.6
1842 — 2nd "	3.34	91.2	2.77	81.4
1843 — 1st "	3.74	94.8	2.80	82.3
1843 — 2nd "	3.35	91.5	2.66	78.2
1844 — 1st "	3.57	97.5	2.78	81.7
1844 — 2nd "	3.43	93.7	2.75	80.8
1845 — 1st "	3.46	94.5	2.79	82.
1845 — 2nd "	3.48	95.	2.76	81.1

this short period. It will be observed in Figures 5 and 6 that rates dropped far more than is reflected in the actual earnings. The latter were 16 per cent lower in the latter half of 1845 than in the same months in 1841. During that time warping rates fell 20 per cent, warp spinning rates 37.5 per cent, carding rates 34 per cent, and weaving rates 35 per cent. Thus if actual wages declined only 16 per cent in the same period, then each operative had to work that much harder at the end of the period to maintain this wage level. The machinery was operated at a faster rate with the expectation that the operatives would make up the earnings by increasing the output. To the extent that there were important technical innovations which contributed to the efficiency of the worker and of the machine, this intensification of effort was obviated. In the absence of direct evidence on this point it is difficult to arrive at a definite estimate of the degree of increased effort required from the operative.

While the need for caution in using these wage averages as a measure of absolute income has been indicated, it may be permitted to make some qualified comment. The price of board was $1.25 per week in the forties. If an operative earned $2.50 per week, her expenses for food and lodging accounted for only half of her earnings. According to present standards that would be a comfortable wage. But if the operative had left $1.00 or $1.50 per

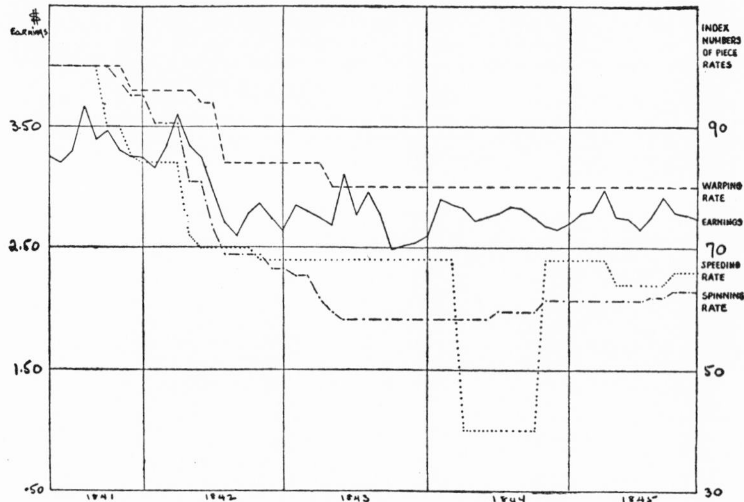

Figure 5. ESTIMATED AVERAGE FULL-TIME WEEKLY EARNINGS OF ALL FEMALE OPERATIVES, EXCEPT WEAVERS, AND INDEX NUMBERS OF PIECE RATES FOR SPINNING, WARPING AND SPEEDING, BY MONTHS, MAY, 1841-DECEMBER, 1845. (MAY, 1841 = 100).

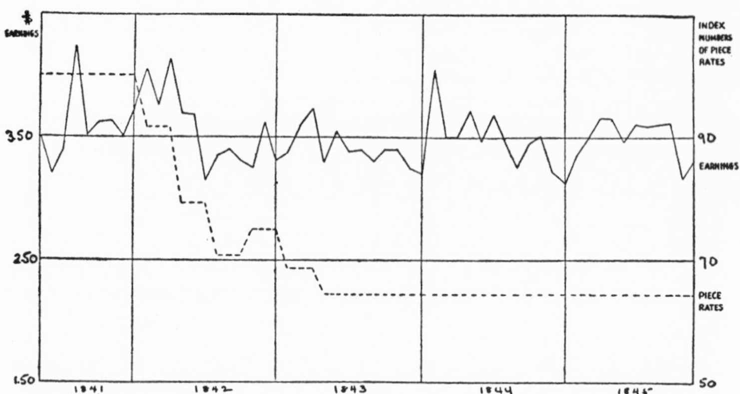

Figure 6. ESTIMATED AVERAGE WEEKLY FULL-TIME EARNINGS OF FEMALE WEAVERS AND INDEX NUMBER OF PIECE RATES FOR WEAVING, BY MONTHS, MAY, 1841-DECEMBER, 1845. (MAY, 1841 = 100).

week after the payment of board, we do not know how far this sum would go for the purchase of clothing and for other expenses, and it is impossible here, to make an examination of the various determining factors. With only herself to support, the operative was probably able to manage well enough, given fairly regular employment. It is probable that the real difficulties associated with standards of living set in after the development of a permanent factory population, and the necessity of contributing to the support of a whole family on mill earnings.

But whether the level of wages in the early forties afforded a fair degree of comfort or not, it was so low, in monetary terms, that a few cents a week change in income meant a considerable percentage change. Furthermore, to the worker, the change seemed greater than it actually was because of the commonly accepted method of calculating wages as the sum of money left to the operative after payment of board. Thus, if a worker received $2.50 per week and paid $1.25 for board, she was likely to consider a 25 cents per week reduction not as a 10 per cent decrease, but as a cut of 20 per cent, counting the surplus of $1.25 per week as her "wages."

Obviously, then, the wage cutting and intensification of work in the early forties was of a serious nature. An examination of the available evidence shows that the reaction to this condition paralleled the general reaction of labor and its supporters throughout the East. The cotton corporations were to come under attack.

At this time the town was served by two newspapers, the *Springfield Republican,* which devoted a column to Chicopee news, and a village newspaper, *the Cabotville Chronicle and Chicopee Falls Advertiser.* The latter was first published in 1840. The *Republican* was a Whig and pro-corporation paper; what stand the *Chronicle* took at the outset is uncertain. It could not have been definitely anti-corporation, but may not have been as completely partisan as was the *Republican.*

In 1843, when the wage cutting had assumed serious proportions, Blossom, the editor of the *Chronicle* sponsored a new publication, *The Olive Leaf and Factory Girls' Repository,* modelled after the *Lowell Offering.* The principal contributors were to be factory operatives.[58] This paper, like its prototype, was to be "devoted to the cause of virtue and morality," and as it might prove difficult to please everyone, the owner's "only course in this

[58] *Olive Leaf,* Vol. I, no. 1, April 8, 1843.

situation is to publish as great a variety of matter as possible, at the same time having it chaste and pure."[59] The prospectus stated that

> The Olive Leaf is a semi-monthly paper, devoted to the interests of the operatives at Cabotville and Chicopee Falls, and throughout the New England States.
>
> The matter will be chiefly original, containing articles—Religious, Literary, and Historical.
>
> *The Paper will ever be free from a party spirit, and nothing will be admitted to its columns with a view to establishing any particular opinion.*[60]
>
> Virtue and Morality will be its leading characteristics, while the chief aim of the Editor shall be to benefit that class, to whose welfare it is devoted, and at the same time endeavor to make it interesting to all.

The editor kept his promise. Not one of the various articles and stories which the girls contributed could even remotely be construed as being controversial. They dealt with Love, Virtue, Truth, Beauty, Friendship, and other sentiments of an exalted nature. One article in particular best illustrates the feeling which promoted such a publication, and is indicative of the wide publicity given to the statements concerning the New England factory system by visitors from Europe.

> During my residence in this village, the perusal of valuable books, reflection and conversation have indeed been of great benefit to me; and suffer me, my friends and associates, to recommend this practice to you. Believe me, we shall then be able to furnish matter for the "Olive Leaf," without murdering the "King's English," and our compositions will be such, that if a Dickens should again visit this country, and go into New England factories, and we girls should happen to be the focus for his eyes, when he returns to his native land, he can speak of us and the "Olive Leaf" in as high terms of commendation, as the author of "Notes on America" has done of the Lowell Offering and the operatives there. It may be that some distinguished writer may visit Cabotville; if so, may he not find a single moping slatternly girl in the mills, wearing "clogs and pattens," but see them, one and all, dressed as neat, clean and looking more tidy than Queen Victoria in all the attire of royalty, together with a cluster of fine trinkets, and a thousand dazzling ornaments.[61]

[59] *Ibid.*

[60] Italics mine.

[61] *Olive Leaf,* Sept. 16, 1843.

A letter from another subscriber supported this position, but at the same time recognized the lack of time for such activity.

> This paper, if we understand its object, is to be devoted to the interest, or more especially, the mutual improvement of that class whose name in part it bears. Now, if others are so much interested in our intellectual welfare, ought not we to be prompt in showing that we appreciate that interest; not only by giving our subscription for the support of the paper, but by devoting some of our leisure moments in supplying its pages.
>
> The time allowed us for mutual improvement, it is true, is extremely limited; but if we are zealous to redeem each moment as it flies, there are but few, we trust, but will have something to offer on the side of virtue and morality, etc., etc.
>
> A FACTORY GIRL.[62]

But while this virtuous paper was being published, a group of girls employed by the Chicopee Manufacturing Company apparently decided that one phase of mutual improvement might be developed by making some protest against wage cutting and the speed-up of machinery. They organized a strike. No report of this strike found its way into the pages of the *Olive Leaf* or the *Springfield Republican.* The only published contemporary report available comes from a New York paper.

> In some cases they are oppressed by a decrease of wages and an increase of labor. This was the cause which led to the glorious turnout of the fair operatives of Chicopee. They formed in solemn column, arrayed in their best bibs and tuckers, and marched to the music of the drum and fife through the streets, and waved their kerchiefs to the girls in the other mills to join them. Failing to enlist reinforcements, they returned to their places. A few days afterwards they mustered their forces again, and with as little success as before, and to add to their discomfiture, when desirous of turning in a second time, they were turned out by their employers.[63]

A less enthusiastic description of this strike was recorded by an eye witness.

> April 28.
>
> The girls in the Factories started on a turnout yesterday and have kept up the spirit of 76. They held a consultation and determined to turn out. They sent for Mr. Carter but he told them

[62] *Ibid.,* April 25; 1843.

[63] *New York State Mechanic,* May 18, 1843. Quoted in Commons, *op. cit.,* Vol. VIII, 219.

they must work out their notice or he would give them no settlement as the cuts would remain the same until the first of June.

May 2.

The girls in the factory show a great deal of uneasiness and threaten to turnout

May 3.

Great turnout among the girls. The weavers met last night at . . . and were advised ?? but what I do not know. But after breakfast this morn. a procession preceded by a painted window curtain for a banner went round the square, the number sixteen. They soon came past again with Mr. . . . They then numbered 44. They marched around awhile and then dispersed. After dinner they sallied forth to the number of 42 and marched down to Cabot under the direction of Mr. . . . They marched round the streets doing themselves no credit. Messrs. Mills and Dwight are up from Boston.

May 4.

Girls on the turnout. They had a meeting at C. last night and were ably addressed by Hosea Kenny Esq. This morning after breakfast they came out and marched round the square numbering 22 and after dinner they were to come out under the direction of Hosea. He went down all dressed in uniform but the girls would not be led by him. Soon the old leaders came on dressed with "Gewgaws" and around him they rallied. After they had formed a procession they marched to Cabot. but it did no good.

May 5.

The girls had no turnout today.

May 6.

The girls have got over their excitement in some degree.[64]

While this was obviously not a mass strike, more girls must have been involved than the foregoing account would suggest, if Edmund Dwight and J. K. Mills came from Boston to look into the matter. Dissatisfaction must have been running high if it was able to precipitate even this demonstration. It required some angry bravery at that time to march "round the streets doing themselves no credit." While these girls were assisted by one or two men in their attempts to protest the wage cutting, they do not seem to have been supported by the male employees of the mill. These, aside from the overseers and their assistants, were mostly skilled

[64] *Taylor Diary*, April 28 et seq., 1843.

wood and metal workers, who were earning fairly high wages, and may not have felt the same pressure that the female operatives did.

If the mechanics of the town did not feel the need of protesting wage adjustments they were interested in the possibilities of a shorter working day. In this they followed the methods of the Fall River and Lowell workers who had petitioned the legislature for relief. The mechanics of the Ames Manufacturing Company presented a petition to N. P. Ames, asking for a reduction in working time, and on receiving the following reply, took no further action.

> The subject of your petition is one that has long been considered by me, and knowing the views of many persons capable of judging on the subject I have formed an opinion respecting it. I know that evening labor does not affect all branches of business alike; in many branches it would not be judicious to employ it to as good advantage as daylight. The variety of business in our works make it difficult to frame a rule that will affect all alike. *I feel it a duty, situated as I am, to adhere to the general rule for labor employed in the vicinity.* It is not our purpose to require more than prudent management in manufacturing would suggest and demand, and we shall always be ready to conform individual cases to circumstances, while we believe a general rule would not be satisfactory to either party.[65]

This esprit de corps maintained by the manufacturers in the matter of hours of work extended to general employment rules.

> On the subject of hiring workmen who I know to be in the employment of neighboring manufacturers or employers, I have ever recognized one course as right, and that is, never to hire away from a neighbor without an understanding on that subject. I have never had any objection to hiring a man, out of employment, who had been employed by a neighboring mechanic, and never had any understanding with any one, that I would not employ men who had been dismissed from their employment.[66]

The letter went on to say that as a general rule employment would not be offered to a man who was temporarily out of work if there was a likelihood that his previous employer might be able to use him in the near future.

[65] *Ames Papers,* Letters, N. P. Ames to his Workmen, Nov. 20, 1843. Italics mine.

[66] *Ibid.,* N. P. Ames to ? (Perhaps the head of the Springfield Armory.)

After these hesitant attempts at labor action on the part of Chicopee wage-earners, the fight passed to the press and to another group. In 1842 the *Hampden Post,* a short-lived Democratic organ published in Springfield, launched a bitter attack on Abbott Lawrence and others who, it was asserted, through their control of the banks and insurance companies exercised undue power over labor.[67] Soon a laborer in the vicinity was writing that "the time when we are to have our 'two dollars a day and roast beef' seems to be yet far distant. In lieu of that we find it hard enough to provide even the necessaries of life for our families and pay our taxes, at present."[68] In 1844 this paper turned its attention to the cotton mills in Chicopee:

> It is seldom that we have so gratifying an event to record as that a manufacturing company has raised the wages of its operatives, but it is our pleasing duty to do so this week. Everybody knows that our manufacturing establishments were never doing better than at present. They are manufacturing largely—crowding their mills to the utmost of performance—are realizing large profits and declaring smashing dividends. Everybody knows all this, but everybody dont know that the corporations in this town have lately raised the wages of their weavers. All incredible as this may seem it is really true. Heretofore they have paid twelve and a half cents a web for weaving, but their increased profits have enabled them to raise the price to fourteen cents. This is honorable! It is highly creditable to the . . . corporations; and it puts an effective damper upon the villainous Locofocos who have all along been loudly protesting that an increase in profits never brought a corresponding increase in wages. We repeat, it is highly creditable to the . . . corporations; but it would have been still more to their honor if they had not at the same time increased the measurement of the webs from thirty yards to forty yards, so that this advance in price really operates as a *reduction of sixteen per cent.* It is truly lucky for the weavers that we have such an excellent tariff, for without it they never would have enjoyed this agreeable episode in the history of their toilsome duties. Who will affirm after this that corporations are soulless?[69]

This report was denied by the *Springfield Republican* which printed wage data relating to various mills outside Chicopee to prove the falsity of the *Post's* position.[70]

[67] *Hampden Post,* March 30, 1843.
[68] *Ibid.,* Nov. 1, 1843.
[69] *Ibid.,* May 15, 1844.
[70] *Springfield Republican,* Sept. 14, 1844.

The *Olive Leaf,* published by the *Cabotville Chronicle,* did not live beyond 1843. Its colorless inanity was at odds with the times. Two years later the publisher of the *Chronicle* was galvanized into sudden anti-corporation activity. His opposition was confined to local problems, and was not part of the anti-Whig propaganda as were the attacks of the *Hampden Post.* His old resolve to steer clear of controversial questions as expounded in the *Olive Leaf* was completely abandoned. He jumped into the fight in 1845, and practically turned the *Chronicle* into a labor paper.

It is hard to know just what happened in those two or three years which so completely changed the *Chronicle's* attitude. The constant pressure on labor must have caused much grumbling and talk in the town. The 20 per cent profits of 1844 and 1845 without an increase in wages must have caused bitterness in the community. The echoes of the factory controversy must have reached Chicopee. At any rate, so far as it has been possible to ascertain from the scattered issues of the paper and reprints of its articles which are extant, the first anti-corporation gun was fired in June, 1845. This article set the mood for further comment on labor conditions.

> The following article so forcibly contrasting the Factory system of Old and New England we take from the Weekly Bee. We wish every one to read it, and think of the matter seriously. Here we have a true picture of the condition of those who work in the Factories. Where is humanity? It is swallowed up in gain—for the almighty dollar; and for this poor girls are enslaved, and kept in a state little better than the machinery, which when it gets out of repair is taken to the repair shop and restored; but not so the *human machinery*—that is kept in constant motion, until the motive power is brought to a stop, and what becomes of it then? it is laid one side, and *new machinery* procured. But what are they compared to the dollar?—Oh, nothing—a little thing—life is not much, and what do they want to live for? they are not fit for *society*—they are *poor,* and perhaps it may be said *ignorant!* But why are they poor? Let the *consciences of others* answer.[71]

At this point a third party entered the controversy. The boarding-house keepers joined the workers in their discontent, for they

[71] Reprint from *Cabotville Chronicle* in the *Voice of Industry,* June 26, 1845.

were in a difficult position. With the price of board set by the corporations and the cost of living going up in the middle forties, they felt that they had to squeeze themselves or their boarders. The unrest in the town must have been great, and the *Cabotville Chronicle,* by its belligerent attitude, gave voice to this unrest.

It was in October, 1845, that the boarding masters, who had the sympathy of the townsfolk, petitioned the corporations for a higher allowance per boarder. They formed an organization, and made the following report:

We, the people of Cabotville, who are the keepers of Boarding houses, on the lands belonging to the several corporations, finding by two years experience, that we were not only not making anything, but actually running behind fast, besides wearing out our beds and household furniture, and having waited until our patience had become exhausted, and our credit in danger, to see if those, who are receiving the benefit of our sacrifice and also the benefit of that which is calculatd to take care of the rich at the expense of the consumer, would not consider us, and so far raise the price of the board of the operatives, that we might by good economy, and unwearied industry, obtain a comfortable living; but we at length come to the conclusion, that if we obtained any help from that source, we must ask for it. Accordingly on the 25th of October last, we presented the Agents of the three Corporations, a Petition signed by some fifty of the Boarding House Keepers, of which the following is a true copy:

To the President, Directors, and Agents of the Manufacturing Companies in Cabotville:

We, the undersigned, keepers of boarding houses, on the lands of the corporations would respectfully represent that in the most favorable time and under the most auspicious circumstances, that the price paid for board was hardly sufficient to pay the first cost of provision, rent, and wear and tear of furniture, to say nothing of the unrecompensed toil which our wives and daughters must endure; and much more is true now, when all kinds of produce provision and groceries have greatly advanced in price, that the rate of board is utterly insufficient to afford us a mere living, though we rise early and sit up late, and eat the bread of extreme carefulness. We therefore most respectfully, yet earnestly ask you so far to raise the price of board, that the keepers of your boarding houses, with hard labor and parsimonious economy, may live and not die.

Whereupon, on the first day of November inst., at 7 o'clock, p. m., a meeting was held at Ferry's Hall, by the Petitioners, to take the subject matter of the Petition into consideration. . . . After some debate on the subject, by several members, it was voted to choose a committee, of one from each corporation, to confer with one or more of the agents on the subject, and ascertain what course they had taken in regard to the subject of the petition, and report at a future meeting. . . .

Monday, Nov 3. Met according to adjournment. The committee reported that they had called on one of the agents according to their mission, and ascertained that the subject matter of the Petition had been laid before Mr. Mills of Boston, who decided that there was no cause existing whereby the price of board should be advanced. After some remarks by several individuals the committee presented the following Preamble and Resolution, which being duly considered, were unanimously adopted, as expressing the views of the members present:

Whereas, finding that after having used all the means in our power to obtain our rights, by requests and petitions, we are still neglected, we deem it due to ourselves, to the community, to justice and humanity, to express our feelings in relation to inequalities which now exist in the community; that those of our fellow beings who have not as yet been led astray by a vain hope of bettering their condition by taking a factory boarding house, may count the cost before they enlist, and so avoid the lamentation which we have to make—"The summer is over and we are in debt." And also to induce, if possible, those who have it in their power so far to order things in relation to our condition, as to do honor to themselves, and justice to us, that we may, by rigid economy, meet our lawful demands, and live as men in the world.

Therefore, resolved, that by three, four, six and eight years' experience, which we have had in keeping boarding houses in this village, we do now know that it is impracticable and impossible to support ourselves unless we resort to unjust measures, either of which would be the height of unjustice.

Resolved, that in our opinion the time has come when the causes which produced the depression of board is done away; that no reason exists why we should not with other classes of our fellow men, experience the benefit of the times, which is causing almost every other class to rejoice.

Resolved, that we still most respectfully request those who have it in their power to control the price of board on the corporations, to take into consideration, and do us that justice which we have a right to expect from men of magnanimity, enterprise, and noble minds.[72]

[72] From *Cabotville Chronicle,* reprinted in Commons, *op. cit.,* VII, 138-140.

The entire proceedings received a full report in the *Cabotville Chronicle.* But a reiteration of the resolutions did not seem to help the boarding masters to achieve an increase on the price of board. The *Chronicle* reported the next step.

A MOVEMENT IN REGARD TO BOARD. Considerable excitement has been created by the late proceedings of the Boarding House Keepers. The agents were sent for to hold a council in Boston, and were absent for several days. They have been compelled to take some action, notwithstanding they had determined to do nothing, for many of the boarding masters have given up their boarders, so that something will be done, and we anticipate a rise in the price of board, fall of rent, or something whereby they may be able to keep square with the world.

A meeting will be held at Ferry's Hall on Monday evening next, by the boarding masters, where we hope to see a goodly number of those whose feelings are enlisted with them to put down the tyranny of the corporations.[73]

In taking this step the boarding-house keepers were supported by public sympathy.[74] Other local newspapers gave wide publicity to the quarrel.

The keepers of Boarding-houses for the corporations complain that they were not sufficiently paid for their services. Their complaints were laid before the proper authorities and received for answer that "There was no cause existing whereby the price of board should be advanced." No cause why the price of board should be advanced? One dollar and twenty-five cents per week, washing included, for female operatives, and a proportional price for males. This is a fraction less than six cents a meal, making no allowance for washing and lodging. Now, where is the man who would open a boarding-house on such terms, unless he calculated in the beginning to starve his boarders or himself, or cheat the grocer and butcher out of their bill. Where is the man who can afford to victual the person who labors twelve hours in a day, for less than six cents a meal? And out of this sum the Cabotville boarding-house keeper must furnish his provisions, pay his help, his house rent and his taxes, must keep his furniture, his beds and bedding good; must clothe himself and family, to say nothing of laying by a store for a rainy day! The thing cannot be done. The closest economy may be studied but loss must accrue to somebody. The man must grow poor in slaving himself and family to death, or he must turn knave and cheat those of whom he pur-

[73] *Cabotville Chronicle,* Nov. 15, 1845.
[74] *Taylor Diary,* Nov. 8, 1845.

chases his supplies out of their dues. The price is inadequate in itself, and should therefore be increased as an act of justice to all concerned.

There is still another consideration which should be brought into the account. The price of board was reduced in 1841. Whether this reduction took place because the manufacturers were seeing hard times or because provisions were cheap, we do not now recollect. Nor is it material, for if either was the cause, it has now ceased to exist. The manufacturers were never doing better than at present, so they can *afford* to be liberal. Neither has there been a time since the reduction, when provisions were so high as at present. They are at least, as a general thing we think, twenty per cent higher than they were last year, and if board could then be afforded for one dollar and twenty-five cents per week, there is the best reason in the world why it cannot now be afforded for that.

No one who takes the trouble to investigate the subject carefully, can doubt that in asking an increase of price, the boarding-house keepers of Cabotville have reason and justice on their side; and we feel confident that those who have the final adjustment of the matter will on reflection come to the same conclusion, will determine accordingly.[75]

The corporations reconsidered their earlier decision, and raised the price of board by twelve and a half cents per week, but not before some of the boarding masters had refused to carry on under the old price. The *Springfield Republican* joined the controversy in the press by supporting the corporations' position in the quarrel.

We understand that the price of board paid by the Factory Corporations at Cabotville and Chicopee Falls, to those who keep their female operatives has been increased from $1.25 per week to $1.37½, to take effect from the first of November. This has been called for by the extraordinary rise in flour and other provisions. With the exception of a similar addition during the years 1837 and 1838, when breadstuffs were exceedingly high, $1.25 per week has always been the price paid for female board by these corporations. The recent movement of the boarding-house keepers in Cabotville, in holding public meetings on the subject, and forming a combination to force the corporations into compliance with their demands, we are informed, were entirely uncalled for, and delayed, in fact, the object which they sought. Those who had the management of the corporations promised early in the month to take the matter into consideration, giving the keepers of the boarding-houses to understand at the same time, that they would comply with their

[75] Reprint from *Tri-Weekly Post* in *Cabotville Chronicle,* Dec. 6, 1845.

requests; but they refused to be driven or forced into it. The combination has therefore been dissolved, and the corporations in making the above advance in the allowance for board, have given them more than they asked or expected. We believe it well for the interests of both parties that a wise and liberal policy should be pursued by the corporations, and such we think the desire and intentions of those who have them in charge. The spirit that would fan a bitter feeling of jealousy between the employer and the employed, for the sake of party purposes, or private ends, is as despicable as it is paltry and mean, and should be scouted by all honorable men of every party.[76]

This account of the affair as it appeared in the columns of the *Springfield Republican* received a scathing attack from the *Chronicle.*

No person in Cabotville, who reads the above article will believe it, and the person who penned it must have done it wilfully and maliciously, or he must have been very ignorant of the matter, for misrepresentation and falsehood characterize the whole, and we have no doubt it was written under the dictation of one or more of the agents in this village. Though the price of board has been increased the trifling sum of 12 and a half cents, it is not sufficient, even at the prices of provisions heretofore, to enable the boarding-house keepers to stand even with the world. This increase in the price of board, the writer says, "had been called for in the extraordinary rise in the price of provisions," as if they had done some great deed of disinterested benevolence, as if there was a *soul* to prompt them to it; but the fact is, it would not have been done but for the recent movements. Here again, is another false statement in regard to their holding public meetings and the writer must have known there was no truth in it.

They have never held a public meeting. Their meetings have been in private, none being admitted but those concerned, and they have even requested those not concerned, to withdraw.

But for this movement, nothing would have been done; for upon the superintendent being presented with the petition, he saw no reason for raising the price of board, and that it should not be raised until flour was twelve dollars a barrel; and it was not till several of the boarding masters went to the counting-room, and gave up their boarders, that anything was done. No, rather than relieve their wants as they would have done, if they had been possessed of the common feelings of humanity, they would have the girls live on so short an allowance of food, that their hard labor would soon bring them to a premature grave. And we have been

[76] Reprint from *Springfield Republican* in the *Cabotville Chronicle,* Dec. 6, 1845.

creditably informed that one of the authorities was heard to say, that rather than do this, they should "Pinch 'em, PINCH 'EM!" Does this sound like alleviation? No; they would not have added the twelve and a half cents if they could have avoided it, and they made as little advance as possible, and it is not true that they gave more than was asked or expected. An advance of 25 cents for females and 50 cents for males was asked for. The question was put to the committee who presented the petition, by one of the agents, "how much would satisfy them?" to which they made answer, "two dollars a week for males and one dollar and fifty cents for females." This is a fair price and will no more than remunerate them.

We again assert, that there was no meeting held by the boarding-house keepers, until it was decided not to raise the board; Dea. Bowles[77] and the agents notwithstanding.

There is another feature in this matter which should not be overlooked, that the writer forgot to mention, that is an endeavor to compel their help to board on the corporation. There are some of such independence, that they *will not* be crowded into the rooms in the blocks, with some half dozen others, knowing that it tends not only to injure the health of the body, but also of the mind. But as they are considered by their employers as mere machinery, what matters it whether *they* enjoy health and happiness? and for this reason every regulation is calculated to oppress.

And to conclude our remarks upon this article, we cannot do better than to use the language of the Post in its concluding remarks on the same, adopting it as our own:

"We concur most cordially with the Republican, that the 'spirit which would fan a bitter feeling of jealousy between the employer and the employed, for the sake of party purposes, or private ends, is as despicable as it is paltry and mean,' and if there is any spirit more despicable, more paltry, more mean, one more utterly to be scouted, it is that of the fawing sycophant, which in every controversy that arises, is the advocate, the apologist, the partisan of the strong and powerful because he is thus strong and powerful for political reasons, *against* the weaker party who in nine cases out of ten has right and justice on his side."[78]

While the boarding-house controversy was in progress, and perhaps encouraged by it and by the attitude of the *Chronicle,* a few girls employed by one of the mills stood out successfully against a threatened wage cut, and won their point. The *Chronicle* commended them for their action.

[77] The publisher of the *Springfield Republican.*
[78] *Cabotville Chronicle,* Dec. 6, 1845.

THE BANNER ROOM. We understand that the young ladies employed in the Spinning Room of Mill No. 3 . . . made a very quiet and successful "strike" on Monday. The Spinning machinery was set in motion, in the morning, but there were no girls to tend it. They had heard the rumour that their wages were to be cut down, upon which they determined to quit. They silently kept their resolve, and remained out until Tuesday afternoon, when they were requested to return to their employment with an addition to their previous wages of fifty cents per week. The Ladies connected with the other Mills, ought certainly to present them with a banner, as a tribute of esteem for thus volunteering as pioneers in the march of increasing compensation.

We also learn that notice has been given to the weavers in the same Mill, that their prices will be reduced twenty cents on a cut, upon which they gave notice to leave. Thus matters stand, and what the result will be we know not.

At the present rate of 90 cents per cut, the weavers are enabled by great exertions, to make enough to feed and clothe themselves, and have a small surplus, if economy is used. The cloth being very fine, it requires a great deal of attention, and ninety cents is not any too much. But the difficulty arises from the fact that it takes the best weavers from the other Mills, and hence the restriction upon their liberties to work where they please.

We think the girls acted rightly, and by way of encouragement, and stirring up their minds by way of remembrance, we say "stick to your text," and pursue a steady course, with a determined spirit, and you will come off victorious.[79]

With the boarding-house controversy settled, the *Chronicle* gave itself over whole-heartedly to the fight against the cotton corporations, and to championing the cause of the operatives. Just what it expected to accomplish is uncertain. The operatives were never advised to attempt some sort of permanent form of labor organization. On the whole the paper personified a mood, rather than a course of action. The editor was belligerent without giving direction to his militancy.

We hope all indebted to us for the Chronicle, will make payment before the first of January next, for we intend then, to make some additions to our office, and improvements in our paper. We shall want every cent that is owing us to be able to make the alterations and improvements which we contemplate. We shall expect that the hard hands and the ???? of our village to stand by (?) their rights and interests, for the corporate power is against us.

[79] *Cabotville Chronicle,* Nov. 15, 1845.

One man said to us not long since, speaking of the character of our paper, "you do wrong to come out against the corporation. If you wish to MAKE MONEY, (as though making money were the *only* thing man lived for) you must keep on the *right* side of them." If they go *right* we go with them, but if they go wrong, woe be unto them. "But," said he, "a poor man cannot be independent."

Whether the gentleman was speaking his *own* sentiments or not, we shall not judge, but our opinion is that a man can be independent and yet poor, for we have experienced it. Give us poverty before a cringing submission to corporate powers for the purpose of "making money."

* * * *

It has been a matter of surprise to many, why we have not before advocated the interests of the operatives. We acknowledge that we have not done that which we now see was our duty some years since. But even now, the curse pronounced upon Cain, was not much more severe than those which have been heaped upon our head for the stand we have taken in the cause of humanity and justice; and we shall continue in our present course. So long as there is a shot left in the locker—amid the gibes and jeers of a purse-proud aristocracy, we raise our standard, and here it shall wave until tyranny and oppression shall be banished from our midst.[80]

After this "declaration of principle" the *Chronicle* attacked the current methods of recruiting labor supplies for the mills.

We were not aware until within a few days, of the modus operandi of the Factory powers in this village, of forcing poor girls from their quiet homes, to become their tools, and like the southern slaves, to give up her life and liberty to the heartless tyrants and taskmasters. Observing a singular looking "long, low black" wagon passing along the street, we made inquiries respecting it, and were informed that it was what we term "a slaver." She makes regular trips to the north of the state, cruising around in Vermont and New Hampshire, and with a "commander" whose heart must be as black as his craft, who is paid a dollar a head, for all he brings to the market, and more in proportion to the distance—If they bring them from such a distance that they cannot easily get back. This is done by "hoisting false colors," and representing to the girls that they can tend more machinery than is possible, and that the work is so very neat, and the wages such, that they can dress in silks and spend half their time reading. Now, is this true? Let those girls who have been deceived, answer.

[80] *Ibid.*, Dec. 6, 1845.

> Let us say a word in regard to the manner in which they are stowed, in the wagon, which may find a similarity only in the manner in which slaves are fastened in the hold of a vessel. It is long, and the seats so close that it must be very inconvenient. Is there any humanity in this? Philanthropists may talk of negro slavery, but it would be well first to endeavor to emancipate the slaves at home. Let us not stretch our ears to catch the sound of the lash on the flesh of the oppressed black while the oppressed in our very midst are crying out in thunder tones, and calling upon us for assistance.[81]

Here again, we find drawn the analogy between southern chattel slavery and northern factory work.

Shortly after this the *Chronicle* stopped publication. It is said that the publisher was run out of town on account of the publication of certain offensive articles, among which was a novel in serial form, entitled "The Mysteries of Cabotville."[82] This story, supposedly dealing with the youth of Chicopee, was said to offend public morality. It is a little odd to find the man who was responsible for the "chastity" of the material in the *Olive Leaf* accused of printing an immoral story. Two installments of the "Mysteries" which could be found are innocent enough judged by any standards. It is interesting to note that they lack the preciosity of style and expression so common to the newspaper stories and articles of the day. We do not know, of course, what appeared in other chapters. If the story gave offense to some, the militant attitude of the publisher on labor problems may have contributed to the desire to dispense with the paper.

With the disappearance of the *Chronicle* it is hard to find any material on labor conditions. One of the merchants reported that there was a strike of Irish railroad workers on account of ill-treatment to which they were subjected by one of the overseers.[83] But obviously, this was an isolated episode.

Another local paper, the *Chicopee Telegraph,* started in 1846, did not follow the policy of the *Cabotville Chronicle.* It either disregarded labor conditions completely, or gave itself over to an elaborate eulogy in the best traditional manner.

[81] From the *Cabotville Chronicle,* reprinted in the *Voice of Industry,* Jan. 2, 1846, and quoted in Commons, *op. cit.,* Vol. VII, 141.

[82] Everts, *op. cit.,* II, 975.

[83] *Taylor Diary,* July 6, 1846.

We would give a passing notice of *one* class in particular—we allude to that class, contemptuously styled by southern aristocrats, *"the white slaves of the north."* As among all other classes of society, there is unquestionably a diversity of character among our female operatives; *but,* we challenge our southern neighbors to produce so great an amount of energy, virtue, intelligence, mental and moral refinement, among the daughters of the south, educated in sloth and indolence, as can be found among an equal number of the female operatives of Cabotville. Don't sneer, Mr. Southerner! —We state facts that are incontrovertible. Our Free institutions have done for *our young ladies* what your *peculiar institutions* can *never* do for yours. Our young ladies—yes, we mean as we say! our young ladies are industrious, and they are not ashamed of it. Their industry makes them *independent,* and they enjoy their independence.[84]

This appeared in 1846. Afterward, the paper kept silent until 1850, when Senator Jare Clemens of Alabama finally referred to the "white slaves of the north" on the floor of the Senate. Now the *Telegraph* came to the "defence" of factory labor, and devoted five solid columns in one issue to confound the Senator. Never before had the paper been so concerned with labor conditions.[85] Letters were received from a few workers supporting the paper's stand, but none of these were written by Chicopee workers. The editor closed the episode with an effusion written, it seems, by a local poet, and symbolic of the attitude of the *Lowell Offering,* Harriet Martineau, and others who had observed and written about the New England "factory idyll." A few verses from this poem follow.

SONG OF THE FACTORY GIRLS

Oh, sing me the song of the Factory Girl!
So merry and glad and free!
The bloom on her cheeks, of health how it speaks,
Oh, a happy creature is she!
She tends the loom, she watches the spindle,
And cheerfully toileth away,
Amid the din of wheels, how her bright eyes kindle,
And her bosom is ever gay.

[84] *Chicopee Telegraph,* June 10, 1846.
[85] *Ibid.,* Feb. 20 et seq., 1850.

Oh, sing me the song of the Factory Girl!
Who no titled lord doth own,
Who with treasures more rare, is more free from care
Than a queen upon her throne!
She tends the loom, she watches the spindle,
And she parts her glossy hair,
I know by her smile, as her bright eyes kindle,
That a cheerful spirit is there.

Oh, sing me the song of the Factory Girl!
Link not her name with the Slave's;
She is brave and free, as the old elm tree
Which over her homestead waves.
She tends the loom, she watches the spindle,
And scorns the laugh and the sneer,
I know by her lip, and her bright eyes kindle,
That a free born spirit is here.

Oh, sing me the song of the Factory Girl!
Whose fabric doth clothe the world,
From the king and his peers to the jolly tars
With our flag o'er all seas unfurled.
From the California's seas, to the tainted breeze
Which sweeps the smokened rooms,
Where "God save the Queen" to cry are seen
The slaves of the British looms.[86]

Four years later another local newspaper was asking, "what is the reason something cannot be done to elevate the condition of the factory girls in Chicopee? Their position is certainly anything but enviable. Now it strikes us that a good reading room, well furnished with suitable productions, would do a great deal to improve them. It would not be necessary to purchase any books; second-hand ones might be contributed, and there are probably a plenty of families who would be willing to do so."[87]

The events recorded above constitute the closing chapter of the Yankee mill population. The *Cabotville Chronicle,* during its brief life as a "grievance" newspaper, must have received the active support and approval of a very considerable part of the working class. When it disappeared, the workers had no voice. It may have been time for their voice to be stilled under any circumstances, for the

[86] *Ibid.,* March 6, 1850.
[87] *Weekly Journal,* Chicopee, Nov. 11, 1854.

general labor movement throughout the state was slowing up. The second half of the forties lacked the turmoil and ferment of the first half. At this time factory conditions were relatively stable. Undoubtedly work now became harder than it had been before. A new group of workers were entering the mills to take the places of many of the Yankees who had endured the pressure of 1841-1845. Most of these new workers were Irish.

CHAPTER VI

A DECADE OF IRISH LABOR, 1850-1860

The labor experiences of the fifties were the experiences of Irish workers. Some of the Irish navvies who had been engaged in railway and canal construction settled down in the neighborhood, many of them securing employment in the various manufacturing establishments and from small employers at unskilled or heavy work.[1] Irish girls, probably the daughters of the men who had built the Erie Canal, were imported from upstate New York in large numbers to take the places of Yankee girls who were leaving the mills.[2] Young Irish boys entered the mills as doffers, and soon were working beside the women in the weaving rooms.[3] As the Irish family population increased the old board-house system changed. Boarding-houses remained, but the puritan discipline disappeared.

Owing to the distinctive differences in the names of the Irish and Yankee workers, it has been possible to make a rough but fairly accurate estimate of the coming of the Irish.[4] Just as a Mehitabel Boston, a Lucinda Pease, and a Wealthy Snow were unmistakably Yankee, so were a Bridget Murphy and a Patrick Moriarty unmistakably Irish. In 1858 at least 60 per cent of the mill population was Irish.

At the beginning of the period, aside from the overseers and their assistants, and the yard and machine shop hands, there was

[1] *Taylor Diary,* March, April, 1852.

[2] *Ibid.,* Nov. 12, 1847.

[3] *Company "C" Papers,* Payroll, passim.

[4] The following transcript from the tenement rolls of one of the Chicopee companies strikingly illustrates the changing nationality of the working population.

Names of tenants and duration of tenancy, No. 21 Cabot Street, back.

Sarah Baxter, 1856-59
Royal Baxter, 1859
Sarah Morley, 1859-60
Ellen Fogerty, 1860-62
John Tuell, 1862-63
John Sears, 1863-80
Henry Adams, 1880
Telesphore Pineau, 1881-82
Marie Lepine, 1882-83
Joseph Lepine, 1883-84
Antoine Bedeau, 1884
Alexandre Lafonde, 1884
Peter Gilbert, 1885
William Nimil, 1885-86
William Gurska, 1886-

TABLE 10. TOTAL NUMBER OF NAMES ON SPECIFIED PAYROLLS AND PERCENTAGE DEFINITELY IRISH, 1841-1854*

Date	Mill 1		Mill 2	
	Total Names	Percentage Irish	Total Names	Percentage Irish
June, 1841	241	2.4	...	....
January, 1842	334	5.	...	....
1843	218	8.7	...	....
1844	224	9.8	...	....
1845	259	18.9	...	....
1846	283	18.	274	7.2
1847	256	13.6	302	13.2
1848	256	19.5	368	9.5
1849	245	30.1	346	16.4
1850	249	35.5	358	21.2
1851	245	30.1	331	28.
1852	243	35.5	340	30.8
1853	243	35.5	...	....
1854	226	47.7	...	....

* Compiled from *Company "C"* Payrolls.

just a scattering of male employees in the mills. From the first young boys had entered the mills for light work, but before long men had taken over the dressing room operations from the women, operated spinning mules, and worked as weavers. Just before the Civil War about 15 to 20 per cent of the operatives were males.[5]

With these fundamental shifts in the constituent elements of the working population, depression periods weighed with increasing severity on the mill hands. Before, even if large numbers of Yankee women were dependent upon the mills, many were able to go back to their parents' homes during bad times, and a great many of them had no other responsibilities, aside from caring for themselves. With the development of a permanent factory population, and the entry of men into mill work, there were whole families dependent upon the prosperity of the mills, and the implications of this situation can be readily seen. While there had been overcrowding under the early boarding-house system, at least it had been the overcrowding of persons of one sex, who had been accustomed to a fairly comfortable standard of life, and understood how to make the necessary adjustments to such conditions. Also it was a literate, an educated population. The new workers were

[5] Compiled from *Company "C"* Payrolls.

massed together, men, women, and children. They were illiterate for the most part, and they were also intemperate. When the mills closed, or ran part time, all income stopped for large numbers of people. They had no farms to which they could turn.

This was the working class group which played the central rôle in the fifties. As in the earlier period, the absentee owners watched the piece rates closely. When it was suggested that a given rate was too high, the agent replied: "I am aware that it is not best to get prices too high to start with, but the usual practise in starting a new kind of work is to put the price high enough to secure good help to start with; then cut them down all they will stand."[6]

However, the changes on the whole were not so drastic as had been experienced in the early forties. Weaving rates, which had been stable from 1843 to 1847 were cut twice in 1848-49. Spinning rates were cut at this time too, but were raised in 1851, only to be reduced again in a few months. But there was a slight net gain. The weavers received an increase in 1852, and the rate remained about the same till after the panic of 1857, when general reductions were instituted.

Figure 7 indicates the trend of female earnings. It will be observed that with the improvement of business conditions immediately after the early forties, earnings moved up somewhat, but that it was not until the fifties that a trend toward substantial gains is evident. These increases in earnings followed increases in wage rates put into effect in 1851-52. In January of 1857 median earnings were 7.7 per cent above the average of the January medians from 1842 to 1846 inclusive, and the average January median of 1855-57 was 11.7 per cent higher. However, in connection with these wage increases, it is necessary to take the price level into consideration. The wholesale commodity index for January, 1857, was about 55 per cent higher than the average January level from 1843 to 1846, and the average January level from 1855-57 was 50 per cent higher.[7] Thus it would seem that as the de-

[6] *Company "B" Papers,* Letter Book, Agent to Treasurer, 1856.

[7] A. Cole, "Wholesale Commodity Prices in the United States, 1843-1862," *Review of Economic Statistics,* February, 1929, p. 31.

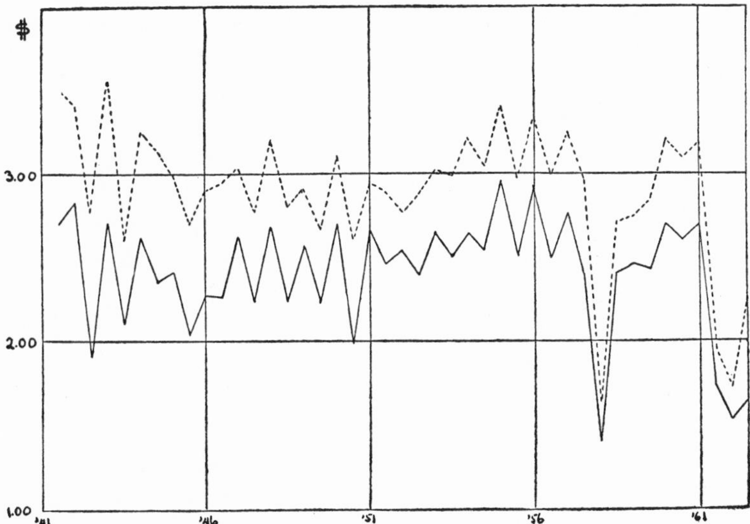

Figure 7. WEEKLY UPPER QUARTILE AND MEDIAN EARNINGS OF FEMALE OPERATIVES, JANUARY AND JULY, 1841-1862.

pression of 1857-58 approached, real earnings were lower than they had been in the forties.[8]

These earnings were even lower in the middle forties, for they had suffered a period of depression before the boom days preceding the panic had pulled them up. The low wage period which started in the previous decade showed no signs of lifting, until work and rates began to pick up in 1851-52. Not only had wage rates been depressed, but work had not been too regular. For this factory population, the middle of the century was not a happy period. "Times for the winter look dark for the manufacturing population," wrote the merchant, Taylor, in October of 1850, "as the mills around here are partially stopping and reducing the wages."[9] A complete section of one mill was shut down for a long time in the latter part of 1851.[10] Again in 1854, Taylor wrote: "In this village it is rather hard for the poor, for provision is very high and

[8] It must be remembered, however, that for large numbers of the workers who lived in company boarding-houses, the cost of living, as determined by the price of board, was stable for long periods, and did not accurately follow the movements of the general price level. To this extent, then, the rising price level was not effective in depressing real wages.

[9] *Taylor Diary,* Oct. 6, 1850. [10] *Ibid.,* Dec. 8, 1851.

work is rather scarce, and outside of the mills the shops are doing as little as possible."[11] Springfield opened a free soup kitchen that winter,[12] and a few months later Taylor recorded that business was still dull. "I stayed in the store all day without much to do and I expect that we shall have quite a number of such days this summer, for Provisions are so high that those who are dependent upon their labor for their money can pay for but little else than provisions."[13] In 1857, when one of the mills went on short time he wrote that "this will be bad for the help for there is a great many of them that just live now."[14]

But there is one factor of importance which must be kept in mind when considering the wage movements of the fifties. The working day was cut to eleven hours. Therefore the wages from 1853 onward apply to shorter working time than had been the case before. The eleven hour day was introduced on November 1, 1853. "Today the Corporation commenced on the 11 hour table. They commence work in the morning at 7 o'clock and come out at 7 during the winter, in the summer half past 6 to half past 6. This will give the help a great deal of leisure especially in the summer, and is the effect of the 10 hour agitation last year, I think."[15] This comment, and that suggested in the selection below, is the only available evidence bearing on the ten-hour movement of 1852 in the town. When the Chicopee Manufacturing Company ran overtime to make up for time lost when the water supply had been low, Taylor wrote that "it will be like to stir up rebellion among the operatives and give us another ten hour furor; and if so there will be more of loss than of gain in the movement."[16] How the workers carried on the agitation in 1852 is unknown, but if Taylor was led to comment that the dislike of overtime work was likely to make trouble for the Chicopee Manufacturing Company, the movement of 1852 must have been quite militant. At any rate, the achievement of the eleven hour day was a positive gain.

[11] *Ibid.*, Dec. 24, 1854.
[12] *Springfield Republican*, Jan. 27, 1855.
[13] *Taylor Diary*, June 13, 1855.
[14] *Ibid.*, Sept. 16, 1857.
[15] *Ibid.*, Nov. 1, 1853.
[16] *Ibid.*, Nov. 29, 1854.

The financial crash of 1857 was keenly felt in Chicopee. The failure of the J. K. Mills Company (selling agents for the local mills) affected the financial position of the Chicopee companies which had to conserve their cash resources, since thousands of dollars were lost. For several months the mills and smaller manufacturing establishments operated at half time, and the latter were very quick to cut wages.[17] When one of the cotton companies adopted a four day week the agent reported to the treasurer in Boston that "the hands take the matter quite hard and it will, without doubt, scatter such of them as have places or homes to flee to." The agent preferred to keep the mills in operation every day at three quarter time, instead of closing down completely for two days, for "there is also another serious evil in our community which will be greatly augmented by two idle days, and that is intemperance. Every holiday we now have breaks us up for a week afterwards, and I fear with two a week this will be greatly aggravated. Intemperance will run riot I have no doubt."[18]

With the treasurer of the company urging the necessity for greater economies, the agent reported: "I am dismissing hands and reducing wages (in all places where it can be done) to the lowest operating point. I have let off some 12 or 15 yard hands and machinists and have dismissed every supernumerary in the mills. I can hardly go much further and keep the mills in a fair operating condition. . . . As we are now running but very few of the operatives will make but a fraction over their board, and there are many that will not make even that. Yet they work on knowing it is as well as they can do and as much as we can afford to pay."[19]

Beginning October, 1857, the median earnings of female operatives were about $1.40 per week for five months. At this time the treasurer of one of the companies urged the agent to cut costs still further by reducing the wage rates, but the latter protested that it was impossible to do this while the mills were running short time, and that a general reduction could be put into effect when capacity production was resumed. However the wages of over-

[17] *Ibid.*, Sept. 16, Oct. 5, Oct. 17, 1857.
[18] *Company "C" Papers*, Letter Book, Agent to Treasurer, Sept. 1857.
[19] *Ibid.*, Oct. 1857.

seers were reduced in December, 1857. The work at this time was inefficient, reported the agent, the overseers were discouraged, and discipline was slack.[20]

One company was not long in resuming full-time operation in some of its mills. "Today a notice was put up that no. 4 mill is to start up December 1 on full time with wages cut down 25 per cent—and I think all of the mills will soon start up at the reduced rates."[21] By March 1st all of the mills were starting capacity production once more with similar pay cuts, and a return to the twelve hour day.[22] These conditions seem to have been extended to the various machine shops in the community as well as to the cotton mills.[23]

But in one company the operatives refused to accept the reductions which the mill owners considered necessary for the full-time operation of the mills. In spite of the fact that they had been working only half time for some months, they announced a strike on April 6th, in protest against the wage reductions. The agent of the company reported the stoppage to his board of directors, indicating that he would not "yield a hair's breadth though it stop every mill for a month. If I yield now we are at the mercy of these people, as it regard wages, ever after."[24]

Immediately after the outbreak of the strike, the strikers sent a delegation to the other mills in order to call out all the workers in the town. Judging from the size of the delegation, large numbers of workers must have already been involved. "This P. M.," commented Taylor, "there was a delegation of 220 girls and 100 men and boys . . . arrived here on a strike on account of the wages being reduced in the mills there, but they did not get anyone to join them from here."[25]

These strikers of 1858 were not respectful as the few strikers of the forties had been. "The idlers hang about the streets howling at, insulting and often assailing the operatives who continue at their looms, but as the novelty of the thing subsides, and a con-

[20] *Ibid.*, Dec. 1857; Jan. 1858.
[21] *Taylor Diary*, Nov. 19, 1857.
[22] *Ibid.*, Dec. 26, 1857; *Springfield Republican*, April 8, 1858.
[23] *Taylor Diary*, Dec. 19, 20, 1857.
[24] *Company "C" Papers*, Letter Book, April 7, 1858.
[25] *Taylor Diary*, April 7, 1858.

tinued idleness draws upon their scanty funds, they become more and more disposed to submit to what is a hardship to themselves but no less a hardship to the corporation. There have been demonstrations of open violence, policemen were stationed at all the approaches to the mills during Monday, and the disaffected contented themselves with shouts and jeers, saying 'the lawyer told them they might do so'."[26] Obviously, strikers were no longer content merely to "wave their kerchiefs" to their fellow workers to come out of the mills. Sixteen special constables were appointed by the board of selectmen to maintain order and protect mill property.[27]

Citizens of the town, many of whom were affected by the curtailment of expenditures in consequence of the stoppage, hoped to effect a compromise of the quarrel by approaching the mill officials, but were not successful.[28] Some of the Irish grocers who were sympathetic to the aims of the strikers contributed financial aid.[29] The press reported the course of events quite fully, but did not offer any encouragement to the strikers, on the assumption that the mills would not have cut wages if they could have afforded to act otherwise, and that therefore it was useless to strike. "We trust the corporation will pay all it can possibly afford, and that the girls may get enough to live well on and have an extra ribbon now and then."[30] It is interesting to note that the strikers were mainly Irish workers; the Yankee minority did not turn out.[31]

The strike lasted for two weeks, and the workers, not all of whom were re-engaged, were obliged to go back to work without having gained any concessions,[32] and probably some lost their jobs, since a number of workers had been imported from other localities. No attempt was made to form any kind of permanent organization. The financial resources of the operatives must have been exhausted before the strike broke out, and it was remarkable that

[26] *Springfield Republican,* April 13, 1858.
[27] *Taylor Diary,* April 15, 1858.
[28] *Ibid.,* April 19, 1858; *Springfield Republican,* April 21, 1858.
[29] *Springfield Republican,* April 13, 1858.
[30] *Ibid.,* April 9, 1858.
[31] *Company "C" Papers,* Letter Book, April 11, 1858.
[32] *Springfield Republican,* April 21, 1858.

over five or six hundred of them should have been able to hold out for two weeks against such odds.

The operatives in the nearby corporation had refused to join the strike. However, after having waited very patiently for the expected increases as business conditions improved, there were signs of trouble at the beginning of 1859. "There was a small turnout in no. 4 weave room today. Some 20 girls turned out, but I believe they go back and work out their notice. The company will have to advance the wages of the common help in order to keep the best help."[33] A little later there were "strong indications of a general turnout in the mills on account of the wages."[34] But at the end of May the Dwight Company gave a general increase of from 10 to 25 per cent and presumably the Chicopee Manufacturing Company followed suit.[35] By 1860 most of the lost ground, swept away by the panic of 1857, had been recovered, but not the eleven hour day.

Throughout this period it had been constantly necessary to recruit new labor supplies to fill the ranks left empty by those who were leaving mill employment. Labor turn-over remained very high. A certain amount of labor in the late fifties came in unsolicited. Company tenements, where rentals were low, were in demand, and were rented, where possible, to families which were able to supply a few workers to the mills. This attempt to have as many workers as possible per family in each tenement was, of course, a contributing factor in the development of the family system. A few transcripts from the tenement rolls of one of the cotton mills are of some interest.

August 28, 1856
John Flanagan of Monson wants a tenement to keep boarders. Has 4 weavers.

Comment: "Supplied."

November 20, 1856
Major Lamont of Middlebury, Schoharie Cy. N. Y. wishes a tenement to keep boarders. Has a family of 5 girls to work in the Mill.

Comment: "Could not come."

[33] *Taylor Diary*, Feb. 14, 1859. [34] *Ibid.*, Feb. 21, 1859.
[35] *Springfield Republican*, May 30, 1859.

December 15, 1856
Elmer Hart of Chicopee Falls wishes a small tenement. His wife is a weaver and spinner.

Comment: "Not worthy."

December 6, 1856
Gideon Saunders of Ashleyville wishes a small tenement to keep boarders. Has no children at home.

Comment: "Not wanted."

February 1, 1858
John . . . of Jenksville wishes a tenement to keep boarders. Has a family of 3 weavers and 3 spinners.

Comment: "Supplied."

But labor supplies coming in this way were insufficient to keep the mills efficiently staffed. In the spring of 1859 a managing agent wrote to his treasurer that it was necessary to increase the labor supply.

> I have engaged a man to go to northern New York next week to look up some fresh girls. He is a man that has been operating in this business for the Great Falls Co., Massachusetts, Boott and Hamilton Mills, and I understand with good success. He thinks he can get me some fifty girls, if I want them. I shall need the whole of this number and most likely more. I suppose it will be two or three weeks before he will arrive here with them. I have arranged with him to pay him for his services $3.00 each girl, he paying his own expenses. The girls to be healthy and robust and from 15 to 35 years old. I am to advance the girls their fare and they to repay the same from their first earnings. But in case they remain in the Company's employ eighteen months, we are to refund the amount to them. This is to induce them to remain *more* than one year which is all that our contract requires of them. They will be worth more to us the last six months than they are the first twelve.[36]

At the same time he sent detailed instructions to the labor recruiter who was operating in New York and Vermont near the Canadian border.

> It is also understood that you may offer to the girls so hired the sum of one dollar per week besides their board for their services the first month, after which time it is presumed they will be competent to go on job work.
>
> A suitable place will be provided for the girls to board and all reasonable and proper care will be shown them in case of sickness.[37]

[36] *Company "C" Papers,* Letter Book, May, 1859.
[37] *Ibid.*

But in spite of these efforts to bring new workers into the mills, the labor shortage persisted into the middle of 1859. This company found that its labor costs were increasing on account of a scarcity of good workers, and the lack of a surplus from which to choose the best, and a "general indisposition" of the hands "to work steady."[38] The agent wrote again to Boynton, the labor recruiter:

I have yours of the 13th and note that you can go at once into the field again to hire more help.

I should be glad to have you devote your whole time to my service until you engage, say, fifty girls.

You had better go to the place where the *quality* of the girls promises the *best* and the *expenses* of reaching here the least. You can judge of this better than I can. I should think the character of the girls in Canada West (Ontario) would be better than in the neighborhood of Montreal. Of this you can judge best.[39]

It is curious that he should have wanted girls from Ontario when he wanted to keep the costs of transportation down. It would have been cheaper to bring them from Quebec, and that is what Boynton did. The agent seemed to be pleased with his first batch of French-Canadian girls for he wrote to Boston: "I had an arrival of eleven girls, 5 Yankee and 6 French, all new hands. They will be of some help to us in a month. I shall expect another and larger lot in two weeks from Canada, and it will be mostly French. The French are better than the Irish when learned. They work steadier and are more ambitious."[40] In October the company was taking all the help that Boynton could send, and now wanted only French-Canadians. "With regard to future operations I will say that I can take some 30 or 40 more girls if they are of the right sort. If you can get those of French origin I think they will prove better than the half-Irish from New York. I have rather bad luck with some of this class of hands. There is a strong disposition to run away to avoid paying their fares."[41]

But this fault did not lie with the new recruits alone. Some were being enticed away by other mills,[42] and this stealing of help by rival companies assumed serious proportions. When the treasurer compared his company's costs with those of the Great Falls

[38] *Ibid.,* July 1859. [39] *Ibid.,* July 14, 1859. [40] *Ibid.,* July 30, 1859.
[41] *Ibid.,* Oct. 1859. [42] *Ibid.*

Company in New Hampshire, and pointed out that the costs of the latter were considerably lower, the agent replied:

> This can only be attributed to the excellence of their help. This feature is noticeable by every one who visits their mills. They are at the doors and homes of a large Yankee population and that of the best kind, while fully two thirds of ours are Irish. But even with the Irish had we but a surplus so as to make a selection of them, I should have no fear but that we could even manufacture as cheap, or nearly so, as the Great Falls. But as it is and has been for a year past, we have been open to a constant drain and we have been as constantly educating help to take the places of those who leave. The result is a diminished product and increased cost. It is an evil of very serious magnitude and one that has exercised more of my thought both sleeping and waking, by night and by day, than any other one subject. It is a growing evil of more than a year, and I suppose it will continue to grow, until the Mills above us are filled. When we are beset by a band of pirates, what can we do? To retaliate and adopt their policy would be as sure death as to submit to their depredations. I have brought from the country within the last fourteen months 230 girls and of these only 115 are now here. Had I but two or three Mills to stock with help, I might be able to keep up my numbers, but having seven, and being open to the plunderers around me, it is very hard and difficult to keep up the supply. To tell the whole truth—though I seldom suffer my spirits to flag—I feel, at times terribly discouraged and think I can see no way to better times.
>
> We are the largest village in the neighborhood and hence if any person wants a house girl or Mill help this place is resorted to at once.[43]

Another factor of local importance was the offer of higher wages by a nearby mill. In the spring of 1860 the agent wrote to Boston: "I am quite short of help, the drain being so great to Indian Orchard. They are now starting up very fast and the drain upon us is large. They offer $4 and $5 per week, by the week, which makes the temptation to leave very great. . . . The starting up of the new Mill at Indian Orchard is really a very serious affair for us. I cannot begin to replace the hands that leave as fast as they come. And besides, I am obliged, in most cases, to take *new* hands to replace the old and experienced (ones) which operates badly in every way."[44]

An interesting consideration presents itself for comment in regard to this labor shortage which was so definitely ascribed to the

[43] *Ibid.*, July 23, 1860.

[44] *Ibid.*, May 18, 21, 1860.

competitive demands of other industrial centers. It may be asked if the mills lost workers to the frontier. No evidence has been found to suggest that such was the case. A recent examination of the rôle of the wage-earner in the movement to the frontier found that very few industrial workers went West, and that they did not leave the East in large enough numbers to have any important effect on labor conditions.[45] The Chicopee evidence confirms one of the conclusions of this study of the westward movement, namely that "if the American wage-earners of the period did in fact have broader opportunities than their fellows in other countries, it would appear that more of the explanation lies in the rapid growth of manufacturing employment than in the presence of a distant frontier."[46]

Judging from the available evidence, there was no conscious attempt to displace the Yankees and then the Irish by lower standard groups.[47] As new labor supplies were tapped, the companies took what they could get. As the Yankees were driven from the mills by the pressure of working conditions, and then the Irish came in, so in much the same way there was a tendency for the French Canadians to come in when the Irish were leaving. To a certain extent, the progression of Yankee, Irish, French-Canadian, in the mills was due to geographical conditions. The first girls to come into the mills were natives of the nearby towns, and as the labor recruiters pushed farther afield the girls came from northern New England. But as the recruiting grounds expanded to the West and to the North, it was only a matter of time before the Irish of upstate New York and the French of Quebec should be reached.

The end of the decade was the end of an era for the Chicopee workers as it was for the rest of the country. The implications of this statement can emerge clearly only when we have examined the labor developments of the post Civil War period.

[45] C. Goodrich and S. Davidson, "The Wage-Earner in the Westward Movement," *Political Science Quarterly,* Vol. 51, pp. 114, 115. (March, 1936.)

[46] *Ibid.,* 116.

[47] After the strike of 1858 the company involved decided to do without more Irish workers, if possible, but in looking for substitutes it was first intended to get English speaking girls from Ontario who would have a higher standard than the French of Quebec.

CHAPTER VII

THE EXPANSION OF LOCAL ENTERPRISE

We have seen that Chicopee had settled down to a routine industrial existence with the development of local middle class enterprise in the years preceding 1860. The number of grocery, clothing and general stores had multiplied, and the owners, so many of whom had migrated to the town from other localities, were building homes, establishing religious congregations, and participating actively in municipal affairs. Some members of this group of merchants were joining forces with other economic interests in the town to sponsor new industrial development.

The local manufactures were prospering. The agricultural tool shops, while catering to a relatively small market, were slowly expanding their production with the extension of farm acreage. The Massachusetts Arms Company had enjoyed a decade of prosperous enterprise, and had weathered the panic of 1857 successfully, as did the other local companies. The Ames shops, while they did not earn the high profits of the forties, had developed a diversity of products and possessed a national reputation. Emerson Gaylord, after working as a contractor for Ames, had recently bought the leather department which he managed, and was starting to build up an independent institution, securing substantial government contracts for mail bags. These local companies were owned by simple business partnerships, or as in the case of the Massachusetts Arms Company, by a closely held corporation. With the exception, perhaps, of the latter company and the Ames shops which were in a somewhat different position insofar as ownership was concerned, they did not earn very high profits, but at least they afforded their managers and owners a comfortable livelihood.

The outbreak of war did not so much change this situation as it intensified the process of business development. The withdrawal of large numbers of men from agricultural and industrial employment throughout the country favored the investment of capital in the manufacture both of machine equipment and consumption goods. The enormous demand for materials of war, a rising price level which assured a profit to almost any undertaking, stimulated investment in large-scale enterprise, and indeed, in enterprise of almost any kind, although the permanent success of the former, in the nature of things, was to be favored. The high price of grain provided a powerful impetus to the expansion of agricultural activity in an effort to increase the product. But at the same time there was a shortage of man power, so that it was necessary to turn to mechanical aids in order to increase the quantity of agricultural produce. In addition to these influences which made for the extension and intensification of agricultural production came the Homestead Act and railroad construction, and the conjuncture of circumstances favorable to the expansion and prosperity of the manufacture of farm machinery was complete.

Thus the various manufacturing companies in Chicopee as elsewhere, began to receive orders which permitted the material expansion of productive capacities. New capital was recruited, and partnerships developed into corporative organizations. New wants and demands paved the way for new partnerships. Profits sought new fields of investment, or were used to extend the original activities of their producers.

Considering all these factors, and the nature of local industry in Chicopee in 1860, the war period could not fail but be productive of greater economic activity than ever before. The Ames and Massachusetts Arms shops which manufactured swords, guns, cannon, and gun-making machinery did not have to wait for the inflationary boom to expand their production to the utmost capacity. The Gaylord company, which made military accoutrements as well as mail bags, was in the same position. The farm implement shops were also favored.

At the end of 1860, the Ames Manufacturing Company, in addition to its other machine shop work, was producing brass cannon. Much of this cannon was being made under contract for the South. In January, 1861, the company decided not to make any further shipments to the secessionist states.[1] It was not long, of course, before the company was swamped with orders from the government, and was working night and day to fill contracts for cannon, shot, swords, and bayonets. Five hundred men were employed in the summer of 1861, two thirds more than at any previous time.[2] As one of the best known ordnance and machine shops in the United States, its production of gun stocking machinery was of importance for other arms makers.[3] By 1864 the company was the largest manufacturer of side arms in the country, and was experimenting with the manufacture of large rifled wrought-iron cannon, although these never saw service.[4]

The Massachusetts Arms Company, which manufactured the Maynard rifle, had 80 men at work at the beginning of the war. The next year this number was doubled, and by 1864 the company gave employment to 200 workers.[5] The profits earned were large. In 1862 a total dividend of 22 per cent was paid to the stockholders, and from January to June, 1865, 40 per cent was distributed.[6]

Emerson Gaylord also benefited from the war activity, and although it was not long since he had started his business with just a handful of workers, he expanded his production of military accoutrements so as to employ 150 men in 1861.[7] In 1863 he incorporated his company with a capitalization of $100,000.[8] Sereno Gaylord, a locksmith, joined the firm at this time, and the manufacture of cabinet locks and trimmings was introduced.[9] In 1865 the company further extended its productive capacity by buying up the Chicopee Malleable Iron Company, an organization which had been incorporated the previous year.[10]

Under the stimulus of the demand for war materials, J. Stevens,

[1] *Springfield Republican,* Jan. 14, 25, 1861.
[2] *Ibid.,* June 18, 19, 1861.
[3] *Ibid.,* Jan. 2, 1863. [4] Clark, *op. cit.,* II, 17, 20.
[5] *Taylor Diary,* Aug. 24, 1861; *Springfield Republican,* Jan. 20, 1862; Feb. 8, 1864.
[6] *Ibid.,* March 2, 1863; May 21, 1865.
[7] *Springfield Republican,* June 18, 1861.
[8] Mass., Sec'y of the Commonwealth, *Abstract of Attested Returns of Corporations Organized in 1863.*
[9] Everts, *op. cit.,* II, 974.
[10] *Ibid.;* Mass., Sec'y of the Commonwealth, *Abstract of Attested Returns of Corporations Organized in 1864.*

the inventor-gunsmith who had been connected with the Massachusetts Arms Company, organized a small shop of his own in 1864. This company started out on a very small scale, with a few men employed, to manufacture breech-loading arms and mechanics' tools, for which, of course, there was a great demand at the time.[11]

In contrast with the rapid and extensive expansion of the war materials factories, the progress of the agricultural tool shops was slower. However the original Belcher company, known as the Whittemore, Belcher Company, was enjoying a good business, and that business was growing. The firm's market area was increasing, and several shipments of farm implements were even exported to South America during the war.[12] B. B. Belcher, who owned the related enterprise, had been operating with a small working capital. In 1863 George Taylor, a merchant, abandoned his mercantile interests and bought a partnership in this firm, to be known henceforth as the Belcher and Taylor Company.[13] The business at this time was quite small, with orders coming from New York and New England, and occasionally some from California and the West.[14] The company was making plows, cutters, shellers, cultivators, and other implements.[15] Belcher and Taylor operated their own iron foundry, and in addition to the material manufactured for their own needs, occasionally accepted small jobs for castings.[16] Taylor devoted all his time to the company, supervising the financial affairs, shipping and selling, while Belcher managed the shops.[17] By 1864 both partners had a $6000 interest in the firm.[18]

With the advance of prices of agricultural tools, and a very considerable increase in their western business, the partners decided to incorporate their enterprise, and enlarge the capitalization.[19] They were not long in putting their plan into effect, capitalizing the

[11] *Springfield Republican*, Jan. 2, 1866; A. M. Copeland, *op. cit.*, III, 500.
[12] *Taylor Diary*, April 30, 1863; Sept. 22, 23, 1865.
[13] *Ibid.*, March 3, 1863.
[14] *Ibid.*, April 10 et seq., 1863.
[15] *Ibid.*, March 17, 18, 1863.
[16] *Ibid.*, June 1, 23, 1863.
[17] *Ibid.*, 1863, 1864, passim.
[18] *Ibid.*, July 9, 1863; July 3, 1864.
[19] *Ibid.*, April 13, August-Sept. 1864; Sept. 28, 1864.

company at $50,000.[20] Taylor and Belcher each took $10,000 worth of stock in the new corporation.[21] Taylor's brothers, who were merchants engaged in business in Chicopee subscribed, and another brother, who was employed in Boston, was able to solicit the investment of some $5000 from business associates there.[22] The first board of directors, in addition to George Taylor and his brother James, consisted of John Wells, a lawyer, E. Blake, agent of the Chicopee Manufacturing Company, Bailey West, who had been employed in the business before, E. O. Carter, and W. P. McFarland, who was a stockholder in the Massachusetts Arms Company, and was employed there in a managerial capacity.[23] Thus the company was facing the close of the war with its expected drop of prices and business disorganization with a fresh start and new capital.

Aside from the expansion of these companies, there is no evidence of any significant establishment of "livelihood" industries which might indicate the transformation of the independent artisan to the status of small manufacturer, or the transference of small mercantile capital to industrial investment. However a few small enterprises which had been established before the war survived, and a few additions to the ranks of petty industry occurred during the war. Thus the manufacture of some boots and shoes, brooms, carriages, bricks, leather belting, bobbins, and weavers' reeds, and the preparation of some food products continued.[24] But they did not show any considerable measure of expansion, and it would seem that for the most part the market for their products was confined to a narrow radius. Immediately before and during the war a bread and pastry shop opened, another boot maker made his appearance, and also a harness and bridle shop, and two enterprises for the preparation of hulled corn and hominy, and soft soap.[25]

The position of the merchant was not so clear during the war. On the one hand the stoppage of the cotton mills, in whole or in part, cut off a considerable source of his income, or subjected it to

[20] *Ibid.*, Nov. 9, 1864.
[21] *Ibid.*, March 2, 1865.
[22] *Ibid.*, Oct. 12, 1864.
[23] *Ibid.*, Nov. 1, 1864.
[24] Mass., Bureau of Labor Statistics, 9th *Annual Report*, 62 (1878).
[25] *Ibid.*

frequent fluctuations. This disorganization of cotton production and the general business uncertainty made 1861 a poor year for retail trade, on the whole. But if cotton earnings fell off, the town was soon employing a greater number of skilled mechanics than ever before. One merchant, at the end of 1861, noted that a poor payment by the Chicopee Manufacturing Company was counterbalanced by the large monthly wage bill of the Massachusetts Arms Company.[26] By 1862 business was picking up in anticipation of a rise in prices, and any stocks that the merchant had on hand were bound to undergo considerable appreciation in value.[27]

Here again we must emphasize what seems to be a significant fact in relation to retail trade. George Taylor had already remarked, at the close of the fifties, that it was then more difficult to earn a living in retail trade than had hitherto been the case. In 1863 Taylor liquidated his mercantile investment and transferred it to a small agricultural tool shop which seemed, at the time, to promise no more than a modest livelihood to its owners. That is all that it had yielded in the past. Moreover this transfer was effected at a time when the prospects for mercantile profits must have seemed brighter than they had been for some years. Under the circumstances it is probably safe to conclude, in spite of the apparent improvement in the lot of the merchant during the war, that the opportunities for mercantile prosperity were to be limited in the long run. Taylor's decision of 1863 supports this conclusion.

The merchant-manufacturer group did not emerge as a wealthy class immediately following the Civil War. A few members of the group achieved some degree of wealth, but on the whole, incomes earned were very moderate.[28] In 1867, when the town resumed its accustomed activity after a brief breathing spell, only 98 persons earned over $1000 per annum, and only 11 of these earned more than $2500.[29] The levels may have been somewhat higher in the latter years of the war, but there is no reason to believe that the distribution was much different. It will be noticed that this group is almost entirely Yankee, and that the largest in-

[26] *Taylor Diary,* Nov. 19, 1862.
[27] *Ibid.,* March 17, 1863.
[28] See Tables 11 and 12.
[29] *Springfield Republican,* April 13, 1868.

TABLE 11. INCOME TAX RETURNS OF ALL PERSONS RECEIVING MORE THAN $1000, 1867 AND 1868*

Income Group	1867	1868
$1000 — $1500	66	62
1501 — 2000	16	17
2001 — 2500	5	10
2501 — 3000	3	1
3001 — 3500	0	2
3501 — 4000	1	1
4001 — 4500	1	2
4501 — 5000	1	2
5001 — 6000	0	1
6001 — 7000	2	0
7001 — 8000	2	0
over 8000	1	1
Total	98	99

* From *Springfield Republican*, April 13, 1868; April 19, 1869.

comes are those earned by persons who had investments in companies which produced materials of war. Roughly 20 per cent of those receiving more than $1000 per annum were merchants. But as there were certainly more than 20 merchants in the town in 1867-68, a good number must have been earning less than $1000. Mercantile enterprise was not conducted on a large scale.

But if this middle class was not a wealthy one during these years, it had at least achieved a position of unparalleled relative importance in the town. Before 1860, the cotton corporations, entirely owned and controlled by outside interests, had constituted the backbone of economic life insofar as the mass of the people were concerned. But when the war came cotton production was completely disorganized. The Chicopee Manufacturing Company had sold most of its raw cotton at an enormous profit in 1861 and had very few looms in operation at the beginning of 1864.[30] The Dwight mills only gave partial employment in 1862, and as late as 1864 had only 400 hands at work. Before the war 1600 had been employed.[31] On the other hand, the Ames Company[32] and the outstanding local firms gave employment to about 1000 skilled

[30] *Springfield Republican*, Jan. 20, 1862; Dec. 19, 1863.

[31] *Ibid.*, Feb. 10, 1862; Feb. 23, 1864.

[32] The Ames Manufacturing Company is grouped as a local concern because of the large stock ownership, the management, and the residence of J. T. Ames.

TABLE 12. INCOMES OF ALL PERSONS RECEIVING MORE THAN $1000 IN 1868, AND THEIR OCCUPATIONS AT STATED INTERVALS*

Name	Income	Occupations		
		1853	1865	1873
A. B. Abbey	$1600	Carpenter		
S. Alvord	1280	...	Doctor	
J. T. Ames	4602	...	Manufacturer	
G. Arms	1817	...	Ames Super.	
S. Babcock	1168			
J. Bartlett	1128			
Benj. Belcher	1707			
J. W. Belcher	1350	...	Manufacturer	
E. M. Belden	1300	Bread Peddler		
E. Belding	1071			
R. E. Bemis	1418	Cotton Mill Agent		
W. P. Bixby	1208	...	Ames Overseer	
W. Blackmer	1149			
E. Blake	4305	...	Cotton Mill Agent and Investments	
H. Boyd	1023			
M. H. Boyden	1120	Gunsmith	...	Mill Employee
I. Bullens	1439	...	Merchant	
E. O. Carter	1865	...	...	Police Court Judge
J. A. Carter	1376	Clerk	...	Merchant
T. W. Carter	3365	...	Manufacturer	
J. Chapin	1061	...	Farmer	
N. Danks	1535	...	Cotton Mill Overseer	
H. Davis	2340	...	Farmer	
N. Day	1304	...	Farmer	
J. A. Denison	1200	...	Merchant	
T. A. Denison	2044	...	Merchant	
L. Dickinson	1138	...	...	Town Clerk
W. P. Elliot	3573	...	...	Cashier, Holyoke Bank
W. B. Fay	1095	Gunsmith	...	Stevens Employee
L. M. Ferry	2474	Ames Overseer	...	Insurance
J. B. Fuller	1145	...	Machinist	
A. Gale	1535	...	Plow Manufacturer	
H. Gates	1400	...	Blacksmith	
E. Gaylord	3172	...	Manufacturer	
W. Gilbert	1345	Machinist	...	Real Estate Broker
J. Goodwin	1079	Probably a Carpenter	...	Builder
A. Graves	1217	...	...	Brass Founder
C. Hadley	1122	...	...	Ames Draughtsman
D. F. Hale	1195			
H. H. Harris	1700	Bank Cashier	...	Bank Treasurer
H. Hitchcock	1918	...	...	Merchant
E. Holcomb	1374	Clerk	...	Merchant
J. E. Hosley	1474	Metal Polisher	...	Merchant
G. Houghton	1143	...	Machinist	
J. F. Hurd	1590	...	...	Cotton Mill Agent
J. S. Jacobs	1123			
C. M. Kendall	1740	...	Reed Manufacturer	
G. H. Knapp	1125			
L. Leppens	1093			
E. Manning	1200			
G. Marsh	1037	Tinner	...	Employee
M. Martin	1620			
C. H. Merrick	1131	...	...	Merchant
J. McClench	1200	...	Merchant	
A. McFarland	1224			
W. McFarland	2031	...	Manufacturer	
R. McKenny	1480	Gas Works Super.		
E. Munn	1093	...	...	Merchant
G. H. Nye	1194			
J. W. Osgood	2020	Cotton Mill Overseer	...	Cotton Mill Agent
A. W. Page	2612	...	...	Needle Manufacturer
T. C. Page	2159	...	...	Manufacturer
E. T. Paige	1250	...	...	Druggist
S. Pattee	1422			
L. M. Pierce	1200			
G. Robinson	2327	...	Lawyer	
G. Rumrill	1423	...	Mason	
J. Sands	1359			

* Compiled from *Springfield Republican,* April 19, 1869 and Springfield *Directories.*

TABLE 12 (continued)

Name	Income	Occupations		
		1853	1865	1873
W. J. Sawin	1392		Doctor	
C. C. Smith	1173			
J. Spaulding	1232		Merchant	
T. W. Stackpole	1065			
Stackpole	1100			Merchant
G. Stearns	1714		Lawyer	
E. Stebbins	4563		Manufacturer	
S. F. Stebbins	1211		Farmer	
P. Stickney	1165		Doctor	
C. S. Styles	1149		Cotton Mill Overseer	
A. C. Taylor	1389		Merchant	
C. A. Taylor	1159		Merchant	
D. E. Taylor	1338	Clerk		
G. S. Taylor	1225	Merchant	Manufacturer	
J. Taylor	2260	Merchant		Manufacturer
M. A. Taylor	1299			
V. N. Taylor	19630		Merchant	
L. Temple	1596	Pattern Maker		Merchant
W. Thayer	1184	Cotton Mill Overseer		
J. S. Tucker	1641	Boarding House Keeper		
W Valentine	1122			Teacher
S. Van Horn	1251		Foreman Machinist	
W. C. Wedge	1597		Baker	
Jerome Wells	4427		Merchant, Banker, Investments	
John Wells	5383		Lawyer and Investments	
G. Wheelock	1036		Printer	
J. R. Whittemore	2105		Manufacturer	
J. Whittemore	2441		Manufacturer	
N. Whitten	1959			
J. B. Wood	1100	Clerk		Merchant
J. Woodard	1633	Hotel Keeper		

workers. But if the cotton companies were less prominent relatively in the life of the town during the war, they were preparing to resume their former position, and were taking advantage of plant shutdown to make alterations which would increase productive capacity. The Dwight mills instituted improvements which were expected to double their capacity.[33] By 1868 these mills once more employed 1500 hands without reaching capacity production.[34] In the same year the Chicopee Manufacturing Company employed some 1200 workers, a good many more than ever before.[35]

Thus at the conclusion of hostilities, the cotton companies once more assumed a dominant position, one which they were to hold for some years, and overshadowed the life of the entire community. In subsequent years production was to be pushed to the utmost. Day and night shifts were inaugurated, and became fairly

[33] *Springfield Republican,* Feb. 10, 1862.
[34] *Ibid.,* March 19, 1868. [35] *Ibid.,* Jan. 13, 1868.

common in the early seventies and again in the eighties.[36] In the latter decade the companies erected new mills and tenements, and made general alterations.[37] Auxiliary steam engines were installed so as to avoid loss of time during low water seasons.[38] By the nineties the Dwight mills employed nearly 2000 workers.[39] Thus expansion was steady to this point, and the cotton mills once more colored the life of the town and conditioned its prosperity as they had done in the days before the war. The interlude in which local industry emerged as an equal with the cotton mills was brief.

While the cotton mills, for obvious reasons, could proceed to extend production rapidly at the end of the war, the problems which faced the local companies were not so simple. Business was depressed in the months following the peace. The Massachusetts Arms Company, and probably the Stevens Arms Company were left with little work. Business in the agricultural tool shops slowed up as buyers postponed their purchases in anticipation of a fall in prices.[40] Mechanics, who had been working night and day during the war, now found their earnings curtailed, and had to limit their expenditures accordingly. The merchants, while adversely affected by this condition, found help from the increasing cotton mill payrolls. But the post-war boom was not long in coming and in making itself felt. The results were apparent in different ways.

While the corporative group of local factories had been equipped to take almost immediate advantage of war conditions, the transition to peace time production was more complicated. The Massachusetts Arms Company, which had more than doubled its rifle producing capacity found that the demand for its product had fallen off sharply, and not having any supplementary product upon which it could fall back, decided to sell its property. The company's water power reverted to the Chicopee Manufacturing Company, and the plant itself was sold to the newly organized Lamb Knitting Machine Company.[41] However T. W. Carter took over

[36] *Ibid.*, Oct. 1, 1873; March 9, 1874; Jan. 30, 1880.
[37] *Ibid.*, Oct. 29, 1881; June 7, 1882; July 14, 1884.
[38] *Ibid.*, Jan. 2, 1877.
[39] *Ibid.*, Aug. 22, 1893.
[40] *Taylor Diary*, April 11, 1865.
[41] *Taylor Diary*, Feb. 11, 1866; Everts, *op. cit.*, II, 972.

the rights to the manufacture of the Maynard rifle, and for a few years continued its production on a much smaller scale than hitherto.[42]

Inasmuch as the Stevens Arms Company had been organized on a modest scale toward the end of the war, and had therefore not been subjected to such rapid expansion as some of the other companies, the firm was able to get off to a good start, and expanded its business slowly, without experiencing any setbacks. In 1867, 20 men were employed in the manufacture of pistols, callipers, dividers, and pruning shears. The half time services of a traveling salesman were secured and in 1868 the plant was enlarged somewhat.[43] In 1872 the company started the manufacture of a breech-loading shot gun, and 40 men found employment in the shops.[44] It was soon necessary to install a larger water wheel in order to secure more power.[45] This was just before the panic of 1873. No doubt business fell off during the next few years, but by 1877-78 orders were plentiful, and it was necessary to start night work in order to keep up with the demand for sporting rifles during the current "rifle shooting craze."[46] With the general improvement of business in 1880-81 it was planned to double the existing productive capacity.[47]

In 1885 the company was incorporated with a capital of $40,000, as the J. Stevens Arms and Tool Company. Joshua Stevens and W. B. Fay each subscribed to 120 shares of stock in the new corporation. Fay had been a gunsmith and had held a position of importance in the company for some years preceding its incorporation; possibly he had been a member of the firm. George S. Taylor, one time merchant, and now connected with the Belcher and Taylor Company took 10 shares. His brother, James, who had also been a merchant and had later been employed in the original Stevens Company, subscribed to 110 shares and was appointed treasurer of the firm. I. H. Page, the book-keeper of the

[42] A. M. Copeland, *op. cit.*, III, 500.
[43] *Taylor Diary*, Aug. 17, 1867; *Springfield Republican*, Jan. 13, Feb. 10, 1868.
[44] *Springfield Republican*, Jan. 3, 1873.
[45] *Ibid.*, June 7, 1873.
[46] *Ibid.*, Oct. 13, 1877; Sept. 29, 1878. [47] *Ibid.*, Oct. 18, 1881.

company took 40 shares.[48] At the time of incorporation, the company employed 40 workers.[49]

The post-war problems of the Ames Company were more difficult of solution than those of the neighboring shops. It represented the investment of some $250,000, and at the end of the war was one of the most important ordnance producers in the country. It was now necessary to diversify production once more, and in looking for business that would keep its large shops busy, it proceeded to manufacture a great variety of products. In 1866-67 in addition to the regular production of machinery, it manufactured skates, mail boxes, and ticket punches.[50] But these were "sidelines." New specialties were developed in the sixties and seventies. Just as after the Mexican War the company had manufactured service swords in war time and then expensive presentation swords for the surviving heroes, now it turned from the manufacture of cannon to the casting of bronze memorial statues, many of which were made from bronze cannon which had seen war service.[51]

A new demand for ornamental swords appeared to make up for the fall in the demand for service sabers. There occurred at this time a rapid development of fraternal lodges such as the Knights of Pythias, the Society of St. Jean Baptiste, the Hibernians, whose members required ceremonial swords, and the Ames Company was readily able to take advantage of this situation.[52] These swords became a staple product. During these years a great deal of contract work was accepted from other firms. The company made brick making machines, screw machines, cartridge boxes, indeed, almost any machine product for which it was possible to secure a contract.[53] But such work, by its very nature, could never assume large proportions.

In 1875 came a sub-contract from a Providence firm for 200,000 bayonet scabbards for Martini-Henri rifles scheduled for Turkey.[54] The next year they filled an order for sabers for South

[48] *Taylor Diary,* Dec. 28, 1885. [49] *Springfield Republican,* Jan. 2, 1886.
[50] *Ibid.,* Feb. 3, 1866; May 4, 1867; Jan. 2, 1868.
[51] *Ibid.,* May 12, 1869; Feb. 19, 1873; Jan. 7, 1875; Oct. 14, 1876.
[52] *Ibid.,* June 18, 1873; Feb. 16, 1874.
[53] *Ibid.,* June 12, 1873; Nov. 5, 1874; July 12, 1878.
[54] *Ibid.,* Sept. 7, 1875.

America, and in 1878 were busy with a large contract for bayonets for Turkey.[55] This seems to have been one of the last large ordnance orders which the company filled.

James T. Ames had resigned from the active management of the company in 1872.[56] In 1875 in spite of a apparently steady production, the financial condition of the firm was not good. The superintendent reported an almost complete lack of working capital which not only prevented the acceptance of some contracts, but also prevented the adoption of certain policies which would have bettered the profit-making potentialities of the company. For instance, if capital were available it would have been possible to buy up large quantities of government swords in order to use the blades for the manufacture of society ceremonial swords. In addition to the fact that it was more expensive to make the blades in the company's shops, the existence of the government blades improved the condition of Ames' competitors who were in a position to buy them. Nor was the situation in regard to the casting of bronze statuary always satisfactory. Government contracts stipulated that the company use condemned bronze cannon which the manufacturer was obliged to buy, but at a low price. While the prices set were very favorable, yet the appropriations of condemned cannon were such that the company had to convert large sums of badly needed cash into more raw material than it was able to use profitably at the time the contract was placed. When the Ames Company had completed the "Minute Men" of Concord, it owed the government $25.74. If funds were available, bronze cannon could be bought up and taken off the market, thus avoiding Congressional generosity when the appropriations were made. It was also recommended that a travelling salesman should be sent out to solicit business, and that cheap turbine wheels should be manufactured to supply the Western and Southern markets, where small-scale enterprise were developing.[57]

There are several important implications in this analysis of the company's condition. The managers of the company no longer

[55] *Ibid.*, Oct. 14, 1876; Jan. 7, 1878. [56] *Ibid.*, Jan. 18, 1872.
[57] *Ames Papers,* Letter Book, March 30, 1875.

seemed to be as ingenious in finding new staple products as had previously been the case. There seemed to be a lack of initiative in investigating new fields of endeavor, and too great a reliance placed on the past reputation of the firm in the expectation that this reputation, in and of itself would bring in new business. Most significant of all is the shortage of working capital just 10 years after the war. There seems to be no reason to doubt that this shortage must be ascribed in large part, to the extravagant payment of dividends during the war years, payments that were made without any thought of either protecting the working capital or of building up a capital reserve.[58]

In spite of these difficulties the company survived the seventies, although the townsfolk seemed to resent the fact that business was not brisker than it was. Their interest in the company was almost proprietary. "They complain that the company are not doing half the work they ought, and that, while business in other places is booming, their pet institution, with such a remarkable history behind it, is rather languishing than otherwise. The complaints are directed rather pointedly to the new head of the company, who, they say, has no interest in Chicopee."[59] But in the late seventies the monument trade was quite good, and in slack periods the foundry turned out "Websters and Clays in bronze, these worthies being a standard commodity."[60] At this time a few turbine wheels were manufactured, and several rapid fire battery guns for the United States and for Russia.[61]

With the coming of the eighties the company seemed to take a new lease on life. Business increased in all departments, and contracts were accepted to manufacture the Eldridge Sewing Machine.[62] In 1881 the company bought the Gaylord Manufacturing Company which had also been making society swords, and incorporated the Gaylord unit with the Ames sword department as the Ames Sword Company. A. C. Woodworth, who was J. T. Ames' son-in-law, managed the two companies.[63] At this time the new

[58] See above, p. 87.
[59] *Springfield Republican*, Oct. 28, 1879.
[60] *Ibid.*, Jan. 9, 1879.
[61] *Ibid.*, Oct. 9, Nov. 15, 1878; Jan. 27, 1879.
[62] *Ibid.*, July 13, April 17, 1880.
[63] *Ibid.*, May 14, 1881.

sword company gave employment to about 125 men, and the Ames Manufacturing Company to 550, of which 150 worked in the sewing machine department.[64] In addition to the swords, sewing machines, and miscellaneous machinery, the company now secured a contract to manufacture the Overman tricycle.[65] While these contracts for the manufacture of tricycles (and then bicycles) and sewing machines were no doubt profitable, they could not be counted upon to continue indefinitely. There was always the possibility that the company tendering the contract might transfer manufacturing rights to a competitor, or might decide to add the profits of manufacture to those of distribution by entering production itself. This is what happened in the case of the Eldridge sewing machine contracts. In 1884, the Eldridge Company bought the Ames sewing machine department and undertook to conduct manufacture itself, renting space in the Ames shop for this purpose.[66] In a case of this kind, while the contract was lost, at least it was possible to dispose of the manufacturing equipment, and obtain an income from some of the floor space. A more serious situation was to occur in the case of the Overman contracts.

Beginning in 1885 Overman began to place increasingly large orders for bicycles with the Ames Company. This production was undertaken on an extensive scale, and the bicycle department soon took an important place in the shops. But it was not without its difficulties. Overman was involved in a patent infringement suit with the Pope Company of Hartford, and pending settlement Ames was obliged to slow down production.[67] In addition, the activities of the company were still hampered by a continued lack of working capital.[68] Fortunately the increasing popular demand for bicycles and the settlement of the legal dispute permitted the shops to resume production.

The profits involved in the manufacture of bicycles were large, but as the business increased enormously, Overman decided to build his own factory. In 1887 he bought the plant of the defunct agri-

[64] *Ibid.,* Sept. 16, 1881.
[65] *Ibid.,* June 5, 1882. [66] *Ibid.,* May 3, 1884.
[67] *Ames Papers,* A. C. Woodworth Letters, July 31, Aug. 22, 1885.
[68] *Ibid.,* March 12, 13, 1885.

cultural tool shops.[69] Thus as the eighties came to a close, an important and profitable part of the Ames Manufacturing Company's business disappeared. If the company had been in difficulties before, its position would now seem to be even more precarious.

The Gaylord Manufacturing Company, which was owned almost entirely by the founder, Emerson Gaylord, had resumed the production of mail bags after the war.[70] The company at this time had a foundry in operation which it had purchased from the Chicopee Malleable Iron Works, and used it for making raw material for the manufacture of steel pens and mail boxes.[71] The production of locks and cabinet locks and trimmings continued, and constituted an important part of the business for some time.[72] In the seventies the Gaylord Company started to make ceremonial lodge swords, entering into direct competition with the Ames Company.[73] In 1881 Gaylord sold the sword business to Ames, and the lock business to a Connecticut firm and retired from business.[74]

The agricultural tool shops experienced slow and steady development after the war. They were favored, of course, by the continued expansion and mechanization of agricultural production. After the reorganization of the Belcher and Taylor Company during the war, 1865-66 came as a critical year.[75] The Company turned to the West for new business, and in expanding its production was not entirely satisfied with the work that B. Belcher performed as the production head of the company, for his work was meticulous and probably not too well adapted to mass production. One of the members of the firm remarked: "I think Mr. Belcher cannot manage the concern as well as it ought to be, for he is too particular about his work, and cannot, or will not, slight it." However, business did not remain depressed for long, responding to improving economic conditions and to greater sales efforts on the part of the firm.[76] But Belcher decided to withdraw from the com-

[69] *Springfield Republican*, Sept. 8, 1889; Feb. 1, 1890.
[70] *Ibid.*, June 8, 1867.
[71] *Ibid.*, Feb. 3, June 16, 1866.
[72] *Ibid.*, March 10, 1868; Oct. 23, 1876.
[73] *Ibid.*, Aug. 31, 1877.
[74] *Ibid.*, April 30, May 12, 14, 1881.
[75] *Taylor Diary*, 1865-66, passim.
[76] *Ibid.*, Aug. 17, Sept. 1-8, 1867.

pany, and he sold all his holdings to James Taylor.[77] The company showed a profit in 1867.[78]

The expansion of the company seemed cautious. Aside from the gradual growth in the ordinary way of business, rights to the manufacture of other agricultural tools were occasionally acquired.[79] The whole period turned out to be a profitable one. From 1869 to 1890 dividends ranged from 6 to 10 per cent, and not more than four years, and possibly only two, saw the passing of dividends. In addition to these profits which were withdrawn from the business comparatively large sums were reinvested in plant and equipment.[80]

In the meantime, the Whittemore, Belcher partnership had been dissolved in 1875, and the business continued as the B. and J. W. Belcher Company.[81] The Whittemores went into business in a small way by themselves.[82] For a number of years these two rival, but smaller companies presented unwelcome competition to the more successful Belcher and Taylor Company.[83] Finally the B. and J. W. Belcher Company was obliged to suspend operations in 1889 not being able to withstand the keen competition of the period. The Belcher and Taylor Company bought the business in the same year.[84] In 1890 the Whittemore shops, which probably were no better fitted to survive than was the B. and J. W. Belcher Company, were sold to Overman, and the patents and patterns passed to the Belcher and Taylor Company.[85] Thus the three tool shops, having originated from one parent company, were consolidated once more at the end of the period.[86]

[77] *Ibid.*, Nov. 8, 1867. [78] *Ibid.*, Dec. 16, 1867.
[79] *Ibid.*, Jan. 2, 1873; Dec. 12, 1879.
[80] *Ibid.*, 1879-90, passim. [81] *Ibid.*, Jan. 2, March 2, 1875.
[82] *Springfield Republican*, Dec. 19, 1884.
[83] *Taylor Diary*, Sept. 2, 1872; Sept. 16, 1878; Oct. 14, 1880.
[84] *Springfield Republican*, Jan. 9, Dec. 25, 1889.
[85] *Ibid.*, Feb. 1, April 2, 1890.
[86] There was a marked decrease in the number of agricultural implement establishments throughout the country after the Civil War. The following figures indicate the trend. From U. S., Bureau of Corporations, *Report on the International Harvester Co.*, 43.

Year	*Establishments*	*Year*	*Establishments*
1849	1333	1879	1943
1859	2116	1889	910
1869	2076	1899	715

But the general business expansion in the years following the Civil War was not confined to the enlargement of pre-existing productive units. There emerged war and post-war profits, some of which, we have seen, were plowed back into established companies. For the surpluses which were withdrawn from production the time was ripe for new and secondary investments. There also developed during the war a surplus of small mercantile profits eager for possible investment in either small manufacturing industry or in more specialized forms of retail trade. The large numbers of skilled mechanics and the increase in the numbers of foremen-mechanics employed steadily from 1861 to 1865 yielded a small group which was able to save money and then in after years invest the same in petty industry or in trade in an effort to secure some measure of economic independence. The growth of the town's population from 7,261 persons in 1860 to 9,607 in 1870, 11,286 in 1880 and 14,050 in 1890, enhanced the possibilities for the multiplication of such small enterprises. The result was a wave of investment of all kinds from 1866 to 1873-74.

It will have been noticed that the group of corporative enterprises described above was controlled by a fairly small number of men. Most of them were primarily interested in one particular company to which they devoted all their time and from which they drew earnings of management, and they invested their savings and some of their profits in their neighbors' companies. This same group of men made investments in the post-war boom.

By far the most profitable of these new investments was the Lamb Knitting Machine Company, established in 1867. This was effected by the union of a Springfield firm with one that had been in operation in Rochester, New York. Chicopee capital was added to the amalgamation.[87] Chicopee was selected as the place of operation because the plant of the Massachusetts Arms Company was available, presumably at a good price, and also because new capital was available in Chicopee.[88] The 1869 board of directors indicates those men who were involved in the transaction. There was T. W. Carter, erstwhile head of the Massachusetts Arms Com-

[87] Interview, Mr. Frank D. Howard.
[88] Interview, Mr. Frank D. Howard; *Taylor Diary,* Dec. 7, 1866.

pany, E. Blake, agent of the Chicopee Manufacturing Company, Emerson Gaylord, E. Chase, C. H. Smith, J. D. Orne, and T. C. Page.[89] No doubt some of the latter and unfamiliar names represented men who had previous connection with the Lamb Company. T. C. Page had operated a machine repair shop in Holyoke. He seems to have converted the profits derived from this business into a large interest in the Rochester company.[90] He was related to Irving H. Page who was to become the dominant figure in the J. Stevens Arms Company. James Taylor, of the latter firm, became a director of the knitting machine company in later years.[91] The new company was capitalized at $100,000.[92]

The Lamb Knitting Machine Company specialized in the manufacture of knitting machines for gloves and mittens. These machines were at first made only for home use, but later were adapted for factory manufacture.[93] In 1868 the company gave employment to 125 skilled workers, including those occupied in the iron foundry.[94] Shortly after, the manufacturing rights for the Dover egg-beater were secured, and many thousands were manufactured.[95] From the first, the export trade absorbed a large part of the company's product. In 1873 Germany took 35 per cent of all knitting machines made, and some exports were made to Japan.[96]

The business collapse of the seventies seemingly had no great effect on the company's fortunes. It is known that 10 per cent dividends were paid in 1874, 1876 and 1879.[97] Other payments may have been made. In 1874 it was necessary to work overtime in order to fill orders, and again in 1877 the company could not produce fast enough.[98] In 1882 the capital stock was doubled, and before long a 15 per cent dividend was paid on this $200,000

[89] *Springfield Republican*, Jan. 26, 1869.
[90] *Biographical Review of Hampden County*, II, 973.
[91] *Springfield Republican*, Feb. 5, 1880.
[92] Everts, *op. cit.*, II, 972.
[93] Interview, Mr. Frank D. Howard.
[94] *Springfield Republican*, Jan. 13, March 2, 1868.
[95] *Ibid.*, Jan. 17, 1872. Mr. Frank D. Howard indicated that this contract was secured because of a marriage relationship of one of the members of the company with a member of the Dover Stamping Company.
[96] *Springfield Republican*, Feb. 5, 1874.
[97] *Taylor Diary*, March 2, 1875; *Springfield Republican*, Feb. 2, 1876; Feb. 5, 1879.
[98] *Springfield Republican*, Aug. 25, 1874; Nov. 5, 1877.

capital.[99] If the seventies had proved to be profitable, the eighties were even more so.

Other investments which the group made were not so fortunate. E. Blake, one of the Carters, E. Chase, and others, organized the Chicopee Falls Hosiery Company in 1868, for the manufacture of woolen knit goods.[100] Whether production ever really got started or not is uncertain, for before long the Bay State Valve and Faucet Company took over the property of the Hosiery company, giving stock in the Bay State Company in payment.[101] This company had not originated in Chicopee, but had moved there in 1869 or 1870 when E. Blake and Carter invested in the enterprise. It seems that the owners decided that a metal goods enterprise stood a better chance of success than their knit goods company. For a while the Bay State Company prospered, but was hard hit by the depression in the seventies. The owners sold out their materials and machinery to Boston and Connecticut firms in 1876.[102]

Another ill-fated venture was the Chicopee Falls Screw Company, organized in 1883 by Jonathan Whittemore, the farm implement maker, G. M. Munn, who had been a machinist and later the superintendent of the Massachusetts Screw Company in Holyoke, T. C. Page, of the Lamb Company, and A. W. Page, who manufactured knitting machine needles.[103] The company achieved very respectable size, employing 85 men in 1885.[104] However, if this firm did not have the depression years of the seventies to contend with, it could not survive the competition of the large-scale screw producers. The plant was sold to A. H. Overman in 1887.[105]

Enough has been said of the corporate enterprises to see that with the development of business and business enterprise in the Civil War and after, there had emerged, as opposed to the comparatively petty nature of other investment, as we shall presently see, a "capitalist" group. Table 13 indicates the ownership of the

[99] *Ibid.*, Jan. 5, 1882; *Taylor Diary*, March 2, 1883.
[100] *Springfield Republican*, Feb. 17, 1868.
[101] *Ibid.*, Oct. 28, 1873.
[102] *Ibid.*, Jan. 29, 1876.
[103] *Ibid.*, Aug. 8, 1883.
[104] *Ibid.*, April 22, 1885.
[105] *Ibid.*, Sept. 8, 1889; Babbitt, *op. cit.*, 14.

companies concerned, and illustrates the duplication of directorates and the grouping of activity. In broad lines it is a striking repetition of the situation found in regard to the Boston associates, striking not only because of its similarity, but because it allows us to see clearly how large, how much more important, were the activities of the Boston merchant-manufacturer-financiers many years before.

TABLE 13. DIRECTORS OF LOCAL INCORPORATED COMPANIES IN SPECIFIED YEARS

Company	Year	Directors
Bay State Valve and Faucet Company	1872	E. Adams E. Blake T. W. Carter J. H. Southworth W. Southworth J. W. Trafton
Belcher and Taylor Company	1864	E. Blake E. O. Carter W. P. McFarland G. S. Taylor J. E. Taylor John Wells B. West
Chicopee Falls Hosiery Company	1868	E. Blake E. Chase E. O. Carter J. B. Pierce
Chicopee Falls Screw Company	1883	T. W. Carter G. M. Munn A. W. Page T. C. Page J. R. Whittemore
Lamb Knitting Machine Company	1880	E. W. Bond E. O. Carter T. W. Carter R. B. Johnson T. C. Page C. H. Smith J. E. Taylor
Massachusetts Arms Company	1862	S. Adams J. T. Ames T. W. Carter J. M. Smith John Wells
J. Stevens Arms and Tools Company	1885	W. B. Fay I. H. Page J. Stevens G. S. Taylor J. E. Taylor

It is in the activities of men such as these that we find the "business leadership" of the community. By and large their activities were duplicated throughout the region. Inasmuch as we are likely to find similar groups in other localities it is well to consider what kind of men they were. They came from simple homes.

Many were farmers' sons; some started as artisans. Many of them were merchants or had worked for merchants at one time or another during their careers. They were the social leaders of their community, and participated actively in municipal affairs. They were the pillars of the church, and the church, for many of them, constituted as important an interest as family and business. Religion was part of their life, and religious precepts, carried over into business activity, were of importance. They were hard-working men, possessed of all the middle class virtues. We find, among them, the ideal of the puritan business man. One member of the group left some interesting and illuminating statements. "I hope the results of last year may show a success not only for my good and the interest of other stockholders, but for the interest of Christ's Kingdom on earth, for I shall aim to be a steward under God for what he gives me. . . . My desire is for success that I may glorify God with my substance. . . . I feel that I have worked hard and have sought direction from God in all our undertakings, and my faith is strong that the year's results will show that he has led and blessed me. I want success in our business so that I may have means to advance God's Kingdom with what I do not now have. . . . God has blessed me in my business endeavors and I pray that he may continue so to do, for I feel anxious to glorify my Saviour as a business man."[106]

But the middle class was made up of a much larger and more varied group of persons than is represented by the upper stratum which we have described. The general increase of population alone increased the possibilities for the expansion of trade and services and petty industry. Judging by the partial list of investments as compiled under Table 14 the multiplication within this group of enterprise was most marked from 1866 to 1874. Con-

[106] Compare these sentiments, expressed in the nineteenth century, with the following passage, written by Richard Baxter, the Puritan writer on religious subjects, in the seventeenth: "If God show you a way in which you may lawfully get more than in another way (without wrong to your soul or to any other), if you refuse this, and choose the less gainful way, you cross one of the ends of your calling, and refuse to be God's steward, and to accept His gifts and use them for Him when He requireth it; you may labour to be rich for God, though not for the flesh and sin." Quoted in Max Weber, *The Protestant Ethic and the Spirit of Capitalism,* 162.

TABLE 14. MANUFACTURING AND MERCANTILE COMPANIES ESTABLISHED, OWNERSHIP, AND DURATION OF BUSINESS LIFE, WHEN KNOWN, 1866-1891*

Year	Kind of Enterprise	Ownership	Duration
1866	Cigars		At least 10 years
1867	Curtain Fixtures	B. Belcher (late of Agric. Tools)	Not very long
	Hairpins and Gadgets	L. M. Taylor	Merged with Conn. firm and left Chicopee
	Brewery		At least 10 years
	Leather		At least 10 years
	Knitting Machine Needles	A. W. Page (Came from Rochester when Lamb Co. came to Chicopee)	Many years
	Meat packing (2)		At least 10 years
1868	Overalls and Sewed Underclothing	A. D. Moore	
	Renovation of Feather Beds	Beckwith (was once railway construction foreman)	
	Carriages		At least 10 years
	Power Loom Harness		At least 10 years
	Soda Water		At least 10 years
	Trusses		At least 10 years
1869	Boots and Shoes		At least 10 years
	Stoves, Tinware		At least 10 years
	Washing Compound		At least 10 years
1870	Coffee		At least 9 years
	Photographer		At least 9 years
	Stoves, Tinware		At least 9 years
1871	Clothing		At least 8 years
1872	Hampden Bleachery	Anderton and Dunn	Still in operation
	Builder		At least 7 years
	Millinery		At least 7 years
	Meat Packing		At least 7 years
1873	Builder		At least 6 years
	Clothing		At least 6 years
	Medicines		At least 6 years
	Stoves, Tinware		At least 6 years
1874	Paper Bags		At least 5 years
	Builder		At least 5 years
	Harness, Bridles		At least 5 years
	Hats and Bonnets		At least 5 years
	Medicines		At least 5 years
	Meat Packing		At least 5 years
1875	Musgrave Alpaca Co.	Anderton and Dunn (of Hampden Bleachery) and E Musgrave, lately employed by Farr Alpaca Co. of Holyoke	Failed in 1881
	Clothing		At least 4 years
1877	Loom Harness	J. Flint (ex-machinist)	
	Sand lots	W. E. Wheeler (was ice dealer and stable owner)	Until 1879
1878	Hosiery	Hatfield (was clerk)	Not long
1881	Lawn Mowers	A. J. Whitcomb (was employed by Lamb Co.)	Sold to Newburgh firm in 1882
	Dry Goods Store	Goldsmith and Shaw (textile foremen)	
	Buck's Arms	Northampton and Springfield Money	Very brief
1883	Laundry		

* This Table is not a complete summary of industrial and mercantile activity. It is compiled from the *Springfield Republican*, Springfield *Directories*, and Mass., Bureau of Labor Statistics, 9th *Annual Report*, 62 (1878).

TABLE 14 (continued)

Year	Kind of Enterprise	Ownership	Duration
1884...	Blake Needle.............	E. Blake, son of Ezekiel Blake (Agt., Chicopee Mfg. Co.) had been employed by Page Needle Co..........	Many years
1885...	Gaylord Mfg. Co. (new firm)	Absorbs Gaylord and Chapin brass works and sword shop. $25,000 capital. Emerson Gaylord, A. F. Gaylord, J. L Pease, (Super. of 1st Gaylord Co.) S. Gaylord, F. B. Doten (bank cashier) J. T. Lyon. (worked for 1st Gaylord Co.)...............	Liquidated 1889
1886...	Nickel Plate............. Harness Trimming.........	O. E. Smith (ex-Ames foreman)....... C. C. Abbey (coal dealer)............	
1887...	Chicopee Falls Bldg. Co. (for construction and sale of houses, lots, on monthly payments)........... Brass Foundry............ Confectionery Store........	G. S. Taylor, J. E. Taylor, J. Stevens, A. Gale (of Belcher and Taylor Co.) A. O. Grout. (Machinist)........... Burdette (formerly employed by Stebbins, Gaylord, and Ames as molder) and Sullivan...................... Textile assistant foreman.............	Several years
1888...	Taylor, Bramley Co. (underwear and sweaters)... Chicopee Falls Wheel Co. .. Olmstead and Tuttle. (Mfr. quilts, mattresses, cotton waste)................	A. Taylor (G. S. Taylor's son) and W. Bramley.......................... H. S. Boyd (insurance) and F. M. Bennitt (doctor)...................... Moved from Springfield.............	Still in operation Not long Several years
1889...	Reed Factory (not new).... Reed factory, as above sold to..................... Tobacco and Candy.......	J. T. Lyon (See 1885 item)........... G. Babcock (formerly employed by Ames)........................... W. T. Powers. (formerly employed by Ames)...........................	
1890...	Dry Goods Store..........	Michael Siske (employed by merchant for many years)..................	
1891...	Nye Truss Co............	S. R. Nye, (had been employed by Belcher and Taylor) G. S. Taylor, J. Stevens, D. Boynton, (Super. of Chicopee Electric Light Co. in 1890) F. W. Patterson, (employed by Lamb Co.) N. R. Wood, (merchant).......	Did not last long

sidering the general situation that was to be expected. It was also to be expected that the rate of increase would slacken during the seventies and revive again during the eighties. There is no special significance to be attached to this growth of small independent enterprise. It is the type of activity to be found in any growing community which is the seat of a resident propertied class, however humble that class may be, and of a group of skilled workers. Growth of population permitted specialization and differentiation of trade and services. General stores, if they did not develop into department stores, split up into meat markets and grocery stores, tobacco and confectionary shops, dry goods, clothing, and hardware stores. Ice and coal and wood dealers appeared, feed stores, repair shops of various kinds. While before the Civil War there was a scattering of store-keepers, in the sixties and seventies the list is longer and more varied.

Petty manufacturing industry as well as retail trade expanded in the period. The owners of petty industry had been small merchants in the town, or artisans who invested their savings in small repair shops. Carpenters and masons sometimes became contractors, foremen and skilled mechanics sometimes opened retail stores. There was some social mobility on the borderline between classes, but it was not very pronounced. One important point must be kept in mind. With rapid railway development and the establishment of a national market, we have the rise of mass production manufacturing industries which undertook to supply goods which had hitherto been made by scattered local producers. The petty manufacturing enterprises, based on individual savings, thrift savings, which sprang up in Chicopee in the seventies and eighties, were for the most part doomed to failure. Thus the expansion of the lower middle class was dependent almost entirely upon the opportunities for small-scale investment in retail trade.

But here a limiting factor becomes apparent in regard to Chicopee. In spite of the expansion of the middle class this was primarily a mill town employing large numbers of semi-skilled workers. Their wages, and therefore the gross income of the merchants, were subject to fluctuation. Even part time work in the mills, to say nothing of a general shutdown, hit the merchant hard. Nor were there compensating expenditures from a substantial salaried group, or fixed income group. The middle class, as a whole, was not wealthy enough, and those who had comfortable incomes were not numerous enough, to support a series of luxury services and trades, the existence of which would be both profitable and afford attractive investment opportunities. In addition, Springfield, a larger trading center, with more goods on display, with a greater variety of fine goods, was nearby. This proximity of Springfield, and the loss of trade to that place, was soon to be intensified by the building of a street railway.[107]

[107] See below, pp. 208, 209, 231 et seq., for a fuller discussion of this whole problem.

For the entire middle class the period was one of expansion and consolidation of positions gained. The upper level, composed of the agents of the cotton mills and the managers of the corporate enterprises, a few professionals and wealthy merchants, constituted the backbone and the "permanent" section of the whole middle class. They had been able to establish themselves firmly, and were the accepted leaders of the community. The lower middle class (and including here a number of skilled Yankee mechanics) was composed of a more shifting group. As early as 1869 it was noticed that several members of one of the Congregational churches were leaving Chicopee.[108] Judging from their church membership these persons were Yankees, and were likely to be skilled mechanics and petty merchants and their sons, members of the lower middle class. These were the very people, one might think, who should have been able to achieve higher and more prosperous economic levels as the result of the war and the post-war booms. But apparently such was not the case. In the seventies this drift from the town was felt still more keenly. "Some of the town's best citizens have left lately," wrote the Chicopee correspondent of the *Springfield Republican,* "the population of the town has changed wonderfully in the last few years, though it has not decreased as much as in other places. The young people who work in the mills have left to seek their fortunes elsewhere, because of the reduction in wages made necessary by the hard times, while many families have left town also. In the Methodist Congregation more than half the faces are different from those seen when Mr. Best began his ministry a little more than two years ago, and in the Congregational and Baptist churches the change has been nearly as great."[109] The places of the Protestants were being taken to a very considerable extent by Roman Catholics. When it began to be noticed, in the fall of 1878, that the movement from the town was checked and that new arrivals were frequent, the same newspaper correspondent remarked that "those who are coming in by no means take the place of those who have

[108] *Taylor Diary,* Feb. 13, 1870.
[109] *Springfield Republican,* April 11, June 10, 1878.

gone. A large number of the older and better class of citizens have departed within a year or two."[110]

While the lower middle class seemed to be gaining ground in numbers, it was losing some of its inherent unity as a social group, and in certain respects was on the defensive. The political leadership of the Yankee middle class was being challenged by the Irish. The latter, toward the end of the period, though still largely a working class group, were making contributions in numbers to the petty bourgeoisie, to the professions, and to the building industry. In 1873 and 1874 there was friction at the town meetings between the Irish and a solid bloc of Yankees.[111] This was more than a division on national and religious grounds; it was Yankee property owner and property tax payer versus Irish worker and poll tax payer. "An American ticket is being worked up for next Monday in which neither the names of Patrick Rourke nor Dr. Mellen will appear. Not a few fear that if the Irish once get a majority in the town's government, they will get complete control, and run things to suit themselves, a large majority of whom, it is claimed, pay only a poll tax."[112]

On the whole, however, the period witnessed the high point of middle class development and fulfilment in the community. Socially, life was fuller than it had ever been. The lyceums and debating clubs did not disappear entirely for a while, but yielded precedence to baseball and rifle clubs.[113] The number of concerts and "readings" increased, brass bands and singing societies were organized. In the seventies amateur theatricals became very popular. Characteristic of the period was the rapid development of the fraternal lodges and societies. Drawing classes, spelling bees, parties of all kinds were frequent. The solid citizenry busied itself with social work, for it was not permitted to forget that it lived in a factory town, and it sponsored reading rooms and lectures, and tried, unsuccessfully, to organize a Y. M. C. A. unit. Their most important activity of this nature consisted of temperance work.

[110] *Ibid.,* Aug. 21, 1878.
[111] *Taylor Diary,* April 7, 1873; April 16, 1874.
[112] *Springfield Republican,* April 4, 1879.
[113] *Ibid.,* Feb. 10, 1862; *Taylor Diary,* 1865, passim.

This was not always completely successful, except as a pleasant diversion for the social workers. "Some of the pledge takers at the temperance meetings last winter have been or are in jail for drunkenness."[114] Organized "self-improvement," the avoidance of empty hands, was still considered a laudable activity. "A 'spare minute circle' was formed at the Methodist church last night, to aid its members toward pleasant use for time hitherto wasted. A course of reading has been selected, and volumes of convenient size for carrying in the pocket will be bought."[115] Regular theatrical seasons in the local opera house were frequent and very well attended in the eighties.

Toward the end of the period amusement was well diversified, and for certain members of the group, began to grow more expensive and more selective. Bicycle clubs made their appearance, and bicycling at that time was an expensive pastime. Then came tennis, and the building of a country club-house by a small section of the solidly established citizenry.[116] The social life of the period was adapted to a wider group of persons of more varied interests than had been the case before. This was especially marked after 1870. This whole social life was not in any way peculiar to Chicopee, but was characteristic of small town life throughout the country at that time.[117]

Certain elements in the position of the middle class throughout the period are worthy of mention at this point. When it had been a much smaller community, Chicopee had supported two newspapers. That was in the fifties. There was no local press of any kind from 1865 to 1890. An attempt to establish a newspaper in the nineties ended in failure. When the street railway development came to Chicopee in the late eighties, no local money was invested in the enterprise.[118] We have already pointed out that there was some drift of middle class elements from the town in

[114] *Springfield Republican,* June 7, 1878.
[115] *Ibid.,* Sept. 16, 1884.
[116] *Ibid.,* July 14, 1890; March 3, 1891.
[117] See L. M. Hacker and B. B. Kendrick, *The United States Since 1865,* p. 241; data on Chicopee social life from *Springfield Republican,* 1865-1890, passim.
[118] *Springfield Republican,* Feb. 20 et seq., 1887.

the seventies, but that there was considerable expansion of middle class activity. But this expansion consisted mostly of multiplication, new investment; liquidations were frequent; productive units did not really grow. It was not enterprise which could be expected to yield profits which would hunt for new investments. The group which became fairly wealthy and really prospered was comparatively small. The members which made up this group were getting older, and there was no sign pointing to the possible rise of a new and vigorous entrepreneurial group.

In the meantime the working class was growing, and as it came to consist of Irish, Polish and French-Canadian workers, it was to change the face of the community under the very eyes of the Yankee middle class which disliked and resented the transformation, but was impotent to deal with the situation. There was one way out for some, and that was by escape, to make their homes in Springfield, if they could, even to transfer their economic interests to that place, depend on it for shopping and amusement facilities. If it was still necessary to work or live in Chicopee, the new street cars furnished half-hour service, and soon the automobile was to appear.

CHAPTER VIII

LABOR IN PROSPERITY AND DEPRESSION, 1860-1890

The three decades following 1860 constituted a formative period for the American organized labor movement. Rapidly changing economic conditions prevented stable growth, sometimes stimulating organization, at other times undermining or impeding it. The rise of prices and lag of wages during the war inflation gave impetus to the growth of trade unions and city trades' assemblies. Falling prices and intensive wage cutting resulted in unrest. We find the development of an eight hour movement in the sixties, producers' and consumers' co-operatives, "Greenbackism," large-scale strikes in the seventies, and in the long depression disintegration of the organized labor movement. Revival of organization which came in 1879 was confined to skilled workers until about 1882. The rapid rise of the Knights of Labor, based on the organization of unskilled workers, was short-lived. Conflict between the Knights of Labor and the skilled craft unions resulted in defeat for the former, and the way was clear for the expansion of the American Federation of Labor.[1]

Chicopee was too small a community to reflect, in all its manifestations, the ferment in the world of labor from 1860 to 1890. But the same economic factors were operative, and there is evidence of restlessness, of attempts to resist or ameliorate the evil consequences of business fluctuations.

Before the Civil War Chicopee's working population had experienced a change in its mode of life from the isolation of the farm to the community life of a factory town. The essential problem for large numbers of workers had been one of adjustment to a rapidly changing factory technique. This working population had been unstable, its constituent elements changing frequently. With the continued and rapid development of a permanent factory

[1] S. Perlman, *A History of Trade Unionism in the United States,* 43 et seq.

population after the Civil War new labor problems became apparent. Depression periods were long and severe and with them came the problem of prolonged unemployment. The effects of unemployment and partial employment were extended to whole families to a much greater extent than ever before. Perhaps we might characterize the period briefly by saying that we have here the story of labor in the business cycle, the experiences of labor during inflationary and deflationary price and wage movements.

We have already seen that in the late forties and fifties Irish workers entered mill employment in increasing numbers, and that the recruiting of French-Canadian labor had started just before the Civil War. By 1875, when 35 per cent of the total population was of foreign birth, the Irish constituted about 21 per cent of the total population; 9.6 per cent were born in Canada[2] and it may safely be assumed that practically all of these were French. In 1885 the French-Canadians had increased to 11.8 per cent of the total population, and in the same year we note that a group of Poles, 205 in number, was living in the town.[3] By the next decade 8.8 per cent of the total population, and 20 per cent of the foreign born population was Polish.[4] As had always been the case, the new workers were imported mainly to keep up the labor supply of the cotton mills.

The entrance of these nationalities, Irish, French-Canadian and Polish, changed many aspects of town life. In the earlier mill days the Yankee workers, speaking the same language, attending the same churches, sharing the same traditions as the merchant and artisan classes no doubt experienced social contact with them, and these circumstances lent solidarity and homogeneity to the entire community. But the religious separation which came with the Irish produced further social classifications, deepened by the language differences that arose with the arrival of the French and the Polish. For a number of years the ranks of the working class itself were divided. In addition to these obviously disintegrating

[2] Mass., *Census of 1875*, Vol. I, 287 et seq.
[3] *Ibid.*, 1885, Vol. I, Part I, 518. [4] *Ibid.*, 1895, Vol. II, 622.

elements, practically all of the newcomers were semi-skilled or unskilled workers, while many of the craftsmen remained Yankees.[5]

The new factory workers did not have to be coaxed into the mills by sets of puritanical regulations as did many of the early operatives, nor were the times such as to perpetuate the early boarding-house system. But if the "system" disappeared the boarding-houses remained. There were still large numbers of unmarried men and women who had to be housed and fed. The arrival of immigrant family groups and, indeed, of considerable numbers of individuals from overseas who regarded the town as their home, since they had no other place to which they could withdraw, was productive of a permanent factory population. By 1878 the Dwight Manufacturing Company ruled that each family renting one of its tenements must have three members who worked in the mills. This ruling even applied to those who already occupied company tenements.[6] Thus we find that whole families, increasingly large groups of persons, were more directly dependent on cotton mill work and wages than ever before. This was the case in spite of the fact that Chicopee was no longer a cotton town in the seventies and eighties in the sense that it had been a cotton town in the years before the Civil War.

With this influx of immigrants, both male and female, we find a large body of workers entering the lower-paid occupations. At the same time there were greater opportunities for skilled labor. The metal industries enjoyed considerable expansion during and after the war, and with their expansion the proportion of male employees in the town increased. This tended to multiply the number of working class families as opposed to large numbers of unmarried and "unattached" workers. Most of these wage-earners continued to be employed in large manufacturing establishments. In 1875, of 2,930 workers none were employed in shops employing less than 20 workers; 259 worked in shops of 21 to 100; 275 in shops of 101 to 300; and the rest, 2,396, were employed in large factories employing over 300 workers.[7] As a result of these tend-

[5] *Taylor Diary,* 1859-60, passim; Nov. 2, 1862.
[6] *Springfield Republican,* Nov. 6, 14, 1878.
[7] C. D. Wright, *A Compendium of the Census of Massachusetts, 1875,* p. 183.

encies depression periods were more serious for the workers than before the War. Then large numbers of single workers were affected; now family incomes were extensively curtailed.

With the coming of the Civil War and the cotton famine textile operatives had to cope with irregular work. Cotton mill production

TABLE 15. AVERAGE DAILY WAGE RATES FOR SELECTED OCCUPATIONS IN MASSACHUSETTS; INDEX NUMBERS OF WHOLESALE PRICES IN THE UNITED STATES AND OF THE COST OF LIVING IN EASTERN CITIES, 1859-1890*

YEAR	MALE WAGE-EARNERS					FEMALE WAGE-EARNERS					Wholesale Price Index 1910-14 Base	Cost of Living Index. 1860 Base
	Machinists	Laborers	Weavers	Slasher Tenders	Loom Fixers	Drawers in	Speeder Tenders	Tenders of Drawing Frames	Spinners	Weavers		
1859.....	$1.63	$ .95	$ .90	$1.04	$1.58	$ .58	$ .52	$ .49	$ .50	$ .66	95	
1860.....	1.65	1.01	.91	1.01	1.56	.57	.55	.49	.50	.66	93	100
1861.....	1.70	.98	.91	.90	1.52	.57	.56	.50	.47	.65	89	104
1862.....	1.83	.99	.88	.91	1.50	.63	.57	.50	.50	.67	104	111
1863.....	2.04	1.11	.90	1.05	1.65	.69	.57	.50	.49	.73	133	128
1864.....	2.03	1.29	.92	1.20	1.59	.66	.67	.55	.61	.71	193	150
1865.....	2.37	1.53	1.20	1.38	2.07	.68	.75	.65	.68	.89	185	163
1866.....	2.56	1.58	1.55	1.60	2.33	.88	.89	.80	.86	1.15	174	173
1867.....	2.58	1.54	1.63	2.11	2.24	1.03	.92	.85	.84	1.27	162	169
1868.....	2.60	1.58	1.53	1.83	2.18	.98	.94	.82	.83	1.22	158	166
1869.....	2.62	1.57	1.62	1.85	2.14	.98	.94	.82	.83	1.21	151	163
1870.....	2.66	1.58	1.58	1.99	2.20	.95	.96	.83	.93	1.19	135	162
1871.....	2.52	1.68	1.78	1.96	2.25	.88	1.02	.82	1.03	1.27	130	153
1872.....	2.62	1.55	1.91	1.98	2.24	1.01	1.02	.82	1.03	1.45	136	147
1873.....	2.74	1.55	1.84	1.92	2.20	.95	1.12	.82	1.03	1.41	133	147
1874.....	2.66	1.49	1.70	1.67	2.21	.94	1.04	.82	1.00	1.33	126	143
1875.....	2.44	1.44	1.58	1.79	1.91	1.00	1.01	.75	.91	1.16	118	141
1876.....	2.38	1.38	1.65	1.64	2.08	.94	.97	.75	.85	1.22	110	134
1877.....	2.19	1.33	1.36	1.61	1.97	.85	.86	.67	.80	1.07	106	134
1878.....	2.14	1.30	1.42	1.55	1.97	.86	.89	.67	.84	1.18	91	127
1879.....	2.09	1.25	1.34	1.53	1.97	.88	.91	.67	.90	1.15	90	128
1880.....	2.16	1.20	1.31	1.52	1.86	.95	.87	.67	.93	1.16	100	131
1881.....	2.28	1.05	1.23	1.38	2.00	.95	.85	.80	.98	1.13	103	......
1882.....	2.30	1.26	1.26	1.57	1.99	.88	.90	.85	.94	1.10	108	......
1883.....	2.22	1.30	1.37	1.42	1.93	.97	.93	.99	.83	1.06	101	......
1884.....	2.28	1.30	1.26	1.48	1.92	.94	.94	.76	.92	.96	93	......
1885.....	2.20	1.22	1.14	1.43	1.82	.87	.82	.89	.91	.94	85	......
1886.....	2.16	1.28	1.17	1.58	1.84	.98	.83	.76	.96	.98	82	......
1887.....	2.19	1.45	1.32	1.64	1.89	.93	.86	.92	.96	1.08	85	......
1888.....	2.24	1.24	1.21	1.69	1.82	.89	1.06	.77	.90	.99	86	......
1889.....	2.26	1.22	1.38	2.09	1.91	.89	1.14	.73	.84	1.29	81	......
1890.....	2.28	1.30	1.39	1.64	1.91	.93	1.00	.80	.96	1.16	82	......

* Wage data from U. S. Bureau of Labor Statistics, *Bulletin* 499, "History of Wages in the United States from Colonial Times to 1928," p. 254 et seq. Price index and cost of living index from G. F. Warren and F. A. Pearson, *Prices,* 26, 194.

was completely disorganized. The Chicopee Manufacturing Company had sold most of its raw cotton at an enormous profit, and was unable to give regular work to all of its employees. Under such circumstances earnings were poor and wage rates slow to rise. But prices rocketed. The cost of living in eastern cities increased 50 per cent from 1860 to 1864.[8] In that time the daily wage rates of machinists in Massachusetts rose 23 per cent; skilled metal workers were in a favored position as regards wages at such a time. The cotton workers were not so fortunate. Not only was work irregular, but rates were slow to rise. In the same period loom fixers and slasher tenders received practically no increases, while those accruing to weavers and spinners were insignificant in relation to the rise of prices. Not until 1869-70 did the wages of the workers in the country at large reach the purchasing power of 1861.[9] It is unfortunate that wage data for Chicopee are not available, but it is probable that the trend was not very different from that for Massachusetts.

With the close of the war the mills resumed capacity production and cotton wages began to move upward, while wholesale prices, but not the cost of living, were receding from the high point of 1864-65. The higher levels prevailed for some time, but in spite of these higher wages a worker reported, at the end of the sixties, that large numbers were in debt, and were obliged to depend upon assistance from the town during bad times.[10]

The twelve-hour day which had come back after the panic of 1857-58 remained in force with the resumption of full time work after the war, and it was not until 1869 that a 66 hour week was again adopted in the cotton mills.[11] At this time a questionnaire submitted by the State Department of Labor concerning the hours of work in textile mills elicited the statement on the part of a Chicopee cotton worker that the long hours previously in force "had a very bad effect. We had no time for anything but work and sleep. . . . Wages are about the same as before the time was reduced; but the men have more time for reading and recreation. I now see a

[8] See Table 15. [9] Warren and Pearson, *op. cit.*, 197.
[10] Mass., Bureau of Labor Statistics, 1st *Annual Report*, 298, 299 (1869).
[11] *Ibid.*, 292.

great inclination among the working class to improve their condition."[12] But even under the eleven-hour day, he said, the worker had little time for reading.[13] According to this observer, recreation for mill hands was of a simple nature. "The married portion of the working class occupy their hours before and after work, in such amusements as sawing and splitting wood, and tending a little garden patch, if they can get one; single folks that board out, in summer, generally walk or ride out, play ball, pitch quoits, play at billiards."[14]

Managers of the cotton mills, brought up in the tradition of hard work, long hours and a sober life, suspected that shorter hours would increase drunkenness, and denied that long hours of work affected the health adversely. The manager of one Chicopee mill said: "I commenced 25 years ago in a cotton mill, and have not had a vacation since (excepting 5 years in the army). I have worked 11, 12, 14 and 15 hours a day, and have felt no bad effects from it, but rather been strengthened. It is not the hours per day that a person works that breaks him down, but the hours spent in dissipation. . . . The effect of the diminution of the hours of labor would be to reduce wages, and in our opinion, increase dissipation."[15] Another cotton mill manager wrote that a reduction in working time "would increase crime, suffering, wickedness and pauperism. . . . Yes, I verily believe, there are a large number of operatives in our cotton mills who have too much spare time now (but not all). I do not advocate an increase in hours; but my observation and experience favor my conclusions. I am not favorable to reducing the present hours."[16] Given this attitude, any possible reductions in working time would come very slowly. Actually, there is no evidence pointing to a shorter hours movement in Chicopee in the sixties; possibly the reductions in 1869 forestalled organized demands. However there was quite a vigorous eight-hour movement in the East during the sixties and early seventies. In 1874 the Massachusetts legislature enacted a ten-hour law for women and minors under the age of eighteen. This law was secured by the efforts of Massachusetts workers.[17]

[12] *Ibid.* [13] *Ibid.*, 266. [14] *Ibid.*
[15] *Ibid.*, 221, 233. [16] *Ibid.*, 226. [17] Perlman, *op. cit.*, 48-50.

The scaling down of inflation wages started in 1867-68. An increase granted by the Chicopee Manufacturing Company in 1866 was followed by an 8 per cent reduction the next year. A small group of spinners struck in protest, but new workers were quickly engaged to replace them.[18] The Dwight Company cut wages at the beginning of 1868, and here also, a handful of spinners walked out "on finding that the amount of their wages at the reduced rates of January 1, did not come up to their expectations, and returned to their work Thursday morning."[19] In each case apparently only a small group of workers were involved. Dissatisfied with working conditions and anxious to maintain earnings they walked out of the mill. These protests were spontaneous. There is no evidence that any efforts were made to broaden the base of organization and disrupt general production throughout the mills. Of necessity, such feeble attempts could not achieve even a modicum of success.

Another and more vigorous attempt to secure wage increases was made by some workers in the Chicopee Manufacturing Company one year after the abortive strike of 1867. "There was quite a sensation at Chicopee Falls, last week, in consequence of a strike of some spinners, mule-tenders, spool-tenders and dress-tenders. . . . Owing to a reduction of wages last fall the operatives have been restive, and two or three weeks ago asked for piece work or for advanced pay, but not getting either, several noisy squads of men, women and boys marched out during working hours on Friday. This strike, like most movements of the kind, was ill advised, and will not materially interfere with the running of the mill."[20] A week later a correspondent of the *Springfield Republican* reported that "the strikers in the cotton mills at Chicopee Falls hold out with wonderful tenacity. Dog-in-the-manger-like, they refuse to allow any one else to work, and a stranger who attempted it was met at the door at the close of his first day and was obliged to flee for safety to his boarding-house."[21] The town appointed special constables to handle possible disturbances.[22] Some days later

[18] *Springfield Republican,* March 21, 1867.
[19] *Ibid.,* Feb. 22, 1868.
[20] *Ibid.,* March 30, 1868.
[21] *Ibid.,* April 9, 1868.
[22] *Ibid.*

it was said that a number of the strikers had returned to work at "moderately advanced rates."[23]

For the next few years work was regular and wages in the cotton mills and other manufacturing establishments moved upward. However, at least one company lowered wages. A cut of 10 per cent was instituted by the Ames Manufacturing Company in 1870.[24] As there do not seem to have been any other reductions of any importance at that time, the Ames cut was probably due to special difficulties which the company was beginning to experience at that time.

But any real gains achieved after the war were to be swept away in the depression years of the seventies. Wage cuts started at the end of 1873, and were continued sporadically in the subsequent years.[25] In addition to the fall of wages there was unemployment and under-employment. The cotton mills cut wages in 1874 and again in 1875.[26] These years were significant not only because they were marked by strikes, but for the first time Chicopee workers began to feel their connection with the general labor movement. A mule spinners' local was organized, and when its members were involved in a strike, contributions were received from textile workers in other Massachusetts cities.

In April, 1874, the mule spinners in the Dwight Manufacturing Company, protesting the 15 per cent wage cut which had been instituted some months before, went out on strike for a restoration of the cut.[27] Some workers came in from nearby towns to take their places, "but owing to the interference of the strikers returned again to their homes."[28] Groups of strikers picketed the mill gates and persuaded a number of boys to join them. Police were appointed to guard the entrances to the mill. The company countered by evicting strikers from company tenements and threatened a general shutdown if the strike spread.[29] The spinners were unable to secure the support of the weavers, and took to picketing the railroad stations in order to prevent other workers from coming

[23] *Ibid.*, April 22, 1868.
[24] *Ibid.*, Feb. 24, 1870.
[25] *Ibid.*, Nov. 18, 1873.
[26] *Ibid.*, April 7, 1874; Jan. 15, 1875.
[27] *Ibid.*, April 6, 1874.
[28] *Ibid.*, April 9, 1874.
[29] *Ibid.*

into town to take their places.[30] Within a few days the weavers were running out of work.[31] Strike meetings were held daily, funds were raised, some help being received from the Father Mathew Temperance Society of Chicopee. More important, contributions were received from workers in Lowell and Lawrence and other mill towns.[32] This was the first strike to occur in Chicopee in which a union was involved. The *Springfield Republican's* local correspondent doubted whether this strike had the whole-hearted support of its members, for he wrote, "Several of the most intelligent of the idle spinners state that they were opposed to the strike, but as they were members of the spinners' union, they could not oppose the majority."[33]

The outcome of the strike followed a modern pattern, indicative of its significance as a *union* strike. For, after a month, when it finally showed signs of collapse, the company announced that the men would not be taken back en masse, but would be re-engaged singly.[34] There was no question, at this time, of any collective bargaining with the union. Women and boys had already been used to take the place of the mule spinners, and the merchants were losing sympathy with the strike as fast as they were losing trade in the general stoppage involved.[35] When the strike collapsed the leaders were not reinstated.[36]

The failure of this strike may, perhaps, explain in part the more hesitant attitude of the employees of the Chicopee Manufacturing Company in dealing with a wage cut which they suffered at the beginning of 1875. The company had been working part time, and following a long-established policy common to the cotton mills, resumed full time operation when the cut was made effective. The *Springfield Republican* felt that "those employed in the mill recognize the good intentions of the company, and accept the cutting down with good grace."[37]

There is no doubt that there was apparent a considerable degree of uneasiness among the workers in the weeks following the cut.

[30] *Ibid.*, April 13, 1874.
[31] *Ibid.*, April 15, 1874.
[32] *Ibid.*, April 16, 18, 30, 1874.
[33] *Ibid.*, April 15, 1874.
[34] *Ibid.*, May 4, 1874.
[35] *Ibid.*, April 23, 30, 1874.
[36] *Ibid.*, May 9, 1874.
[37] *Ibid.*, Jan. 15, 1875.

They were not prepared, however, to take any positive action in order to secure wage increases. The press comment on the situation follows:

> It seems that the trouble with the weavers in the Chicopee Company's mill has been considerably exaggerated, and that although there has been considerable dissatisfaction among the hands ever since the reduction of wages in January, there has been nothing like a general effort to secure a remedy. Several of the weavers presented a request to the overseer . . . for an increase of pay, but resumed work immediately, on being assured by him that, if they did so, an attempt would be made to arrange matters satisfactorily. The average pay of the weavers, according to the record of the books, is now $5.48 a week, while some of the men get as much as $1.44 a day, which are certainly living wages, with the present price of board in the village. It is still true that there is considerable uneasiness among the hands, and there are some apprehensions of trouble, but it will probably be avoided. The hard times and the condition of the river have operated against the mill company, this winter, but they have shown a disposition to treat their employees as well as possible, which the hands should not be slow to recognize and to repay with forbearance."[38]

As the depression deepened, wage cutting continued; further reductions came in 1876. George Taylor, of the Belcher and Taylor Tools shops wrote: "Business is so dull and prices have come down so low on agricultural tools that we are thinking of another reduction of wages. It is hard to be obliged to do it, but our business compels us to do it."[39] When the wage cut was announced a few days later he recorded: "We gave notice of the reduction of our wages today. So far I have had no complaint, still no doubt the help would prefer the old prices, yet they must see that wages must come down."[40] For at least part of the year the Belcher and Taylor Company worked only 8 hours per day.[41] In 1879 came another cut and the 10 hour day.[42] At the beginning of 1876 the Ames Company made a "further reduction" of 15 per cent, and the Chicopee Manufacturing Company reduced their rates by 5 per cent.[43] The Dwight Company also cut wages again at this time, and the *Springfield Republican* commented that "the proposed re-

[38] *Ibid.*, March 12, 1875.
[39] *Taylor Diary*, July 27, 1876. [40] *Ibid.*, Aug. 11, 1876.
[41] *Ibid.*, Dec. 29, 1876. [42] *Ibid.*, March 4, 1879.
[43] *Springfield Republican*, Jan. 27, 1876.

duction of wages in the Dwight mills strikes many of the employees rather disagreeably. Some of them have all they can do now to keep body and soul together, even with strict economy."[44] In 1878 the cotton mills cut wages again in the weaving departments.[45] The next year the weavers in the Musgrave Alpaca Company struck against a 10 per cent wage cut.[46] In the same year wage reductions were extended throughout the plant of the Ames Manufacturing Company.[47] It was estimated that in 1878 average wages in Chicopee were 25 per cent above the 1860 level, and that the cost of living was 17 per cent higher, leaving a small net gain for the period.[48] This estimate applied to the possible full time earnings of 1,354 workers for whom there was data available for both 1860 and 1878.[49]

French workers began to come to the mills in increasing numbers in the late seventies.[50] But it appears that the supply of French-Canadians was not too steady at this time. The Canadian government was settling natives of Quebec in the West, and was offering to repatriate émigrés. Some who had settled in Chicopee were taking advantage of this offer.[51] But at the same time other French-Canadian families were coming to Chicopee. Some returned to Canada of their own accord. "Some of the Frenchmen, who were induced to come down from Canada by rather big promises from irresponsible parties, have returned because they could not earn as high wages as they expected."[52] It was not indicated who the "irresponsible parties" were. In 1880, when a number of French-Canadian families were leaving, a group of girls were brought in from Nova Scotia.[53] The next year Polish workers began to make their appearance.[54]

With the improvement of business conditions in the eighties the cotton mills gave 10 per cent wage increases.[55] A small strike in the Dwight mills hastened the appointment of 18 special con-

[44] *Ibid.*, Jan. 12, 1876.
[45] *Ibid.*, Oct. 21, Nov. 23, 1878.
[46] *Ibid.*, April 3, 1879.
[47] *Ibid.*, Jan. 29, 31, 1879.
[48] Mass., Bureau of Labor Statistics, 10th *Annual Report*, 84 (1879).
[49] *Ibid.*, 78.
[50] *Springfield Republican*, April 1, 9, 1879.
[51] *Ibid.*, April 12, 1879.
[52] *Ibid.*, Oct. 29, 1879.
[53] *Ibid.*, March 24, 1880.
[54] *Ibid.*, Jan. 18, July 15, 1881.
[55] *Ibid.*, Jan. 13, 30, 1880.

stables, probably in the expectation that the strike might become general.[56] At the same time the night hands of the Musgrave Alpaca Company struck for a 10 per cent wage increase.[57] Workers elsewhere were growing restive. One employer wrote: "Our foundrymen are quite uneasy and we have been obliged to advance their pay a little," and later said, "Our men in the machine shop have been uneasy and want more pay. Some of them I advanced and others I shall let go."[58] Another small strike occurred in the Dwight mills when a group of weavers who had been working at night at higher than day rates, demanded the extension of night rates for daytime work when they changed shifts.[59] "About 40 of the striking French weavers gathered at the office of the Dwight mills yesterday and made such noisy demonstrations that the services of a police officer were needed to keep them quiet. The company paid them off and many drew their earnings from the bank and went to Canada. A number will return to their work, as it is probable that all who desire to return can do so."[60]

The prosperity of the early eighties did not last long. Depression set in again and with its serious unemployment and wage reductions.[61] These conditions were especially serious for a

TABLE 16. DURATION OF UNEMPLOYMENT IN 12 MONTHS PRECEDING MAY 1, 1885*

Duration of Unemployment	Male	Female	Total
Any Time	1651	765	2416
1 month	91	69	160
2 months	294	115	409
3 "	469	341	810
4 "	244	54	298
5 "	88	17	105
6 "	240	79	319
7 "	44	14	58
8 "	76	17	93
9 "	45	23	68
10 "	24	19	43
11 "	28	17	45
12 "	8	....	8

* Mass., Bureau of Labor Statistics, 18th *Annual Report*, 58, 59 (1887).

[56] *Ibid.*, Jan. 30, Feb. 4, 5, 1880. [57] *Ibid.*, Feb. 3, 1880.
[58] *Taylor Diary*, April 14, 15, 1881.
[59] *Springfield Republican*, Nov. 17, 1881.
[60] *Ibid.*, Dec. 1, 1881.
[61] *Ibid.*, 1883-84, passim. See also Tables 16 and 17.

TABLE 17. PRINCIPAL OCCUPATIONS OF THE UNEMPLOYED AND AVERAGE DURATION OF UNEMPLOYMENT, 1884-85*

Occupation	Total Persons Engaged in Industry	Number Unemployed	Average No. of Months of Unemployment
TOTAL	5176	2416	4.07
MALE	3329	1651	4.18
Farmers	119	26	6.00
Farm Laborers	217	130	4.94
Gun Makers	28	24	3.04
Sword Makers	44	27	3.74
Carpenters	133	85	3.65
Masons	53	52	5.08
Painters	55	32	4.09
Cotton Workers	957	452	3.75
Machinists	245	160	3.61
Machine Shop Workers	54	40	4.98
Sewing Machine Workers	40	34	4.44
Knitting Machine Workers	12	12	3.58
Iron Workers	84	67	4.18
Blacksmiths	42	17	3.47
Brass Workers	17	13	4.69
Needle Makers	14	13	3.92
Screw Makers	13	9	3.67
Laborers	100	80	4.96
Others	1102	378	4.46
FEMALE	1847	765	3.81
Teachers	49	35	3.71
Dressmakers	76	36	4.69
Milliners	14	7	5.00
Cotton Workers	1369	604	3.61
Others	339	83	4.86

* Mass., Bureau of Labor Statistics, 18th *Annual Report,* 183 (1887).

community whose labor force contained so large a proportion of immigrant workers. An increasingly heavy burden of poor relief fell upon the town. The municipality raised seriously the question of requiring corporations which imported labor to post a bond of $300 to prevent a person so imported, or his dependents, from becoming a public charge within two years of his arrival.[62] As the depression lifted in the middle eighties the cotton workers once more showed signs of restlessness. A few went out on strike for wage increases at the end of 1885, but to no avail. Two months later wage rates were raised.[63]

Practically all the strikes of this period were poorly organized

[62] *Ibid.,* March 10, 1884.
[63] *Ibid.,* Dec. 18, 19, 1885; Feb. 12, 1886.

and ineffective attempts to prevent a reduction of wages or to demand wage increases as depression periods lifted. Except for one or two unimportant exceptions they were confined to the cotton mills. All were closely connected with the movements of the business cycle. Unfortunately the data available are insufficient to permit any correlation of price and wage movements, and of the incidence of strikes. However, some observations may be noted. As wage rates were revised downward during the business recession of 1866-68 we find strikes against wage cuts. They were not successful. As business activity started to increase in 1868 a strike for higher wages seems to have achieved its objective—the only successful strike of the period. The mule spinners' strike against a wage cut in 1874 failed, as was to be expected in view of the general business situation. With the return of prosperity at the end of the seventies workers began to grow restless and struck for wage increases. The strikes as such failed, but increases were granted in the months following the disputes. Exactly the same thing occurred during the business revival of 1885-86.

The mechanics and metal workers had not been exempted from the wage adjustments of these years, but either suffered them in silence, or perhaps were able to arrange satisfactory settlements by negotiation. Aside from the mule spinners, there is no record of any trade union organization among the textile workers. From 1884 to 1887 there were two local units of the Knights of Labor, with a few hundred members, probably many of them cotton workers, but these locals seemed to be social organizations rather than labor unions.[64] In 1888 a workers' mutual benefit lodge was organized.[65]

During three decades of unsettled times the Chicopee workers had made occasional efforts to organize and to improve their conditions. Their real wages were somewhat higher at the end of the period than in 1860. They had not yet made their power felt politically in any way. They still worked long hours. Large numbers of mill workers were still living in crowded tenements. Very few indeed had been able to emerge from the working into the merchant class. Savings accumulated during the good years were

[64] *Ibid.*, 1884-87, passim.

[65] *Ibid.*, Feb. 2, 1888.

eaten up in the frequent and severe depression periods. These workers were less patient than had been their predecessors, but they were unable to achieve permanent organization by themselves. While they were learning to make positive demands for the improvement of conditions, as well as to protest the lowering of standards already achieved, they were not often successful in their efforts.

CHAPTER IX

BUSINESS ENTERPRISE AT THE TURN OF THE CENTURY

The industrial expansion of Chicopee proceeded rapidly as the nineteenth century drew to a close. A search for patterns of development indicates that the decades preceding and following the turn of the century were marked by the culmination of old, and the beginning of new trends. The process of small investment continued, new shops came into being, established companies prospered and grew. But the expansion of local middle class activity does not seem to have kept pace, in this period, with the development of the community as a whole. We find that new large-scale industrial investment was sponsored by outside interests, with the result that the sphere of absentee ownership was extended and became of greater importance than it had been for many years. The growth of population was largely conditioned by the arrival of immigrants who came to work in the various manufacturing enterprises. The population of Chicopee reached the 20,000 mark in 1905, and for the first time the proportions of males and females were about equal.[1] Hitherto there had always been a preponderance of women, indicating the importance of the cotton mills in the economic and social life of the community. By 1905, however, other industries, and the cotton mills too, were offering enough employment to men to make the balance. The foreign-born, who already in 1875 had constituted 35 per cent of the total population increased to 43 per cent from 1890 to 1895, and were just under 40 per cent from 1905 to 1915. In the latter year there were some 30,000 persons living in Chicopee.[2] The small Yankee middle class group could not, by itself, keep pace with this expansion in point of numbers. The natural increase of the foreign-born working class was augmented by new arrivals. It is true that

[1] Mass., *Census* of 1905, I, 170, 171.

[2] Mass., *Census* of 1895, Vol. II, 84, 85, *Census* of 1905, Vol. I, 170, 171, *Census* of 1915, pp. 200, 201, U. S., 11th *Census,* "Report on Population," Part I, 534.

in the middle class there were recruits from the ranks of the Irish, but the old homogeneity of the group was lost. The activities of the local manufacturers tended to fade into insignificance when compared with the growth of the new large corporations. The economic and social position of the former, in these years, would depend upon their relationship to the industrial and mercantile enterprise in the town, and the relative importance of their activity in municipal and business affairs.

The investment of small sums of money continued in much the same manner as before. Two or three men would pool their savings, and try to start the manufacture of some commodity, in the production of which at least one of them was likely to have had some experience as a skilled workman, or as a foreman or supervisor. Thus of the three men who invested in a knit goods shop in the early nineties, two had been employed by the Chicopee Manufacturing Company, while the third was a clerk in the Overman Wheel Company.[3] At this time we find occasional small investments made by French and Polish residents in petty manufacturing enterprise. These nationalities had already entered the mercantile field, and were trying to extend their activities. However there is no record of any manufacturing concern started by immigrants which survived for more than a short period. As a matter of fact practically none of the small-scale manufacturing investments of this period proved to be permanent. The exceptions were the Taylor-Bramley Company, first organized in 1888, and the Knit Goods Specialty Company, started in 1899.[4] The former company started out on a small scale to manufacture men's underclothing, later adding silk and worsted sweaters and women's wear.[5] One of the partners of the company was Albert Taylor, son of George S. Taylor, of the Belcher and Taylor Agricultural Tool Company. The other partner, Walter Bramley, previously managed the knitting department of a Springfield firm.[6] The

[3] *Springfield Republican,* March 15, 1893; Springfield *Directories,* passim.
[4] Spence, *op. cit.,* 111, 112; *Springfield Republican,* Jan. 17, 1891.
[5] Babbitt, *op. cit.,* 16.
[6] *Springfield Republican,* Jan. 17, 1891; *Biographical Review of Hampden County,* II, 891, 892.

company enjoyed steady expansion, received new capital from at least one New York investor, perhaps the sales agent for the firm, and is still in operation at the present time.[7] The Knit Goods Specialty Company was a smaller enterprise, and for a long time concentrated on the manufacture of gas mantles.[8] Later the company proved itself most adaptive to changing conditions by specializing in the manufacture of "fad" products.[9] There were other investments of a similar nature, not always so successful, or so long-lived. But in spite of the fact that small-scale investments continued to occur, it seems that they were not so numerous as they had been in the past, and they were overshadowed by the new large investments of the period.

The activities of the small group of men who had sponsored and built up the local corporative enterprises tapered off in the nineties. Some of these men died, others were old, and no longer able to take an active part in business affairs. Most significant of all, there does not seem to be any record pointing to the rise of a new group of entrepreneurs comparable in any way to that which had been a characteristic feature of the preceding years. Sufficient time had passed to permit the emergence of such a group to perpetuate the activities of the original entrepreneurs, or to open up new fields of endeavor. Those who were left of the old group, together with a few newcomers, made some further investments, but small in amount. The Nye Truss Company, for instance, organized in 1891, was initiated by George Taylor and Joshua Stevens of the original group. Other investors were David Boynton, who had been the superintendent of the Chicopee Electric Light Company, F. W. Patterson, who was employed by the Lamb Knitting Machine Company, and N. R. Wood, a merchant. The capital invested was small, and the company did not remain in business very long.[10] S. R. Nye, the inventor of the truss, received royalties for the manufacturing rights to the product, and he supervised its production.[11] An entirely different project undertaken

[7] A. M. Copeland, *op. cit.*, III, 504.

[8] *Springfield Republican*, Aug. 20, 1914. [9] Spence, *op. cit.*, 111, 112.

[10] *Springfield Republican*, Jan. 8, 1891; Nov. 29, 1893; Springfield *Directories*, passim.

[11] *Springfield Republican*, Jan. 8, 1891.

by the group, marking a departure from their usual type of investment, was a building and real estate company, the Chicopee Falls Building Association. The directors in 1892 were G. S. and J. E. Taylor, Joshua Stevens, Andrew Gale, T. C. Page of the Lamb Knitting Machine Company, and H. N. Lyon, the book-keeper of the latter company.[12] These were the last new investments of the old merchant-manufacturer entrepreneurs.

In the case of the long established corporations both old and new trends were apparent. All of them continued production along established lines and in some cases made important innovations. The Belcher and Taylor Tool Company, now an amalgamation of all the agricultural tool shops, prospered, occasionally adding new products; its affairs were entrusted to the same management as before.[13] On the death of W. P. McFarland, his seat on the board of directors was taken by F. N. Withrell, the book-keeper of this company and of the Chicopee Falls Building Association.[14] The Stevens Arms Company also expanded its business, and in 1898 was employing a night shift in order to keep up with orders which may have been stimulated by the Spanish-American War demands.[15] But the Ames Company did not profit from war orders as it had in the past. When the Overman Wheel Company, which had furnished the bulk of its business decided to start large-scale manufacture in its own plant, the Ames Company found itself in serious difficulties. With the increasing importance of heavy steel artillery, it could no longer maintain its position as an ordnance producer, and it is possible that the exploration of possibilities for the manufacture of subsidiary products was neglected during the capacity production of bicycles. In 1898 the property of the company was offered for sale; its land and buildings, bronze and iron foundries, machinery and water power, were placed on the market.[16] The bronze foundry was purchased by J. C. Buckley, the superintendent under Ames' ownership. He operated the foundry for a short time, and then sold the property to the Spald-

[12] *Ibid.*, Oct. 14, 1892. [13] *Ibid.*, passim.
[14] *Ibid.*, July 13, 1903; Springfield *Directories*, passim.
[15] *Springfield Republican*, Aug. 9, 1898.
[16] *Ibid.*, Jan. 1, 1898.

ing Company.[17] For a time part of the abandoned factories were used as warehouses and some space was rented to small manufacturers.[18] The Ames Sword Company, specializing in the manufacture of society regalia, remained in operation.

It was the concentration on the manufacture of bicycles that induced the investment of new capital derived from outside sources. We have already seen that A. H. Overman, a bicycle maker, had given extensive contracts for the manufacture of his product, the "Victor" Wheel, to the Ames Manufacturing Company. In 1883 Overman moved his offices from Hartford to Chicopee.[19] The largest bloc of stock in this new concern was held by Overman and his associates, though some shares were owned by Chicopee men, notably A. C. Woodworth, of the Ames Company, L. M. Ferry, and Luther White, a lawyer.[20] In 1887 Overman bought up the plant of the Massachusetts Screw Company in Chicopee Falls, with the intention of starting to make the Victor bicycle under his own roof. Two years later he built a large new factory.[21] Still the demand for bicycles mounted, so that in 1890 more plant was bought and a new building erected. The company gave employment at this time to from 400 to 600 men, working in day and night shifts.[22] Before long the company was manufacturing rubber tires, and later, by the addition of the production of cork grips and other accessories, the plant became one of the most highly integrated bicycle factories in the country.[23] In 1894, when the bicycle craze was near its height, 1,200 men were employed, and were hard pressed to meet the enormous demand.[24]

But with the manufacture of bicycles established on an extremely profitable basis, other producers entered the field, and made serious inroads into the rate of profit. This was evident in

[17] *Ibid.,* Oct. 17, 1906.
[18] *Ibid.,* Sept. 11, 1903; Jan. 6, 14, 1904.
[19] *Ibid.,* Oct. 4, 1883.
[20] *Ames Papers,* Memo. Signed by Sec'y of the Overman Wheel Company, 1885.
[21] *Springfield Republican,* Sept. 8, 1887; May 3, 1889.
[22] *Ibid.,* Feb. 21, March 25, May 12, 1890.
[23] *Ibid.,* Oct. 6, 1891; Sept. 30, 1897; Davis, *The New England States,* I, 415.
[24] *Springfield Republican,* April 25, 1894.

Chicopee itself. In 1889-90 the Lamb Knitting Machine Company started to make bicycles when it accepted a contract from Overman for the manufacture of a lower priced product.[25] The Lamb Company furnished the plant and equipment. Before long Overman began to feel not only the general competition that was rapidly developing in the trade, but the direct competition of A. G. Spalding, a new maker. Spalding, a manufacturer of sporting goods, had been Overman's western sales agent, and in 1893 or 1894 was left at the end of the season with a number of Victor bicycles on his hands. At this time Spalding started to manufacture a wheel of his own, and he proceeded to dump the overstock of Victor Wheels on the market.[26] As the Lamb Company was already filling contracts for the Spalding machine,[27] the time was ripe for expansion. In 1893 the Lamb Company was reorganized as the Lamb Manufacturing Company, with an increase in capital contributed by Spalding and his associates, who gained a controlling interest in the company.[28] The new firm continued the manufacture of knitting machines, but this turned out to be a minor department, when the production of bicycles boomed. Local investors still had a considerable stake in the reorganized company, but the control had passed from them to the absentee owners.[29]

Enormous expansion occurred in the bicycle industry in 1895-96 with keen competition and price cutting which reached its height in 1897.[30] The competitive behaviour of the bicycle makers was not confined to price cutting. Large sums of money were spent for advertising of all kinds. Otherwise prices might have declined more than they actually did.[31] Overman seems to have been one of the first of the makers to inaugurate extensive advertising campaigns, and his lay-outs and slogans were varied, and far superior in writing and appearance to almost any advertising which had hitherto appeared in the pages of the *Springfield Republican.* He

[25] Interview, Mr. F. D. Howard.
[26] *Springfield Republican,* March 15, 1894.
[27] *Ibid.,* Jan. 13, 1891.
[28] *Ibid.,* Oct. 6, 1893; Interview, Mr. F. D. Howard.
[29] Interview, Mr. F. D. Howard.
[30] A. S. Dewing, *Corporate Promotions and Reorganizations,* 257.
[31] *Ibid.*

also made an arrangement with the Dwight Manufacturing Company to carry the Victor trade mark on some of its cloth. Racing teams were financed to attend the bicycle meets, and brass bands were sent to important races and shows.[32] More directly, Overman continued his feud with Spalding, and started to manufacture sporting equipment in order to carry the fight into Spalding's own territory. It is possible that in so doing he weakened the capital structure of his company.[33]

The experience of the profit-destroying competition of the nineties made the bicycle makers decide to apply the same cure as was being attempted in other industries—combination. Spalding was asked to organize a bicycle combine, and the result was the incorporation of the American Bicycle Company in 1899.[34] Forty-eight companies joined the combination, among them, of course, Spalding's Lamb Manufacturing Company, the sales offices of which were moved to New York, emphasizing still further the break between the control of the company and the location of its plant.[35] The Overman Wheel Company did not join the trust.

But in spite of the fact that the combination held 65 per cent of the bicycle business in the United States in 1895, and concentrated production in only 10 of the most efficient of its 48 plants, the trust collapsed.[36] Actually it was the collapse of an industry with the cessation of demand for its product. "The causes lay primarily not in inefficient management or unwise financial policy, but in the practical cessation of a manufacturing industry employing machinery not readily readjusted to other uses."[37] The Overman Wheel Company while not in the trust, was affected in the same way. The company was already in difficulties by 1898, and tried to strengthen its position by disposing of its athletic equipment department to the superintendent in charge, who operated it independently for a while.[38] Work in the bicycle departments picked up the next

[32] *Springfield Republican,* June 8, 1891; Aug. 18, 1892; Jan. 26, 1893; and passim.
[33] *Ibid.,* April 25, 1894; letter from Mr. A. H. Benton.
[34] Dewing, *op. cit.,* 257; U. S. Industrial Commission *Report,* XIII. 688.
[35] Dewing, *op. cit.,* 257; *Springfield Republican,* Dec. 6, 1899.
[36] U. S. Industrial Commission *Report,* XIII, 690; Dewing, *op. cit.,* 257.
[37] Dewing, *op. cit.,* 268.
[38] *Springfield Republican,* Jan. 3, March 23, 1898.

year, but the Overman Company could not survive the general collapse of the industry.[39]

The Lamb bicycle shops had been obliged to shut down in the spring of 1901.[40] Since a considerable part of the payment for the property transferred to the American Bicycle Company was in the form of stock, the local owners of the Lamb unit suffered a severe loss when the company went into receivership. Although the bicycle business was ruined, there was still the knitting machine department, the operation of which could be continued, if the financial means could be found to do so. A new company was organized to buy this business, assuming once more the name of the Lamb Knitting Machine Company. Mr. F. D. Howard, of Chicopee, who had been connected with the earlier company was one of the prime movers of the reorganization. Other important investors were Robert Russell, of Holyoke, an original stockholder, H. P. Norris, of Springfield, J. T. Herrick of Hyannisport, and the Chicago sales agent of the company. Fifty thousand dollars in all was invested.[41] In subsequent years the company concentrated once more on the manufacture of knitting machines, and later started general machine shop jobbing and foundry work.[42]

Thus for a period of years the companies engaged in the manufacture of bicycles offered employment to large numbers of men, but these were thrown out of work with the disappearance of the industry. However new factories appeared which reabsorbed these men, and the bicycle industry, although itself of a transitory nature, led to further industrial developments.

When A. G. Spalding became interested in the Lamb Company, he moved his sporting equipment plant from Philadelphia to Chicopee.[43] Organized sport and athletics were becoming increasingly popular amusements throughout the nation. By 1902 the Spalding factory in Chicopee employed about 200 workers.[44] Expansion was steady, and the company bought the old Ames factories, most of which were lying idle, made extensions, and acquired a bronze

[39] *Ibid.*, March 15, 1899. [40] *Ibid.*, May 27, 1901.
[41] Interview, Mr. F. D. Howard; *Springfield Republican*, July 27, 1904.
[42] Interview, Mr. F. D. Howard.
[43] *Springfield Republican*, Oct. 19, 1893.
[44] *Ibid.*, Oct. 23, 1902.

foundry[45]—the original Ames foundry, in fact. But the Spalding plant did not offer as many opportunities for skilled workers as did the metal industries.

Another innovation came with the introduction of the manufacture of automobiles. Charles E. Duryea had built and operated the first American gasoline car about 1892, taking it for its first run in Springfield.[46] In the nineties the development of the kerosene-steam car and the electric car showed signs of forging ahead of the gasoline car, and indeed, in 1900, at the first American automobile show, they received most attention.[47] In view of the fact that much of the early automobile experimentation was carried on in small machine shops, and that those machine factories which were already adapted for the production of standardized interchangeable mechanical parts were already well established in Chicopee, it is not surprising to find local manufacturers interested in the possibilities which the new product presented. It was in just such shops experienced in the production of sewing machines, bicycles, and other machinery, that it was often possible for small automobile companies to get their start.[48] Chicopee was a bicycle centre, and with the disorganization of the bicycle market it was natural to turn to another form of locomotive agent. Accordingly we find that A. H. Overman was making a steam car at the end of the century, and even had orders on hand waiting to be filled.[49] He had already rented factory space and started to organize the plant necessary to manufacture on a commercial scale. But with the bicycle business shattered, and its sustaining profits gone, he had lost the means which could have been used to finance the automobile business and to perfect the model.[50] Things might have been simpler if he had been working on a gasoline model. He did shift to the latter type of car in 1902, but nothing came of it, for reasons which it has not been possible to ascertain. He

[45] *Ibid.*, Jan. 14, 1904; May 17, 1907; July 23, 1909.
[46] Arthur Pound, *The Turning Wheel*, 35.
[47] Lawrence H. Seltzer, *A Financial History of the American Automobile Industry*, 17, 18.
[48] *Ibid.*, 19, 20.
[49] *Springfield Republican*, June 12, Aug. 12, 1899.
[50] *Ibid.*, March 14, 1900; Jan. 31, April 2, 1901.

finally made some business arrangement with the Locomobile Company in Bridgeport, severing all connections with Chicopee.[51] It is interesting to note that even when the bicycle business was at its height Mr. Overman had never resided in Chicopee.

In the meantime the Stevens Arms and Tool Company, makers of machine tools among other things, had been working on the Duryea automobile. It is not known whether or not this machine shop helped to finance Duryea's early experiments. At any rate, in 1902, the company advertised that the Stevens-Duryea autoobile was ready for sale.[52] There were no important technical difficulties which remained unsurmounted, and the Arms Company was prosperous enough to look after the financial needs involved. The plant of the defunct Lamb Manufacturing Company was acquired, and further expansion came in 1904 and 1905.[53] The Stevens-Duryea Automobile Company was incorporated in 1906 as an independent institution, with the importation of new capital.[54]

The existence of Chicopee as an important bicycle centre influenced its emergence as a seat of the rubber tire industry. When bicycle manufacture was at its peak in 1896, there was organized the Spaulding and Pepper Rubber Company. C. L. Pepper had worked for the Ames Company and later for the Overman Wheel Company.[55] The largest investor in this company organized to manufacture bicycle tires, was T. H. Spaulding, head of the Spaulding Machine Screw Company of Buffalo, New York, a firm which had a plant in Chicopee for a time.[56] By 1898 the rubber company was insolvent and was bought up by N. W. Fisk who continued the manufacture of rubber tires for bicycles.[57] The decline in the production of bicycles was more than compensated for by the rise of the automobile industry. The Fisk Rubber Company, owned and controlled by outside interests, grew rapidly. By 1904, after extensive additions had been made, some departments were obliged

[51] *Ibid.*, May 21, Oct. 10, 1902.
[52] *Ibid.*, Nov. 12, 1901; Oct. 17, 1902.
[53] *Ibid.*, Aug. 16, 1902; March 22, 1904; Aug. 26, 1905.
[54] Moody's *Manual of Industrial Investments,* 1923.
[55] *Springfield Republican,* Mar. 12, 1897; Spence, *op. cit.*, 77.
[56] *Springfield Republican,* Sept. 23, 1898.
[57] *Ibid.*, July 13, Oct. 29, 1898.

to work in two shifts, and the company had received orders from most of the important automobile makers of the day.[58] In 1910, when 600 hands were employed, it was decided to double the producing capacity, and again in 1912 the plant was extended so as to make use of 2,000 workers.[59] It was not long before the rubber company was employing more workers than the two cotton companies combined.

Other factors influenced industrial enterprise in Chicopee. As Springfield and Holyoke grew in size, and became congested, some firms which had been conducting business there found it profitable to move to Chicopee, where larger manufacturing quarters were available at the same or lower prices than could be obtained in the larger cities. Thus the B. F. Perkins Company, a machine manufacturing corporation was attracted by cheap land, the Burtworth Carpet Company came from Springfield, and the C. F. Church Manufacturing Company of Holyoke moved its plant to Willimansett so as to get roomier quarters at a lower price.[60] Other companies followed, making use of cheap land and good railroad loading facilities. These were comparatively small firms. In a few cases large nationally organized corporations established branches in Chicopee which was in the center of a fairly thickly populated region. Thus the Swift Packing Company and Standard Oil established distributing points, handy either to Springfield or to Holyoke, as did the Paper Makers' Chemical Corporation, the latter in order to be near Holyoke's paper mills.[61] A number of manufacturing companies were later established on the outer fringe of the city limits, so that in certain respects Chicopee came to be an industrial suburb of Springfield and Holyoke.

As the city grew, townspeople were apt to correlate the number of industrial firms with municipal prestige. A board of trade consisting mostly of merchants, occupied itself with trying to induce firms situated elsewhere, to locate in Chicopee. It induced the

[58] *Ibid.,* Aug. 1, 1902; Nov. 16, 1904; Feb. 17, 1905.
[59] *Ibid.,* Aug. 2, 1910; Aug. 3, 1912.
[60] Spence, *op. cit.,* 124; A. M. Copeland, *op. cit.,* III, 504, 505; *Springfield Republican,* Sept. 22, 1912.
[61] *Springfield Republican,* Aug. 19, 1892, Aug. 20, 1908; Springfield *Directories,* passim.

municipality to promise public improvements which would be to the direct advantage of the desired company. Men of property were sometimes persuaded to invest in the prospective firm which, if it happened to need ready cash, might find the injection of new capital attractive. The National Scale Company was moved from Pennsylvania to Chicopee under these conditions.[62] When the Page-Storms Drop Forge Company moved in, the city promised to build a railway underpass and to furnish water to the new company.[63] In making these improvements the city was competing against other municipalities who were also angling for selection as the seat of new enterprise. Improvements were undertaken, of course, with no assurance that the company would stay in Chicopee permanently, and therefore it was often difficult to plan carefully for the amortization, and even interest charges, of the public debts incurred. This was to become a tangled problem for numerous towns and cities in the twentieth century. The existence of industrial enterprise owning taxable property does not guarantee indefinitely a property valuation which will yield a tax return commensurate with the burden of public improvements undertaken at an earlier period.

Enough has been said about these developments to show that Chicopee was experiencing an expansion of industrial activity similar to that which was prevalent throughout the country. Large sums of money were invested and reinvested from 1890 to 1910, in spite of the occasional set backs. Significant, however, is the waning relative position held by local industrial owners compared with the economic importance of that portion of the town's business controlled by an absentee ownership. The period of ascendancy of local middle class interests was over. The town was once more, as it had been in the early days of the cotton manufacture, first and foremost, a "mill town." With the extreme division of labor introduced by the manufacture of interchangeable metal parts in the bicycle trade, skill and experience were no longer so important as had been the case before. Increasing mechanization

[62] *Springfield Republican,* Jan. 15, March 25, 1909.
[63] *Ibid.,* Feb. 19, 1909.

called for semi-skilled labor, as did the rubber and sporting goods industries. This is a factor to be reckoned with in considering the fortunes of the merchant class and of the purveyors of services.

Workers who earn small annual incomes can support retail stores only for the satisfaction of the simplest of economic wants. Luxury stores cater to skilled workers and to the middle class. By the nineties there had accumulated, in Chicopee, a large working population which did not have much money to spend, and the middle class itself was a small one. This situation limited, to some extent, the possibilities of mercantile expansion. It also modified the rate of profit to be derived from pre-existing mercantile investment, and tended to prevent the accumulation of savings which could be reinvested in other lines of business. In the nineties, when trade in Chicopee Center, the seat of the Dwight Manufacturing Company, was much depressed, this condition was ascribed in part to the preponderance of cotton workers. "Chicopee Center can have no great hope for prosperity if it is simply to be a cotton mill town. The cotton mills are not to be disparaged, as they are the foundation of Chicopee and to them is due the greater part of whatever prosperity the city has enjoyed. But if the city is to depend on this alone for the future the prospect is gloomy. In the first place the cotton mills do not employ a great deal of a high type of labor. A man cannot earn high wages at it, his wife must work to support the family, and at an early age the children must join the ranks."[64] The writer felt that new enterprises offering better employment opportunities should be attracted to the town as one way of solving the problem. It is highly significant that the writer thought of attracting *outside capital,* and that he did not suggest that local investment perform this function.

Another complication was the fact that not only was there an exceptionally large number of working class consumers and low wage groups, but these were mostly employed by a few large factories. The danger of a temporary or permanent shutdown meant that even if the merchant was able to build up a steady clientele, his gross income might at any moment be seriously curtailed. It is

[64] *Ibid.,* Aug. 1, 1897.

very likely that this prospect made the would-be merchant think twice before investing his money in Chicopee. This factor also influenced housing. In the early years of the twentieth century there was a shortage of tenements. By 1907 it was observed that many worked in Chicopee and commuted to homes outside the city limits. It is quite probable that people were right when they ascribed this state of affairs to the shortage of houses, but it is also possible that some preferred to live elsewhere because of business connections of other members of the family or for other reasons. But even if one makes allowance for such possibilities one is forced to the conclusion that investors were slow to start building, partly because of the fear that one important plant shutdown might be sufficient to ruin a housing project.[65]

The result of this curtailment of middle class opportunities was that while workers flocked to the town, there is little evidence that petty traders or manufacturers came. Indeed occasionally younger members of the group went elsewhere to look for work which offered possibilities of "advancement."[66]

It is probable that conditions such as these would be found in almost any factory town. But they were accentuated in Chicopee on account of a special set of circumstances peculiar to it. Chicopee itself is not a compact economic unit, and Chicopee lies between and immediately adjacent to, two larger cities.

We must not forget that the City of Chicopee is made up of two principal manufacturing centers, that is, Chicopee and Chicopee Falls, and of a few minor settlements. Except in the former, population is sparse. Willimansett, the third most important unit is nearer to Holyoke than to Chicopee Falls or Chicopee Center. The Brightwood area, a part of Chicopee, is as much a suburb of Springfield. Thus the consumers are scattered, and specialty stores, even clothing stores, which must depend upon reasonably large numbers of persons passing their doors find it hard to exist without this requisite density of population. The scatter of consumers tends in the first instance to prevent the opening of certain kinds

[65] *Ibid.*, Sept. 12, 1903; April 14, Aug. 29, 1907.
[66] *Ibid.*, Aug. 1, 1897, and passim.

of stores, and established merchants find it difficult to vary their stocks sufficiently to attract customers from outlying sections. In addition, many residents would find it more convenient to trade in Holyoke or Springfield, even if it were possible to find a large variety of goods in the Chicopee stores. Holyoke and Springfield, even at that time, were larger and more compact units. For one reason or another, then, people developed the habit of making some of their purchases in these adjacent cities. With the development of convenient street car service, the habit became fixed. In 1890 it was noted that "there is a growing tendency among the townspeople, especially at Chicopee Center, to run to this city (Springfield) for every little thing that is needed in their household economy. The merchants carry as good a stock as they can under the circumstances, but are of the opinion that it does not pay to invest their money in a supply of goods and have no chance to dispose of the stock. The street railroad makes it very convenient for people to come to this city for everything."[67] Two years later there was talk—even if idle talk—of enacting some sort of a measure which would force residents to trade in Chicopee, as the merchants were finding it more and more difficult to meet Springfield competition.[68] Again in 1906 it was said that merchants could not afford to carry good stocks because of this drift of money to Springfield.[69] By this time the complaint had become chronic, and has remained such ever since.

In the old days the leaders of the middle class were accepted as leaders of the community in more ways than one. This middle class was made up completely of Yankees who experienced social contact with their fellow-Yankees who happened to be workers. They were thus the accepted leaders of the community in business, religion, and social affairs. This situation lent cohesion and "sameness" to the community which changing conditions made it difficult to maintain. The arrival of large numbers of immigrant workers established a cleavage between workers and merchant-manufacturers. Afterwards some of these foreign-born residents were able to enter mercantile ranks and divide even the merchant

[67] *Ibid.*, Sept. 22, 1890. [68] *Ibid.*, Nov. 6, 1892. [69] *Ibid.*, April 8, 1906.

class, because of differences in language or religion, or both. While it is true that the merchants multiplied, we do not find that there arose from their ranks leaders of business enterprise such as flourished—in small numbers it is true—in the earlier years of the life of the town. We find that as the town grew in size, and as new large-scale investment poured in, the local business men were overshadowed by the weight of the big corporations and by the sheer numbers of the workers. They had always lived very modestly and as they became a smaller group relatively, their social life and their every day activities were less obvious than had formerly been the case. In reference to the most important enterprises, it is also noticeable that except in the case of the Taylor and Carter families there were no sons who carried on the industrial and mercantile activities of their fathers. The result of these conditions was the recession of the social and economic position of the most vigorous section of the middle class, increasingly apparent at the end of the nineteenth century. For reasons already stated, the merchant class, as a whole, could not expect to assume a dominant position.

With the growth of the town, social and political life became more complex, and tended to assume many of the unpleasant characteristics of a poor city community. Overcrowding in the cotton tenements was most serious in the Polish districts.[70] There were frequent complaints of rowdyism in the streets, there were many arrests for drunkenness, occasional raids resulted in the closing of brothels and gambling houses.[71] The adoption of city government in 1891 brought with it the inauguration of ward politics, the rise of political machines which utilized the votes of conflicting nationalities to achieve power. Preoccupation with municipal politics was intense at this time, with occasional accusations and counter-accusation of graft and "deals."[72] By 1903-04 there was a Good Government League, and a women's club was discussing civic affairs.[73]

There is little record in the press of concerts and lectures dur-

[70] *Ibid.*, April 27, 1897.

[71] *Ibid.*, 1903-1910, passim.

[72] *Ibid.*, 1898-1908, passim.

[73] *Ibid.*, Jan. 16, Nov. 24, 1903.

ing these years. But sport and dancing were popular, there were numerous athletic clubs, and the fraternal lodges were very active.[74] The town continued to rely upon Springfield newspapers, but the space devoted to Chicopee in the press was more and more given over to the recording of police court news.[75] More attention than hitherto was paid to the social life of the workers by that very paper which in the early years had completely disregarded labor activities. This was symptomatic of the changing character of the community.

[74] *Ibid.,* 1890-1910, passim.

[75] *Ibid.*

CHAPTER X

INDUSTRIAL RELATIONS, 1890-1916

Chicopee's labor history of the period 1860-1890 was characterized as the story of labor in a rapidly changing economic situation. The outstanding experiences of labor in the twenty-five years following 1890 also lend themselves to generalization in that they constituted an education in industrial relations for the workers of those years. It was only natural that the large and differentiated labor force which the factories had brought to Chicopee should, to some extent at least, have been drawn into the labor movement of the times. The process of labor organization presented new problems. When strikes occurred in the earlier years the issues at stake were clear-cut and well-defined—wages had to go up, or wages must not come down. On the whole, workers' demands were not associated with union organization. In the nineties and after, conflicts were complicated in many cases by the desire of the workers, on the one side, to achieve organization and then recognition of their union, and on the other side by the refusal of the employers to recognize the existence of workers' organizations. This impasse, even when there was no fundamental dispute concerning wages or working conditions, was to induce industrial conflicts and all of the various experiences attendant upon them. With union organization came a greater degree of solidarity among the workers, including some co-operation among different occupations.

Except in cases in which unionization was openly fought by employers there is no evidence available showing step by step the progress of the organization of the workers. There had been some organization in the eighties and early nineties, but the greatest strides were made from 1897 to 1904.[1] In the latter year a number of cotton operatives were affiliated with the United Textile Workers of America, being organized according to crafts. Locals existed or were formed among weavers, slasher-tenders, nappers

[1] These years, of course, witnessed a great increase in the membership of the American Federation of Labor. Perlman, *op. cit.,* 163.

and drawing-in hands. The mule spinners were also organized on a national basis.[2] It was reported that the Polish workers had joined the union in very large numbers in 1903, and that there were 2,000 textile workers in the organization.[3] The textile workers union bought a bakery in order to supply its members with bread at cost price, and employed union labor. This resulted in the unionization of workers employed in other bakeries.[4] Other crafts which had achieved some measure of organization by the early part of the twentieth century were the bartenders, barbers, allied metal mechanics, metal polishers, painters and decorators, carpenters and joiners, iron and brass molders, and wire weavers.[5]

In the early nineties occasional disputes had occurred in various plants, but never developed into extensive strikes, and they represented the dissatisfaction of small groups of workers, rather than the organized protest of a whole working force.[6] Then came the depression, with wage cuts and extensive unemployment. In these circumstances effective organization was difficult. And yet, at least in the case of the textile workers, it seems that they were ready for some kind of action. In 1893 the Dwight Manufacturing Company had given notice that it would be necessary to institute either a 10 per cent wage cut or a complete shutdown.[7] The workers' reactions indicated that they were more experienced in such matters than had been their predecessors. Some said that they preferred to accept a complete lay-off rather than a wage cut, since once rates were reduced it would be extremely difficult to have them restored to their previous levels. On the other hand some felt that even after a partial or complete shutdown, capacity production would be resumed at reduced rates.[8] As a matter of fact in all previous deflationary periods it had been customary to cut the rates after a period of short time operation. The company decided to cut wages, and within a few days a strike started when some 200 weavers walked out.[9] In spite of the fact that the press had said that the Polish workers did not seem to understand the seriousness

[2] *Springfield Republican,* Dec. 18, 1896; May 3, 1903.
[3] *Ibid.,* Jan. 5, 1903.
[4] *Ibid.,* Jan. 5, Feb. 19, 1903.
[5] *Ibid.,* May 3, 1903.
[6] *Ibid.,* 1890-1892, passim.
[7] *Ibid.,* Aug. 15, 1893.
[8] *Ibid.,* Aug. 23, 1893.
[9] *Ibid.,* Aug. 24, Sept. 5, 1893.

of the situation, large numbers were quick to participate in the strike, and by the evening of the first day the Poles constituted a majority of the strikers.[10] The next day the company closed three mills entirely, throwing more people out of work, and announced that those who were willing to accept the new wage scale would be re-engaged. But strike leaders would not be re-employed and boarding-house keepers were ordered to evict them. However the action had been so spontaneous that it was almost impossible to locate the leaders.[11] The lockout lasted for 10 days, during all of which time the agent was absent from the town, as an indication that there was no intention of negotiating a settlement. The strike failed completely.[12] It is obvious that the company's tactics were more drastic and more determined beginning with the first announcement of the wage cut than had been its practice before. In the case of the Chicopee Manufacturing Company which was not affected by the strike, the workers' prediction that partial operation would be followed by wage reductions was correct.[13]

As the depression lifted organization of the textile workers proceeded and union activity was noticeable among other workers. In 1895 a number of polishers employed in the Overman plant went on strike to attempt to force the discharge of a non-union hand, a typical trade union demand, but no attempt was made to organize any but the highly skilled workers. Conflicts cropped up from time to time from 1895 to 1898, negotiations were conducted by a national officer, and finally a boycott was imposed on Overman products.[14] From the scattered reports available the fight centered about the maintenance of a closed shop in the skilled trades in the plant. This seems to have been the first important occurrence of a strictly "union" conflict.

Other union activity at the outset of the twentieth century was directed mainly toward the achievement of a shorter working day. Grocery clerks were supported in such a demand by the bartenders' union which decided to fine any member if he or his family pat-

[10] *Ibid.*, Aug. 23, Sept. 5, 1893.
[11] *Ibid.*, Sept. 6, 1893.
[12] *Ibid.*, Sept. 9, 10, 18, 1893.
[13] *Ibid.*, Oct. 11, 1893.
[14] *Ibid.*, Dec. 24, 25, 1895; Jan. 16, 1896; Oct. 14, 1897; April 30, 1898.

ronized what was considered an "unfair" store.[15] In 1901 organized carpenters and plumbers secured the eight hour day without corresponding reductions in wages. It was not always necessary to strike in order to secure these gains.[16] The Stevens Arms Company, the Buckley Bronze Foundry, (formerly the Ames bronze department) and the Spalding Company all granted the nine hour day without pay cuts in 1903.[17] All of these gains of 1901-1903 seem to have been won by strength of organized labor.

Vigorous organization of the textile workers occurred from 1901 to 1903, and wage negotiations came to be handled by national officers of the union.[18] There is no evidence pointing to active opposition toward unionization on the part of the textile companies at this point. When a few Portuguese workers were imported from New Bedford some thought that this was to be the spearhead of an attack on the union. However only a few Portuguese came, and they did not receive a very cordial reception from the Poles who feared an undermining attack on their wages.[19] In 1904 it was reported that the union was not as strong as it had been. Many Poles were going back to Europe because of the irregular work, and some were supplementing textile earnings by doing farm labor during the summer months.[20] It is also possible that during the first enthusiasm which attended the organization campaign many members were swept into the union who could not be depended upon to remain members in good standing.

On the whole the organized labor movement was quite vigorous from 1900 on. Much space in the Springfield press was devoted to labor news, and the *Republican* commented that strikes were gaining public sympathy as a rule.[21] This was not so much a change in attitude for the *Republican,* perhaps, as a changing conception of what constituted the "public." At the beginning of 1904 some ten local unions organized the Chicopee Trades' Council. Two previous attempts to do so had ended in failure.[22]

[15] Mass., Bureau of Labor Statistics, 32nd *Annual Report,* 47 (1901).
[16] *Ibid.,* 140; *Springfield Republican,* June 3, 4, 7, 1901.
[17] Mass., Bureau of Labor Statistics, 34th *Annual Report,* 354 (1903).
[18] *Springfield Republican,* Feb. 21, Dec. 20, 1902; Jan. 31, Feb. 11, 1903.
[19] *Ibid.,* Sept. 28-30, Oct. 2, 1903.
[20] *Ibid.,* May 12, July 24, 1904.
[21] *Ibid.,* Aug. 18, 1904.
[22] *Ibid.,* May 3, 1903; Feb. 16, 1905.

Industrial disputes started to increase in 1904 and it became apparent that employers were beginning to resist unionization more actively than hitherto.[23] For the first time, there occurred a strike in regard to working conditions. A small group of nappers in the Chicopee Manufacturing Company struck against what they considered was excessive heat in the napping rooms. The manager said that the room had to be hot, to which the workers replied that not only was the room hotter than was necessary, but that the ventilation was bad.[24] A settlement of some kind was effected, but when the men went back to work they found that their machine load had been increased, upon which they walked out again. Not long after the men were ordered to return to work or to vacate company tenements, the strike was broken, and all returned to work at the company's terms, and the thermometers were removed from the napping rooms—a complete defeat. All the men went back to work. The boss napper had not joined the walkout, but he had refused to train new men taken on during the strike.[25] As a result, he lost his job.

A group of spool girls were more successful than the nappers. The spoolers received a rate cut without notice when a new machine was introduced which, it was alleged, made the work easier and faster. There followed the usual claims on the part of the girls that earnings under the new conditions would be lower, and on the part of the company that they would be higher. The girls held out firmly for several days until the mill began to be tied up. A union organizer suggested the appointment of an arbitration committee, but the girls refused to hear of it, insisting that the dispute be settled by direct negotiation. This might perhaps be considered a logical union demand at that stage of the strike, and it is interesting that it should have come from the inexperienced Polish operatives rather than from the union organizer. Conferences were conducted with the assistance of a Polish intrepreter. The girls demanded the old rates with the aid of the new machine for difficult yarns.

[23] As a rule such resistance was directed more against demands for union recognition rather than against other demands which usually accompanied organization.

[24] *Ibid.*, Sept. 14-16, 1905.

[25] *Ibid.*, March 3 et seq., 1905.

The company now offered to submit the quarrel to an arbitral committee, then offered the higher rate with the old machine pending settlement by arbitration, then offered to let the girls pick their own committee from the citizens of the town. The strikers refused to accept any of these terms, and within a few days were called back to work on their own terms.[26] The spoolers emerged from the strike with a permanent organization as did the spinners, even though the latter had not been concerned in the dispute.[27] Not long after a group of Polish weavers were striking to prevent the lowering of rates with mechanical innovations and were successful in gaining concessions in spite of the company's move to start evictions. Again unionization was encouraged by the successful conclusion of the strike.[28] Other groups of textile workers were involved in wage disputes in 1906, and considerable gains were made in rates or working conditions.[29]

A prolonged controversy occurred in the Stevens Arms shops at this time in which the company refused to recognize or to deal with the union. This conflict was marked by the company's employment of tactics with which the Chicopee workers were as yet entirely unfamiliar, although they were common enough in industrial disputes elsewhere. A disagreement concerning piece rates had resulted in a walkout by the metal polishers who immediately organized strike headquarters, and set up a picket line. The company began to employ some girls to perform light polishing and imported strikebreakers from Boston and other cities. In order to destroy the effectiveness of the picket line the company arranged to house and feed the strikebreakers on their own premises.[30]

For some days the point at issue seemed to be the question of wage rates, but the company officials made public a statement which presented the real controversy. "It would be idle," they said, "to discuss the strike on other grounds than simply an attempt to unionize our polishing department . . . as long as this shop is run under the present management, it will be run as an open shop." The statement went on to say that the hiring of new workers to replace

[26] *Ibid.,* June 2 et seq., 1905.
[27] *Ibid.,* Sept. 11, 1905.
[28] *Ibid.,* Jan. 27 et seq., 1906.
[29] *Ibid.,* Feb. 13 et seq., 1906.
[30] *Ibid.,* March 6 et seq., 1906.

the strikers had been a permanent arrangement, and that in consequence, it would be impossible to reinstate many of the strikers.[31] The union replied that it was not asking for more than a preferential shop, and charged that the company refused to negotiate the dispute.[32]

After this exchange the strike settled down and seemed to win the sympathy of the townspeople. The Trades' Council rendered some financial assistance.[33] Some of the polishers took jobs elsewhere, in order to conserve the union's funds, it was said. Others remained on picket duty.[34] Negotiations undertaken by the officers of the national union were hampered by the refusal of the company to delegate a representative with authority to act, and by the process of referring union spokesmen from one man to another. The union finally decided to recommend that the firm be placed on the unfair list of the American Federation of Labor.[35]

The picket line, in the meantime, was active, and was often successful in persuading newcomers to leave their jobs.[36] The company's answer was to secure a temporary injunction against the union, which was to remain in effect for about five weeks until a hearing was held. The defendents were restrained from "posting or maintaining pickets or patrols on sidewalks or streets in front of or in vicinity of plaintiff's premises for the purpose of inducing or compelling any persons who are now or may hereafter be in or desirous of entering the plaintiff's employ, to leave such employ, or to refrain from entering such employ; from any threatening, intimidating or annoying, or otherwise disturbing or interfering with such persons; from following any products of the plaintiff's business for the purpose of learning what persons have bought the same, for the purpose of inducing such persons not to buy these goods, or from posting or displaying in any manner placards applying to any persons in the employ of the plaintiff the name of 'scab' or other term or epithet calculated to induce any person to leave the company's employ."[37] The injuction caught the strikers

[31] *Ibid.*, March 27, 1906.
[32] *Ibid.*, March 28, 1906.
[33] *Ibid.*, April 1, 2, 1906.
[34] *Ibid.*, April 12, 1906.
[35] *Ibid.*, April 16, 1906.
[36] *Ibid.*, April 18, 1906.
[37] *Ibid.*, April 29, 1906.

by surprise, and they decided to remove the picket line, as they did not wish to incur contempt proceedings. The press and the townsfolk were likewise surprised that the injunction was secured, for it was asserted that the picketing had been entirely peaceful.[38]

The injunction hearings and charges were of the usual order. The company claimed that the picketers threatened and intimidated the workers, using such expressions as "get your blocks knocked off" and "it will not be safe for you to cross the bridge." The company also charged that placards had been posted which advertised their products as being manufactured by scabs, and that customers were followed and asked not to purchase these products. Strikers made "threatening faces," it was said, and followed strikebreakers home. One of the latter testified that a picketer had displayed a "semi-belligerent method" which frightened him. Pickets were said to look like "muzzled bulldogs," and one had a "look on his face like Iago in Othello when Iago was handcuffed." The expression on another picket's face was "dogmatic."[39]

The union, of course, denied any conspiracy to harm the company, admitted persuasion, and admitted that posters were used to inform newcomers of the existence of a strike. A strikebreaker had once been followed to Holyoke, it was said, but that anyone was ever intimidated was denied.[40] The hearings dragged on for two months, with the injunction still in force. By that time most of the strikers were absorbed elsewhere, and the whole dispute seems to have petered out. The episode added further to the education of organized labor in Chicopee.

In the meantime, the affairs of the textile workers were not running smoothly. 1906 was a turbulent year, and strikes seemed to be almost fashionable. Mill hands were restless and impatient for wage increases. Sporadic strikes occurred, and the dissatisfaction of the Polish worker was not allayed by the importation of a small group of Greeks to act as strikebreakers.[41] At the end of the year an unauthorized strike was called off pending investigation by national officers of the union.[42] The officers came to an

[38] *Ibid.,* May 1, 11, 1906.
[39] *Ibid.,* June 2, 9, 1906.
[40] *Ibid.,* June 2, 9, 14, 1906.
[41] *Ibid.,* May 2, 7, 1906.
[42] *Ibid.,* Nov. 26, 1906.

agreement with the two cotton companies which increased wages so as to bring the wage scales into agreement with those prevalent in other cotton centers, but these increases did not meet the original demands of the workers.[43] A large number of weavers refused to accept the settlement and struck for greater increases in spite of the advice of the Central Trades' Council and the national executive of the textile union, to whom the Chicopee Manufacturing Company appealed. The strikers were told that no support would be forthcoming from the national union.[44] This action divided the ranks of the union; the spinners, carders and weavers remained in rebellion, while the loom fixers, nappers, spoolers and slasher tenders supported the official union settlement. The strikers criticized the union leaders and threatened to form an independent organization if they were suspended.[45] After some days the strikers went back to work under the union agreement.[46] The president of the national union ascribed this "rank and file" action to inexperience with union discipline.[47] Textile strikes flared again from 1907 to 1909. The Poles, industrial newcomers, and hampered by language difficulties, usually acted as the leaders.[48]

As the years passed opposition to unionization stiffened; the larger the corporation concerned, the more stubborn the resistance. It was more difficult to obtain union recognition from the very large manufacturing enterprises such as the Fisk Rubber Company and the Westinghouse Electric Company[49] than from the cotton mills.

Organization of the employees in the Fisk Company seems to have started in the early part of 1906. At that time a wage cut had been followed by a small strike and the appointment of a committee to bargain with the company officials. The men claimed that the immediate cause of the strike was the dismissal of their spokesman. While they did not achieve the restoration of the desired wage rates, some of the heavy work which prevented good earnings was elim-

[43] *Ibid.*, Dec. 24, 30, 1906.
[44] *Ibid.*, Jan. 9, 1907.
[45] *Ibid.*, Jan. 11, 12, 1907.
[46] *Ibid.*, Jan. 19, 22, 1907.
[47] *Ibid.*, April 11, 1907.
[48] *Ibid.*, 1907-1909, passim.
[49] The Westinghouse Electric Company took over the plant of the Stevens Arms Company at the beginning of the War.

inated, and the discharged worker was reinstated.[50] Little more was heard from Fisk workers until 1914 when it was known that some were affiliated with the International Rubber Workers of America, a constituent member of the American Federation of Labor.[51] While organization was being consolidated a strike occurred which arose out of the demands for certain improvements in working conditions and for recognition of the union. The former demands were granted, but union recognition denied, and the men accepted a settlement on this basis. The settlement included the statement that "the employees fully recognize the employer's right to hire and discharge, and when necessary, to inflict a penalty—such as laying off for a stated time. But the case of a penalized or discharged employee may be made the subject of negotiation like any other real or fancied grievance. There shall be no strike or lockout. In case of a controversy that fails of mutual settlement the matter shall be submitted to the state board of conciliation and arbitration."[52]

The dispute cropped up again two years later when the machinists employed by the Fisk Company struck for an eight hour day, the reinstatement of a discharged union man, and higher rates for overtime work which must have been frequent in 1916. At the same time moves were made to organize the tire workers.[53] On the day after the walkout, the company announced an elaborate welfare scheme. They proposed to create an industrial relations department, and to employ doctors, nurses, visiting nurses and safety inspectors. Free legal advice was to be made available for the workers. A sick benefit of $1.00 per day would be paid to men and women workers, without levying contributions. Free life insurance up to $1000 was to be given.[54] The striking machinists who felt that this announcement was timed to forestall general unionization said that welfare plans were nice enough, but had nothing to do with the organization of the workers.[55] This walkout did not last very long, but in a few weeks the tire makers demanded an eight hour day and wage increases, and found that their

[50] *Ibid.*, Feb. 1-3, 1906.
[51] *Ibid.*, May 2, 1914.
[52] *Ibid.*, May 1, 1914.
[53] *Ibid.*, May 15, 1916.
[54] *Ibid.*, March 16, 1916.
[55] *Ibid.*, March 17, 22, 1916.

committee was not received. Plans were laid for the organization of women and unskilled men in the tire departments. About 1,700 persons stopped work on the first day of the strike, and they were soon joined by the workers in the shipping departments.[56] The company offered a number of concessions and reinstatement of those machinists who had been striking six weeks before and were still unemployed.[57] But the deadlock continued as the men decided to insist on recognition of the union, in spite of the urgings of the president of the Central Trades' Council who was "disturbed" because of the men's refusal to accept the offered concessions.[58] The company now offered further concessions in the matter of working conditions and higher wages for overtime work, and suggested that the proposed shop committees would be tantamount to union recognition. The strike was finally settled on this basis.[59]

In the same way skilled workers employed by the Westinghouse Electric Company were unable to secure recognition of their union. The company refused to deal with officers of the tool makers' organization which claimed that it wanted, not a closed shop, but equal standing with non-union men. Direct demands made at this time were for recognition, reinstatement of a worker discharged for "neglect of duty," and a minimum wage scale.[60] The intervention of the state board of conciliation and arbitration resulted in the settlement of the strike. It was recommended that the men go back to work and that the company reinstate all without discrimination.[61]

With this fairly intensive experience in industrial relations sustained over a number of years, there came some interest in political affairs. This was not so much the general interest in "politics" of the day, but in politics as they affected the interests of the working man.

Chicopee workers had been accustomed to cast their votes for

[56] *Ibid.*, May 11, 12, 1916.

[57] *Ibid.*, May 14, 1916.

[58] *Ibid.*, May 17, 1916.

[59] *Ibid.*, May 20-22, 1916.

[60] *Ibid.*, Dec. 22, 1915.

[61] *Ibid.*, Jan. 1, 1916. It is interesting to note that four months before the strike the company had secured permission, not without pressure, it was said in the press, for the maintainance of armed guards who were not residents of Chicopee. *Springfield Republican*, Sept. 2, 14, 16, 1915.

the traditional political parties. A meagre handful of votes had been cast for the Socialist Party in state elections since 1891.[62] In 1898-99 a permanent Socialist group was organized under the leadership of John J. Kelly, a worker who was said to have received his inspiration from Edward Bellamy, author of "Looking Backward," for some years a resident of Chicopee.[63] Several meetings sponsored by the new group were very well attended, but they received only 28 votes in the municipal election of 1899.[64] But by 1902 Kelly secured election to the city council as alderman.[65] From 1903 to 1905 the Socialists held two seats on the city council in spite of the avoidance in the latter year of a three-cornered fight in one ward by the Republicans and Democrats.[66] In 1906, at the height of the strike movement, Kelly almost secured election to the mayoralty. But the Democrats, it was said, had sponsored a weak candidate so as not to split the anti-Socialist vote. It must also be noted that in this election, as in the preceding ones, Kelly ran far ahead of the rest of the Socialist ticket, and probably was receiving a good many votes as an individual, and not as a Socialist.[67] The Socialists received a great deal of publicity in the pages of the *Springfield Republican.* Possibly this was due to the correspondent's misunderstanding of what Socialism was, for after a while the paper began to complain that Kelly was willing to work for the interests of the workingman rather than for the interests of the "city," and this was explained as a bid for popularity. The paper also began to object to the fact that a Socialist candidate was obliged to obey the orders of his party.[68] In the 1907 election the major parties combined to defeat the two Socialist aldermen, and Kelly made a poor showing in the mayoralty race. "The election marks the downfall for the present of the Socialist party and the rise of the French, backed by the old republican machine, to power."[69] By 1909 the Socialists were no longer participating in municipal elections.[70] In that year the labor unions,

[62] *Ibid.,* Dec. 14, 1902.
[63] *Ibid.,* Dec. 14, 1892; Dec. 1, 1898; March 27, 1899.
[64] *Ibid.,* Oct. 6, Nov. 7, Dec. 13, 1899.
[65] *Ibid.,* Dec. 10, 1902.
[66] *Ibid.,* Nov. 21, 1905.
[67] *Ibid.,* Nov. 31, 1906.
[68] *Ibid.,* Nov. 24, 1907.
[69] *Ibid.,* Dec. 11, 1907.
[70] *Ibid.,* Nov. 12, 1909.

through the Central Trades' Council, followed the policy of the American Federation of Labor of "rewarding friends" and "punishing enemies."[71] In no other way did the unions concern themselves with political affairs.

It has been shown that considerable progress was made in shortening the working day. This, together with a greater preoccupation with labor problems, permitted a fuller social life for large numbers of people than had previously been the case. The development of fraternal societies and lodges absorbed a good many workers as well as members of the middle class. Skilled workers made up a very substantial portion of society officers in 1905.[72] Related to organizations of this type, in certain respects, were the national societies of the French-Canadians and the Poles, organizations which were of importance in the social life of these national groups. The unions, especially active from 1902 to 1909, contributed to the social life of their members. The Overman Wheel Company had pioneered in organizing workers' clubs and "social evenings," and no doubt the same was done in other factories, although perhaps on a smaller scale. Most of the companies had workers' baseball clubs. Sport was quite an important item in the recreational life of the workers. It could not have become important, however, until they had the time and energy to devote to it. This they had in some measure, from the eighties and nineties onward.[73]

On the whole it may be said that for labor the period was one of amelioration in spite of the depression set-backs. Some positive gains seem to have been achieved. We must not forget, however, that there were still large numbers of textile workers living in crowded quarters, and that whole families were working in the cotton mills because the wages of one were not always sufficient to meet family needs. But at least life for the worker in this period seems to have been fuller than it had been for a long time. If he wished to participate in the organized labor movement he was able

[71] *Ibid.*, Feb. 27, Nov. 22, 1909; Nov. 21, 1910.
[72] Springfield *Directory*, 1905.
[73] *Springfield Republican*, 1890-1910, passim.

to do so. If he did, he was likely to find himself involved in industrial disputes. Such conflicts, although basically concerned with working conditions, were also inextricably bound up with demands for union recognition. While the union organizations were often able to secure concessions relating to work and wages, their most fundamental objective, recognition and the closed shop, usually failed of attainment.

CHAPTER XI

A FACTORY CITY

At the close of the nineteenth century a change in the direction of Chicopee's economic development as a community was apparent, which became more clearly defined as the years passed. Population increased, and except for the depression periods capital investment increased and industrial expansion was marked. But the "normal" or balanced community of the middle period was becoming purely a factory city, marked by the recession of the middle class and of middle class enterprise. The decline of the middle class has of necessity adversely affected many of the features of social and economic life which can thrive only where there exist income groups capable of supporting them.

When we examine the fortunes of the various companies in this century we find that most of them were expanding operations, at least until 1929. The greatest strides were made by the largest corporations. With the war-time demands and the growth of the automobile industry the production of the Fisk Rubber Company soared, and the company became the largest employer of labor in the city.[1] At the same time the production of the cotton companies was pushed to capacity. The Westinghouse Electric Company which took over the Stevens Arms plant soon became an important employer.[2] This purchase continued the process of the alienation of local companies started when Spalding secured control of the Lamb Manufacturing Company. The Westinghouse Company bought the capital stock and property of the J. Stevens Arms and Tool Company and the plant of the Stevens-Duryea Automobile Company in 1915, no doubt to meet the immediate pressure of war production. The New England Westinghouse Company was incorporated to operate the acquisitions.[3] After the deflationary

[1] *Springfield Republican,* March 12, 1917.
[2] *Ibid.*
[3] Moody's *Manual of Industrial Investments,* 1917.

period of 1920-21 general production expanded again, reaching a high point in 1926.[4]

All the companies in Chicopee did not participate in the industrial expansion of the twenties. Some did not survive, and others were affected by the alienation of ownership and control to which we have referred. The Stevens-Duryea Company had been a successful producer of automobiles for nearly twenty years. The company manufactured an expensive car and was preparing to expand production before the crash of 1920. It was forced into liquidation in 1922.[5] It has not been possible to ascertain just

TABLE 18. STATISTICS OF MANUFACTURES IN THE CITY OF CHICOPEE, 1875-1934*

Year	Population	Number of Establishments	Average Number of Workers Employed	Total Wages Paid $000	Capital Invested $000	Value of Materials $000	Value of Product $000
1875....	10,335	146	3,521	1,570	2,051	2,340	4,035
1885....	11,516	111	3,547	1,061	6,040	2,128	3,586
1895....	16,420	84	4,926	2,167	7,175	2,938	6,667
1899....	19,167	46	4,085	1,558	5,967	2,700	5,389
1904....	20,191	40	4,670	1,935	6,829	4,330	7,716
1909....	......	58	7,260	3,696	14,803	10,952	19,219
1910....	25,401	39	7,266	3,782	19,256	13,674	20,477
1911....	......	42	7,266	3,817	18,317	12,462	19,979
1912....	......	39	7,662	4,300	19,507	13,961	24,076
1913....	......	40	9,043	5,390	23,069	17,336	31,126
1914....	......	62	8,426	5,130	23,500	17,117	28,869
1915....	30,138	49	8,924	6,110	28,472	17,967	30,384
1916....	......	49	12,656	9,293	39,624	24,902	42,451
1917....	......	52	16,426	14,639	40,536	37,124	66,695
1918....	......	47	11,796	12,557	58,493	37,300	76,276
1919....	......	60	10,068	12,592	69,411	46,458	89,772
1920....	36,214	54	10,978	14,992	77,341	43,046	82,118
1921....	......	56	8,332	9,731	....	23,042	48,525
1922....	......	54	10,351	12,199	59,735	32,380	64,914
1923....	......	57	10,118	13,884	......	38,897	68,551
1924....	......	56	9,217	11,454	44,827	37,431	69,661
1925....	......	49	10,536	13,660	......	47,470	87,057
1926....	......	48	10,419	13,486	56,189	55,650	91,320
1927....	......	50	9,558	12,298	......	42,955	72,859
1928....	......	50	10,483	13,584	54,198	44,614	78,201
1929....	......	56	10,766	14,211	......	40,350	75,964
1930....	43,930	53	8,179	10,502	61,401	28,865	59,500
1931....	......	54	6,530	8,017	......	17,578	43,545
1932....	......	45	5,029	5,229	43,405	10,922	24,981
1933....	......	45	4,768	4,270	......	11,755	23,950
1934....	......	47	6,440	6,719	31,129	16,453	31,587

* Compiled from Mass., *Census of Manufactures* and U. S. Thirteenth *Census* Abstract, Mass. Supplement, 678.

[4] See Table 18.

[5] *Springfield Republican,* April 16, 1920; *New York Times,* May 10, 1922.

what was responsible for the failure of the company. It may have been due to problems peculiar to itself, or the company may have shared the fate of the New England automobile industry which could not meet the competition of the concentration of the industry in the middle West.[6] The Belcher and Taylor Agricultural Tool Company which was reported to be employing about 300 men in 1923 was sold to an outside producer, and the Chicopee plant was closed some time after the sale.[7] The Stevens Arms Company which had been in the hands of the Westinghouse Electric Company during the war was sold to the Savage Arms Company in 1920, and has since been operated as a subsidiary of that firm.[8] The Ames Sword Company, a very small concern during these years, has been purchased by the owners of the Lilley Company, of Columbus, Ohio, manufacturers of regalia. Only a handful of workers have been employed in recent years. The Page Needle Company, operated by local capital for many years was sold to another firm, operated as a branch plant for a while, and then discontinued production.[9] The Chicopee Manufacturing Company, while owned by outside interests from the beginning, had always been an independent company. In 1916 it was purchased by the Johnson and Johnson Company of New Jersey, manufacturers of surgical supplies.[10]

In 1894 the Dwight Manufacturing Company had expanded its productive capacity by establishing a mill in Alabama.[11] It was one of the first of the New England cotton mills to make such an investment. In 1924 the Johnson and Johnson Company built a mill in Georgia. Ironically enough, from the point of view of the Chicopee employees who might have hoped that expansion of the

[6] The localization of the American automobile industry and the failure of New England to keep its early important position present interesting problems which have not yet been thoroughly analyzed. While New England had the inventors, skilled labor, the technique of interchangeable parts, the middle West did not lack these requisites and had the advantage of being near the sources of raw materials. See Selzer, *op. cit.*, 26 and Pound, *op. cit.*, 100, 101.

[7] *Springfield Republican*, Jan. 7, 1923; Interview, Mr. F. D. Howard.

[8] Moody's *Manual of Industrial Investments*, 1923.

[9] Interview, Mr. F. D. Howard.

[10] Moody's *Manual of Industrial Investments*, 1917.

[11] Clark, *op. cit.*, III, 174.

company would benefit them, the new mill town which was built in Georgia was called Chicopee.[12] In 1927 the Dwight Company closed its Chicopee mill entirely and concentrated all of its production in the southern plant. It has not been possible to secure an explanation of this move to the South. As in the case of the automobile industry, it is part of a wider problem. For Chicopee the loss of the Dwight Company was disastrous. The mill had employed about 2,000 workers, and in many cases whole families had been entirely dependent on cotton earnings. A large proportion of the workers affected by this shutdown lived in a compact area, and the traders who served it also suffered. The city lost one of its largest taxpayers. But at least this shutdown occurred in 1927 when it was more or less possible to secure employment in other manufacturing establishments or in Holyoke and Springfield. When the depression came the weight of the unemployed textile workers constituted a serious problem and contributed to the general economic demoralization of the community.

The depression would have been serious for Chicopee under any circumstances. Production fell off rapidly and severely after 1929. The Fisk Rubber Company was involved in financial difficulties and was obliged to suspend operations for a time. The company has recently been reorganized and production has been resumed.[13] The Lamb Company and the National Scale Company, among others, were unable to survive. Other companies were crippled. Table 18 indicates the drastic collapse of production and the degree of unemployment which the city experienced. But Chicopee entered the depression under the handicap of a recent major shutdown, and the number of workers on relief seems to have increased more rapidly as the depression deepened than in other comunities which had not suffered similar catastrophes. By 1933 twenty-five per cent of the total population in Chicopee was receiving relief.[14]

The interesting question arises as to whether the community suffered more in the depression because of the heavy preponderance

[12] Interviews, Mr. N. P. Ames Carter, Mr. P. O'Toole.
[13] *New York Times,* Feb. 12, April 5, May 11, 1933.
[14] K. D. Lumpkin, *Shutdowns in the Connecticut Valley,* 168, 169.

of absentee-owned industry than would have been the case if there had been an important resident-employer class. This is a moot point. A citizens' unemployment committee has suggested that home industries might have been of greater assistance to the Chicopee workers.[15] This suggestion rests on the assumption that locally owned industry will operate at a loss in order to maintain employment for a longer period than will a corporation owned by distant stockholders. It is hard to believe that such assistance could be maintained long enough to alleviate the unemployment situation to any appreciable degree. It might be argued that the Dwight Manufacturing Company would not have moved to the South had it been owned by Chicopee residents. But even absentee owners do not quickly scrap a valuable piece of property unless there is excellent reason, as they see it, for so doing. Resident owners of large-scale industry must act in much the same way as any other owners if they are to continue profitable operation of their properties. On several occasions, for instance, we have seen that local companies were sold to outside interests with no guarantee that they would continue production in Chicopee.

Chicopee is now primarily a working class community. As it completes the cycle from company town to balanced community to factory town, the rôle of the middle class and the forces affecting it emerge very clearly. The recent position of Chicopee's middle class is worthy of further analysis at this point.

It is so easy to think of a town or minor city as the miniature counterpart of a metropolis, reproducing, on a smaller scale, all the characteristics of the latter. There are many communities which bear this resemblance to larger centers. If so, it is the result of an orderly economic evolution accompanied by some degree of industrialization together with the development of trade and services and the professions introduced and controlled by the middle class. When this has happened we are likely to find that as the metropolis has its captains of industry and important bankers and wealthy rentiers, the small town has its small independent manufacturers and local bankers and a circle of minor property

[15] Mass. Joint Committee on Unemployment, Connecticut Valley Branch, *Report on Chicopee*. Mss. 1932.

holders. The ramifications of big business are often found to be duplicated by relatively petty capitalist enterprise controlled by a small group of men who together with their wives and families constitute the "best elements" of the community and the leaders of "polite society." Under them are grouped the larger numbers who make up the lower middle class.[16] These people are numerous enough to furnish a demand for luxury goods and services of various kinds sufficient to perpetuate the conditions favorable to the expansion or maintenance of middle class positions. In their comfortable residential and thriving business districts, in their social activities, they fix the character of the community, maintain its middle class façade. The factories and working class homes, if they happen to exist in large numbers, are likely to be on the "other side of the tracks."

But if we are dealing with a factory town, especially one in which a major part of the industry is controlled by absentee owners, the situation is different. Such a town has smoke stacks and factories which are far from decorative. It has numerous shabby streets and tenements which are quick to catch the eye. Its stores and theatres and houses are poor, its streets not too well paved. It offers few "attractions" to the middle class observer. Chicopee is such a community. The local middle class has been unable to keep pace in economic activity and numbers with the expansion of non-locally owned industry and with the working population. The heavy proportion of manual workers does not provide a condition favorable to the growth of mercantile investment, as does the existence of a balanced community. It is in relation to this situation which is intimately connected with the problem of the middle class that we must again emphasize the proximity of Springfield and Holyoke.

It must be remembered that the territory under the municipal jurisdiction of Chicopee is not an economic unit but is made up of several more or less self-contained sections. Some farms are still worked in the Chicopee Street area. The main line railroad passes

[16] It will be recognized that Chicopee most nearly approximated this "normal" in the years immediately following the Civil War.

through this region and several factories, lumber and coal yards have made their appearance along the tracks. In the eighties and nineties the section known as Willimansett experienced considerable development. This village lies across the river from Holyoke, and no doubt has drawn a number of residents from that city, attracted by lower rentals and land values. Chicopee Falls and Chicopee Center constitute separate units. Other residential districts are spread out over a wide area between these principal producing centers.

This decentralization of population and business interests, we have already indicated, is of importance. The scatter of the retail stores and houses gives the town the appearance of having a much smaller population than it actually has. It has prevented the concentration of retail trading localities into a substantial business district. The scatter of customers, so many of whom are as near Holyoke and Springfield shopping centers as they are to Chicopee stores prevents the local merchants from keeping varied stocks of goods. Springfield, furthermore, a large and easily accessible city, is a good shopping center, and attracts customers who live and work in the heart of Chicopee. If all the villages and scattered streets which make up Chicopee constituted a compact area more and larger stores would find it possible to exist because of the concentration of consumers.

We must also take into consideration the attraction that a larger city has for its smaller neighbor, especially when that neighbor is poor. Fine theatres, amusement facilities of all kinds, draw trade, and correspondingly limit opportunities for such investment in Chicopee itself. The availability of these facilities in Springfield, combined with the existence of fine residential districts and large stores constitutes an inducement for some middle class families with Chicopee business connections to live in Springfield. For the same reasons the removal during the past twenty-five years, of some Springfield and Holyoke firms to Chicopee did not result in a change of residence of the owners of the enterprises. In 1930, of 144 officers of incorporated establishments doing business in Chicopee, 48 were listed as residing there, 37 lived in Springfield and vicinity, 23 in Holyoke, 23 elsewhere, and the homes of 13 were not listed.[17]

The influence of the proximity of Springfield and Holyoke is strikingly reflected in Table 19. Per capita expenditure in Chicopee retail stores is very low, even when compared with other factory towns, and there are fewer stores in relation to the total population than are found in other cities. If we examine per capita food expenditures, Chicopee still falls behind other factory

TABLE 19. STATISTICS OF RETAIL DISTRIBUTION IN SELECTED LOCALITIES IN MASSACHUSETTS IN THE YEAR 1929*

City	Population 1930	Total Sales $000	Per Capita Sales $	Per Capita Food Sales $	Number of Stores	Persons Per Store
Brockton.....	63,797	35,004	548	150	888	72.2
Chicopee.....	43,930	8,814	200	112	522	84.1
Easthampton.	11,323	3,319	293	140	156	72.5
Fall River....	115,274	45,997	399	121	1,551	74.3
Holyoke......	56,537	29,141	515	169	1,028	54.9
Lawrence.....	85,068	36,916	433	124	1,220	69.7
Lowell.......	100,234	44,650	445	131	1,535	65.2
Lynn........	102,320	51,714	505	162	1,445	70.8
Pittsfield.....	49,677	32,204	648	163	698	71.1
Springfield....	149,900	107,587	717	160	2,233	67.1
Westfield.....	19,775	10,011	506	162	309	64.

*Compiled from U. S. Fifteenth *Census,* "Retail Distribution in Massachusetts," 1930, p. 78 et seq.

communities. Of course, we cannot be sure that all food purchases were made at home, but it seems fair to assume that by far the bulk of such purchases were made in neighborhood stores. What we have, then, is the result of a large factory population living on a lower food standard than is usual in communities which have a larger middle class element. There are likely to be fewer expenditures on luxury foods in Chicopee than in other communities.

We must come to the conclusion that not only is the middle class numerically small but it is not a wealthy class. We know that its members are confined mostly to small trade which is incapable, under existing circumstances, of yielding a high income. This state of affairs is immediately obvious if we examine the individual income tax returns filed in Chicopee in comparison with those filed in other Massachusetts cities in recent years.[18] In 1929

[17] Springfield *Directory,* 1930. [18] See Table 20.

the proportion of persons who were obliged to make federal income tax returns was lower in Chicopee than in any of the other representative cities listed.

TABLE 20. INDIVIDUAL INCOME TAX RETURNS AND THEIR RATIO TO 1930 POPULATION IN SELECTED CITIES OF MASSACHUSETTS, 1929-33*

City	Population	1929		1930		1931		1932		1933	
		Total Returns	Percent of Population	Total Returns	Percent of Population	Total Returns	Percent of Population	Total Returns	Percent of Population	Total Returns	Percent of Population
Brockton	63,797	2,751	4.31	2,697	4.22	2,456	3.84	3,375	5.29	3,221	5.04
Chicopee	43,930	979	2.22	759	1.72	692	1.57	797	1.81	703	1.60
Fall River	115,274	2,580	2.23	2,625	2.27	2,425	2.10	3,100	2.68	2,936	2.54
Greenfield	15,500	827	5.33	559	3.60	783	5.05	989	6.38	906	5.84
Holyoke	56,537	2,623	4.63	2,477	4.38	2,399	4.24	3,009	5.32	2,701	4.77
Lawrence	85,068	2,414	2.83	2,453	2.88	2,376	2.79	2,776	3.26	2,782	3.27
Lowell	100,234	2,906	2.89	2,951	2.94	2,846	2.83	3,682	3.67	3,519	3.51
Lynn	102,320	4,868	4.75	4,447	4.34	3,998	3.90	5,218	5.09	4,900	4.78
Northampton	24,381	1,498	6.10	1,350	5.53	1,284	5.26	1,879	7.70	1,737	7.12
Pittsfield	49,677	2,877	5.79	2,712	5.45	2,575	5.18	2,895	5.82	2,681	5.39
Springfield	149,900	8,390	5.59	8,054	5.37	7,423	4.83	9,863	6.57	9,662	6.44
Westfield	19,775	674	3.40	647	3.27	609	3.07	574	2.90	618	3.12

* Data furnished by Bureau of Internal Revenue, U. S. Treasury Department. From 1929 to 1831 the lowest net incomes for which returns had to be filed were $1500 for single persons and $3500 for married persons. In 1932 these were reduced to $2500 and $1000.

There is other concrete evidence which points to the underdevelopment of middle class activity and status.[19] In 1930 there were comparatively fewer persons in Chicopee whose occupations were listed under the professional services The explanation lies in the fact that a small middle class does not require extensive professional services, and that fact, in turn, reduces the size of the middle class still further because of the limitation of opportunities for the development of such services. A similar situation is found in regard to the domestic and personal services. This was most marked in the case of female servants, a classification which includes other than household servants, although the latter seem to comprise by far the majority of this grouping. In other words, fewer families in Chicopee can afford to employ household servants than in any of the other listed communities, except Lawrence. It is very probable that if servants who live in Chicopee and work in

[19] See Table 21.

Holyoke and Springfield were weeded out of the classification, the Chicopee total would not differ much, proportionately, from the Lawrence figure. The median position which Chicopee holds in relation to clerical workers is probably due to the fact that many of the latter find employment in the neighboring cities. The proportion of proprietors, managers and independent enterprisers, aside from the large group of those engaged in the retail trade is even more striking. The evidence which indicates the position of the middle class in relation to that of other industrial communities seems to be clear enough, and substantiates the general contention that this class is under-developed in relation to the total population of the town.

TABLE 21. OCCUPATION STATISTICS FOR SELECTED CITIES IN MASSACHUSETTS, 1930*

City	Population 1930	Professional Services		Domestic and Personal Services		Female Servants		Retail Dealers and Managers		Clerical Workers		Other Proprietors and Managers**	
		Number	Percent of Population	Number	Percent of Population	Number	Percent of Population	Number	Percent of Population	Number	Percent of Population	Number	Percent of Population
Brockton....	63,797	1,832	2.87	2,329	3.65	716	1.12	1,099	1.72	3,098	4.85	1,145	1.79
Chicopee.....	43,930	730	1.66	1,017	2.31	321	.73	562	1.27	1,513	3.44	335	.76
Fall River....	115,274	3,109	2.69	3,422	2.96	989	.85	1,553	1.34	2,758	2.39	1,170	1.01
Fitchberg....	40,692	1,222	3.00	1,492	3.66	525	1.29	537	1.31	1,370	3.36	526	1.29
Holyoke.....	56,537	1,860	3.28	2,172	3.84	833	1.47	914	1.61	2,423	4.28	802	1.41
Lawrence....	85,068	1,929	2.26	2,394	2.81	566	.66	1,316	1.54	2,523	2.96	823	.96
Lowell.......	100,234	2,868	2.86	3,497	3.48	1,086	1.08	1,519	1.51	3,295	3.28	1,190	1.18
Lynn........	102,320	2,921	2.85	4,251	4.15	984	.96	1,397	1.36	5,457	5.33	1,571	1.53
Pittsfield.....	49,677	2,102	4.23	2,051	4.12	704	1.41	790	1.59	2,529	5.09	702	1.41
Springfield...	149,900	5,631	3.75	7,936	5.29	2,345	1.56	2,624	1.75	9,433	6.29	3,048	2.03
Taunton.....	37,355	1,095	2.93	1,184	3.16	392	1.04	549	1.46	1,240	3.31	439	1.17

* Compiled from U. S. Fifteenth *Census*, 1930. "Occupation Statistics of Massachusetts," 7 et seq.

** Consists of manufacturing managers and officials, manufacturers, independent shoemakers, tailors, garage owners and managers, truck and taxi owners and managers, bankers, brokers and money lenders, insurance agents, hotel keepers and managers, restaurant keepers, proprietors of trading establishments not listed elsewhere.

Chicopee's middle class had to decline relatively if it did not reproduce itself and if few new recruits appeared. These conditions were not fulfilled. Few workers were able to move into the middle class groups. For instance, of 51 officers of fraternal lodges who were workers in 1905, 45 had the same status in 1917, two became foremen, one became a milk dealer, one a merchant, one achieved a high municipal position, and one moved back from the independent position of insurance salesman to a foremanship in a factory.[20] These men were mostly highly skilled workers and were therefore in a favorable position to achieve economic independence. It is possible that some were able to set up members of their families in retail trade. Not only was it difficult for additions to the middle class to appear, but some of its members moved to Springfield. Trade opportunities were poor, and it is through trade and trade expansion that the first steps toward middle class status are often taken.

Considerable emphasis has been placed on the importance of trade and the repressive effect on its growth in Chicopee exercised by the neighboring cities of Springfield and Holyoke. This has been done because it raises a problem which is not really peculiar to Chicopee alone or to Chicopee's middle class. There are innumerable communities throughout the country which are "suburban" to other larger communities, and to a greater or lesser degree almost any town makes use of the trading, recreational and cultural facilities of another. The rapid growth of motor transport makes it possible for the population of the fringes to respond to the attractions of the more brilliant urban centers. "Fully one-half of the people of this country now live within an hour's motor journey of a city of 100,000 or more."[21] This is a recent development and involves many problems of fundamental importance, as of government, for instance, that cannot be discussed here.[22] But what we should note is the fact that the possibilities for the existence of thriving retail trade and of a prosperous middle class in "suburban" communities must vary with the degree of that community's dependence on another town or city. The growth of "metropolitan areas" is an important factor affecting the fortunes of the middle class.

Chicopee remains an important manufacturing center. Though

[20] Springfield *Directory,* 1905, 1917.
[21] President's Research Committee on Social Trends, *Recent Social Trends in the United States,* I, 492.
[22] See *Ibid.,* 443 et seq.

the effects of the depression have been unusually severe, if we consider the trend of production and investment up to 1929 there is no reason to think that Chicopee will not maintain its relative importance as a manufacturing area. A frequently met attitude in the region, intangible evidence to be sure, implies that Chicopee is not the important community that it once was. The growth of this mode of thinking coincides with the definite re-emergence of Chicopee as a factory town. The facts do not seem to justify such a judgment. It is true that Chicopee's middle class has declined in importance, that it has not maintained its relative position compared with other middle class groups, but its industrial activity continues at the same rate as hitherto. All we can say of this attitude is that the "prestige" of an American community seems to be based on the prominence of the middle class in its life. Chicopee is no less important economically, than it ever was, but it is different. What for a few decades had been a balanced community has become a "factory city."

Chicopee differed from most other communities from its beginning in that it did not experience gradual industrial development in slow stages under the leadership of local men. But if Chicopee varied in this regard from other contemporary communities, its course of development was not peculiar to itself, but was typical of other cotton textile towns which came into being with the rise of the modern cotton textile industry. The latter, at its inception, was a highly integrated undertaking, and was sponsored by a group of the most outstanding and wealthiest financial and mercantile figures of Boston. These men, in their multifarious activities which have been examined in considerable detail, conducted a highly sophisticated and certainly very modern type of business enterprise. This important phase of the industrial revolution was the work, not of the middle class, but of the "big bourgeoise." We have but to compare the activities of the local middle class, when it finally emerged, with those of the real founders of industrial Chicopee, to realize that they had nothing in common, that they did not, in fact, represent the same kind of economic activity. Considering the scale of the operations of the

Boston associates and the extent of their interests, one may safely say that in many respects the capitalist enterprise which they pursued was more in keeping with the spirit of post-Civil War developments, almost with "finance capitalism," than with the usual developments of their own time. Certainly, if the period 1820-1860 was the day of the small shop operator and the apprentice, these large-scale manufacturers and financiers were not representative of their times. But these were the men who were responsible for the introduction of large-scale enterprise, for the very introduction of the industrial revolution in America to a great extent, and it is highly significant that they did it in that way at that time, and we must think twice, certainly in reference to New England, before placing the Civil War as the dividing line between small workshop and large factory. It is true that the large cotton mills and allied machine shops did not dominate the economic life of the nation, or even of sections, yet they constituted a characteristic part of early industrial development. The existence of such a fully-developed, modern business type at this early period is perhaps worthy of greater emphasis than it has hitherto received.

The founders of industrial Chicopee were not merely investors. They developed a technique of manufacture, devised a system of selling their product, recruited and trained a labor force; they organized an industry. In doing these things they founded new communities, the predecessors of modern "company towns." Chicopee was one of these.

In creating Chicopee the absentee owners followed the model of Waltham and Lowell. In searching out the power site they found a farm community which they transformed by the building of the mills. This community grew by leaps and bounds, because for the first time large numbers of workers assembled under one roof, and had to be housed nearby. The development of the cotton textile industry was of fundamental significance, for it created for the first time in this country a large and concentrated labor force and the conditions which made for its perpetuation. Because of labor shortage and early repugnance to factory work a mode of life was outlined by the mill proprietors which accentuated those social customs and conventions which were considered good in any puritan New England community. As has been suggested, it may well have been that these textile towns merely followed the social usage of the times. But any possible relaxation of the rules which might have been caused by the stimulus of change and new life and contacts was precluded by the policy of the cotton corporations, which attempted to perpetuate the puritan tradition. Thousands of men and women flocked to the new industrial centers to enter the mills. The movement involved a great social change. In the case of women we have the abrupt shift from household chores to the factory discipline, the withdrawal from family life on isolated farms to non-family existence in the industrial community. New recruits came in to take the places of those who left mill employment. The natural labor turnover of women occasioned by marriage was hastened by the intensification of work and the reduction of wage rates in the thirties and forties. In this period Yankee factory operatives gave way before the steady downward pressure, and the "genteel tradition" failed to maintain an adequate supply of native-born labor. The Irish took the places that were being abandoned by the Yankee "young ladies."

In its first years as a factory town Chicopee consisted largely of Yankee men and women who worked in the cotton mills and lived beside them in the boarding-houses owned and controlled by the corporations. In the first stages of industrialization there were practically no merchants or small manufacturers, few persons of property except the farmers of the neighborhood. But as the mills and houses and canals and machine shops made their spectacular appearance, springing out of nowhere, merchants began to make their way to the "boom" region, coming from other towns, some of them from farms, bringing capital with them. With the merchants came a few men who engaged in small-scale manufacturing, catering to the needs of the cotton mills, or making consumption goods for the new settlement. As these men prospered there emerged from their ranks a small group of men who began to diversify their investments, to transfer capital from mercantile to industrial pursuits. Their activities expanded with the growth of the town.

When with the rise of the middle class Chicopee had begun to assume the character of an "average" New England town, most of the population, mill operatives, merchants, artisans, constituted a homogeneous group. All were Yankees, all Protestant in religion. They came from much the same homes, most of them directly related to farmers, all of much the same social status. Under these circumstances social life was similar for most people, and the community was compact, bound together by strong ties. Such, at least, is the impression that one gains from the contemporary press, and from the records left in the county histories. All hard working and God-fearing men were held in esteem; those who achieved financial success were held in admiration. The successful men, the managers of the cotton mills, some representatives of the old farming families, became the accepted leaders of the social, religious and political life of the community.

The middle class was in the ascendancy in the forties and fifties. Merchants and others were becoming prosperous, sponsoring independent industrial developments, building homes and schools and churches. There was a vigorous local press and the *Springfield Republican* devoted a daily column to Chicopee affairs. There were large industrial establishments of which the citizenry and others could be proud because of their size; the Ames Company probably enjoyed a national reputation. The town had a place in the sun, the citizens were conscious of it, and neighboring towns recognized and acknowledged Chicopee's status as a "coming" community, and no doubt enjoyed the reflected "glory."

In this very period of the rise of the middle class occurred the repression of the factory operatives. Frequent depressions, an increasingly competitive situation in the cotton industry, factors inherent in the nature of the new industry and its management, contributed to the sporadic lowering of wage rates and the increase of the machine load per worker. Some gains made in the middle fifties were swept away in 1857-58. Loss of status on the part of the workers was closely connected with the fact that the character of the working population underwent radical change. Irish immigrants replaced Yankee mill hands, and with their arrival came the establishment of a permanent factory population, and one of the first signs of division in the ranks of the citizenry. It is perhaps a mistake to speak of a division—it was rather a manifestation of increasing social complexity which was to become more pronounced as workers of different nationalities and languages made their appearance. With this change the social contact between workers and middle class elements was broken.

The Civil War found a number of locally owned concerns ready to take advantage of the industrial expansion that attended and followed the conflict. For a time local industry was of equal importance with the cotton mills, and was instrumental in recruiting many skilled workers whose spendings were of profit to the merchants. The middle class grew, and as the population increased there were more numerous opportunities for small investment, for example, in specialized forms of retail trade. Investments were numerous from 1860 to about 1885 and established companies prospered. From almost the beginning of local investment in manufacturing, however, it was noticeable that a comparatively small group of men controlled the important companies and the local banks, and that these men had been merchants, cotton mill managers, and men with technical experience in the particular line of business concerned. The companies in which they were interested enjoyed comparatively long and prosperous life. Other establishments, founded after the war, and operated by only one or two men, were not so stable, and for the most part afforded their owners a livelihood in return for work performed rather than a profit on capital invested.

Thus the rise of the middle class was in the first place contingent on the establishment and expansion of the cotton mills, but later it was able to go ahead under its own power during a favorable conjuncture of circumstances, and one group at least was able to consolidate its position in the years following the Civil War. The entire middle class, made up largely of small merchants and purveyors of services was dependent on the prosperity of the large manufacturing corporations, and the shutdown of a cotton mill was a serious affair for many merchants, as it was for the workers. In the middle period the machine shops employed many skilled workers whose expenditures were able to support traders quite comfortably. But as the years passed and as machine shop work became more and more mechanized, as the cotton mills expanded and employed more men, the proportion of skilled workers to the unskilled fell, and with it opportunities for mercantile expansion.

The coming of the nineties brought two important new developments. There came a wave of new investment from the outside, and as the original merchant-enterpriser group became older there did not emerge another and younger group to take its place. After the primary establishment of the community as a factory town middle class elements experienced fairly rapid development to the point when Chicopee, during and after the Civil War almost approximated other balanced industrial communities. The rapid infiltration of new capital after 1890 upset this balance, and the community reverted to the position of a purely factory town, although it is not a company town in the sense that the early cotton mill community had been. It remains one of the important manufacturing centers of western New England. Because of its configuration and location it is subjected to special problems which vary in degree only from those of other factory towns.

Appendix A

FINANCIAL AND TRANSPORTATION INTERESTS OF THE BOSTON ASSOCIATES

I. Banking[1]

Boston Banks in Operation in 1848, Paid Up Capital, Directorates, and Capital of Boston Associate Banks

Bank	Capital	Directors	Boston Associate Capital
Atlantic Bank................	$500,000		
Atlas Bank..................	$500,000		
Boston Bank................	$600,000	N. Appleton D. C. Bacon J. I. Bowditch J. Bradlee Samuel Cabot T. B. Curtis J. M. Forbes R. Hooper J. C. Howe R. G. Shaw H. Upham P. Upham	$600,000
Boylston Bank..............	$200,000		
City Bank..................	$1,000,000	W. T. Andrews C. W. Cartwright C. C. Chadwick D. Chamberlain J. B. Glover I. Livermore S. R. Payson P. S. Shelton	$1,000,000
Columbian Bank.............	$500,000	William Amory S. A. Appleton J. T. Coolidge G. W. Lyman J. Tilden J. G. Torrey	$500,000
Eagle Bank.................	$500,000		
Exchange Bank..............	$500,000		
Freemens' Bank.............	$200,000		
Globe Bank.................	$1,000,000	A. Adams S. Fairbanks H. Hall J. Lamson P. Perrin I. Sargent	$1,000,000
Granite Bank................	$500,000		
Grocers' Bank...............	$250,000		

[1] Compiled from *Mass. State Record,* 1847, p. 213 et seq. and 1849, p. 228 et seq.; J. Winsor, *op. cit.,* IV, 161; Mass., 1830 *Private and Special Statistics* C. 144.

I. BANKING (continued)

Bank	Capital	Directors	Boston Associate Capital
Hamilton Bank	$500,000	G. Brewer T. G. CARY D. Denny W. Dwight W. Phipps WILLARD SAYLES S. W. Swett T. Wigglesworth, Jr. M. P. Wilder W. APPLETON (1831) J. Bryant " H. CABOT " E. FRANCIS " A. LAWRENCE "	$500,000
Market Bank	$560,000		
Massachusetts Bank	$800,000		
Mechanics' Bank	$120,000		
Merchants' Bank	$3,000,000	E. BROOKS N. F. Cunningham Luke Fay F. C. Gray D. Henshaw S. HENSHAW S. Hooper J. B. Jones J. K. MILLS W. P. Winchester I. Whitney	$3,000,000
New England Bank	$1,000,000		
North Bank	$750,000		
Shawmut Bank	$500,000		
Shoe and Leather Dealers' Bank	$500,000		
State Bank	$1,800,000		
Suffolk Bank	$1,000,000	J. Balch J. Belknap E. CHADWICK J. W. EDMUNDS A. A. LAWRENCE W. LAWRENCE J. A. LOWELL B. R. NICHOLS J. Richardson N. P. Russel H. B. Stone W. W. Tucker N. APPLETON (1818) W. APPLETON " J. W. BOOTT " E. FRANCIS " G. Greene " A. Heard " P. T. JACKSON " A. LAWRENCE " AMOS LAWRENCE " L. LAWRENCE " W. LAWRENCE "	$1,000,000
Traders' Bank	$400,000		
Tremont Bank	$500,000		
Union Bank	$800,000		
Washington Bank	$500,000		
TOTAL	$18,980,000		$7,600,000

II. INSURANCE[2]

INSURANCE COMPANIES IN BOSTON AND MASSACHUSETTS, CAPITAL, AND BUSINESS CARRIED IN 1846. (Boston associate companies are starred)

Boston Companies	Capital	Marine Insurance Carried	Fire Insurance Carried
*American Insurance Co.	$ 300,000	$4,683,528	$3,086,651
*Boston Insurance Co.	300,000	2,180,311	....
Boylston Insurance Co.	300,000	2,189,792	3,210,463
*Firemen's Insurance Co.	300,000	....	10,824,495
Franklin Insurance Co.	300,000	1,672,675	3,711,883
Hope Insurance Co.	200,000	492,265	....
*Manufacturers' Insurance Co.	400,000	1,954,411	12,391,773
Mercantile Marine Insurance Co.	300,000	1,639,071	....
*Merchants' Insurance Co.	500,000	7,247,702	13,856,305
*National Insurance Co.	500,000	4,239,462	7,867,453
Neptune Insurance Co.	200,000	6,933,110	4,331,882
Suffolk Insurance Co.	225,000	1,022,658	542,815
Tremont Insurance Co.	200,000	4,734,337	1,338,786
U. S. Insurance Co.	200,000	1,128,866	372,850
Warren Insurance Co.	150,000	1,992,270	....
Washington Insurance Co.	200,000	2,365,778	....
Total, Boston Companies	$4,575,000	$44,476,236	$61,535,356
Other Massachusetts Companies	1,200,000	4,264,252	78,190
TOTAL	$5,775,000	$48,740,488	$61,613,546
Boston Associate Totals	$2,300,000	$20,305,414	$48,026,677
Boston Associate Totals as Percentage of Massachusetts Totals	39%	41%	77%

DIRECTORATES OF BOSTON ASSOCIATE INSURANCE COMPANIES IN 1846-47.

American Insurance Co.

J. S. Amory
S. APPLETON
E. Austin
J. I. BOWDITCH
T. Chase
R. B. Forbes
B. A. Gould
H. Gray
S. May
CHARLES H. MILLS
P. P. Pope
B. Rich
R. G. Shaw

Boston Insurance Co.

T. C. Amory
J. C. Collamore, Jr.
A. Cotting
J. Crane
P. R. Dalton, Jr.
A. Davis
W. G. Eaton
J. G. Hallett
J. Hay
T. Nichols
I. SARGENT
B. Seaver

[2] Insurance data compiled from official returns printed in *Massachusetts State Record*, 1847, p. 223 et seq.; *Ibid.*, 1849, p. 242 et seq.; Mass. 1831 *Private and Special Statutes*, C. 11.

Incorporated in 1831 by

T. C. Amory	H. G. OTIS
S. APPLETON	T. H. PERKINS
W. APPLETON	E. G. Prescott
J. Collamore, Jr.	W. PRESCOTT
H. Curtis	I. SARGENT
W. G. Eaton	L. M. Sargent
J. S. Ellery	J. TILDEN
AMOS LAWRENCE	W. Willett

Manufacturers' Ins. Co.

E. T. ANDREWS	T. P. Cushing
W. T. Andrews	O. Daniel
A. Binney	H. Hall
C. W. CARTWRIGHT	G. Morey

Merchants' Insurance Co.

D. C. Bacon	H. Hall
J. Balch	R. Hooper
J. Belknap	ABBOTT LAWRENCE
E. CHADWICK	J. A. LOWELL
J. W. EDMUNDS	W. Rollins
R. B. Forbes	J. Williams
P. Grant	W. P. Winchester

National Insurance Co.

W. AMORY	D. Kimball
D. Denny	GEORGE H. KUHN
J. W. EDMUNDS	J. Lawrence
S. FROTHINGHAM	I. LIVERMORE
J. L. Gardiner	J. A. LOWELL
W. H. GARDINER	B. R. Nichols
O. GOODWIN	W. SAYLES
T. Gray	S. W. Swett
N. Hooper	N. Thayer
G. Howe	I. Whitney

Mass. Mutual Insurance Co.
(newly organized)

E. T. ANDREWS	W. LAWRENCE
J. Austin	J. Lovering
G. Bartlett	J. A. LOWELL
H. Codman	S. May
C. P. Curtis	Charles Wells
E. FRANCIS	J. D. Williams

New England Mutual Life Ins. Co.

Charles Brown	T. Parsons
C. P. Curtis	W. Perkins
T. A. Dexter	W. Phillips
GEORGE H. KUHN	W. W. Stone
W. R. Lee	S. Tappan
F. C. Lowell	B. Wainwright

Mass. Hospital Life Ins. Co.

J. R. Adam	P. C. BROOKS
W. AMORY	J. Hooper
S. APPLETON	S. Hubbard
W. APPLETON	C. Jackson

P. T. JACKSON	J. Quincy
ABBOTT LAWRENCE	I. SARGENT
G. W. LYMAN	W. STURGIS
W. Minot	J. TILDEN
T. H. PERKINS	T. B. WALES

III. RAILWAYS[3]

DIRECTORATES AND MILEAGE OF BOSTON ASSOCIATE RAILWAYS AND TOTAL SINGLE TRACK MILEAGE OF RAILWAYS IN MASSACHUSETTS, JANUARY 1, 1850. (INCLUDES ROADS WHICH EXTEND INTO ADJOINING STATES)

Company	Directorates	Mileage
Boston and Lowell	E. CHADWICK (1847) J. A. LOWELL G. W. LYMAN W. STURGIS J. TILDEN	26
Boston and Providence	W. APPLETON (1847) J. Barstow J. Bryant, Jr. J. Grinnell J. K. MILLS W. STURGIS C. H. Warren	53
Connecticut River	H. W. Clapp (1848) N. H. Emmons S. HENSHAW E. Hopkins L. Pope E. H. Robbins I. SARGENT	52
Nashua and Lowell	D. Abbott (1849) J. Bowers C. F. Gove T. B. WALES H. Timmins	14
Stony Brook	Operated by the Nashua and Lowell Road	13
Taunton Branch	W. A. Crocker (1837) J. F. Loring J. K. MILLS G. W. PRATT T. B. WALES S. FROTHINGHAM (1849) J. F. Loring S. Quincy T. B. WALES	11
Western	George Bliss (1837) EDMUND DWIGHT J. Henshaw J. Quincy, Jr. R. Rantoul, Jr. T. B. WALES A. Walker J. K. Mills was the largest individual subscriber. Most of the Boston associates invested in the Western road.	156
All Other Roads		810
TOTAL		1135

[3] Compiled from *Mass. State Record,* 1847, p. 228; 1849, p. 258; 1851, p. 253; Mass., *Annual Reports of Railroad Corporations,* 1837, 1848; J. Winsor, *op. cit.,* IV, 131, 132.

Appendix B

STATISTICAL DATA USED IN CHAPTERS V AND VI

Semi-Annual Estimates of Operating Profit and Cash Dividends Paid for Three Chicopee Cotton Companies, 1836-1864

Date	Company "A"		Company "B"		Company "C"	
	Estimated Profit	Cash Paid	Estimated Profit	Cash Paid	Estimated Profit	Cash Paid
1836.........	$48,662	$27,000	$......	$......	$......	$......
....	40,171	22,500	......	......	......	......
1837.........	32,038	18,000	......	......	......	......
....	14,677	......	4,128	......	......	......
1838.........	40,897	22,500	14,069	......	......	......
....	45,224	45,000	27,464	25,000	......	......
1839.........	53,431	30,000	38,118	25,000	......	......
....	13,567	15,000	15,099	......	......	......
1840.........	— 2,225	......	7,643	15,000	......	......
....	32,145	25,000	36,987	15,000	......	......
1841.........	24,901	20,000	23,974	......	......	......
....	21,031	15,000	20,803	......	......	......
1842.........	17,064	10,000	11,062	15,000	13,980	15,000
....	12,321	......	5,327	30,000	11,100	......
1843.........	18,246	20,000	18,597	......	22,874	20,000
....	44,798	35,000	38,307	50,000	50,606	35,000
1844.........	72,494	50,000	71,767	50,000	73,374	56,000
....	49,574	50,000	61,157	50,000	77,766	70,000
1845.........	51,530	50,000	55,000	50,000	69,253	70,000
....	56,617	50,000	52,002	50,000	67,246	70,000
1846.........	64,268	50,000	48,803	40,000	72,184	56,000
....	34,857	30,000	20,891	25,000	54,053	56,000
1847.........	21,651	20,000	27,911	25,000	50,878	35,000
....	9,214	......	27,054	20,000	36,795	28,000
1848.........	11,580	15,000	17,258	15,000	27,802	21,000
....	13,301	15,000	17,668	15,000	33,879	21,000
1849.........	24,092	15,000	12,834	10,000	49,238	28,000
....	24,455	20,000	16,770	15,000	35,734	28,000
1850.........	20,287	15,000	16,108	......	44,719	28,000
....	8,583	15,000	11,834	......	22,009	21,000
1851.........	—14,363	......	8,616	15,000	26,373	14,000
....	— 8,874	......	5,743	......	6,064	......
1852.........	11,927	......	18,698	15,000	32,973	21,000
....	15,120	......	23,773	30,000	33,280	21,000
1853.........	......	......	40,081	20,000	37,819	......
....	......	......	41,045	20,000	45,466	28,000
1854.........	......	......	42,160	30,000	36,944	21,000
....	......	......	35,984	......	29,555	14,000
1855.........	......	......	33,444	20,000	36,812	......
....	......	......	38,821	20,000	37,968	21,000
1856.........	......	......	......	......	95,013	51,000
....	......	......	......	......	70,599	51,000
1857.........	......	......	......	......	56,327	34,000
....	......	......	......	......	3,323	......
1858.........	......	......	......	......	19,089	......
....	......	......	......	......	85,137	......
1859.........	......	......	......	......	96,736	51,000
....	......	......	......	......	75,596	51,000
1860.........	......	......	......	......	102,286	68,000
....	......	......	......	......	79,330	68,000
1861.........	......	......	......	......	58,413	34,000
....	......	......	......	......	111,016	68,000
1862.........	......	......	......	......	157,666	68,000
....	......	......	......	......	300,000	85,000
1863.........	......	......	......	......	53,597	68,000
....	......	......	......	......	72,478	51,000
1864.........	......	......	......	......	10,966	51,000
....	......	......	......	......	50,840	51,000

Weekly Lower Quartile, Median and Upper Quartile Earnings of Female Cotton Mill Operatives as Compiled from the Payrolls of Company "C", 1841-1862

Date	Lower Quartile	Median	Upper Quartile
April, 1841	$1.72	$2.49	$2.98
May	1.16	2.31	2.82
June	2.07	2.87	3.55
July	1.66	2.71	3.51
August	1.78	2.90	3.87
September	1.73	2.58	3.46
October	1.79	2.64	3.35
November	2.22	2.77	3.25
December	1.82	2.67	3.31
January, 1842	2.08	2.84	3.41
February	2.15	2.81	3.43
March	1.77	2.80	3.57
April	1.61	2.83	3.68
May	1.98	2.83	3.44
June	1.89	2.78	3.37
July	1.09	1.91	2.76
August	1.51	2.29	2.86
September	1.66	2.35	2.93
October	1.23	2.12	2.72
November	1.60	2.30	2.96
December	1.60	2.40	2.82
January, 1843	2.26	2.70	3.56
February	2.14	2.75	3.16
March	1.77	2.46	3.14
April	1.41	1.85	2.47
May	1.89	2.56	3.09
June	2.12	2.71	3.67
July	1.38	2.11	2.60
August	1.81	2.45	3.08
September	1.51	2.33	2.86
October	1.76	2.38	3.10
November	1.94	2.51	3.26
December	1.41	2.25	2.96
January, 1844	2.14	2.62	3.25
February	1.95	2.29	2.75
March	2.03	2.68	3.45
April	1.94	2.55	3.38
May	1.91	2.64	3.39
June	1.71	2.45	3.18
July	1.44	2.35	3.14
August	1.39	2.33	3.04
September	1.43	2.30	2.91
October	1.96	2.58	3.11
November	1.65	2.48	2.78
December	1.81	2.43	2.95
January, 1845	1.85	2.45	2.99
February	1.86	2.34	2.76
March	1.82	2.40	2.89
April	1.66	2.42	2.98
May	1.48	2.37	2.99
June	1.43	2.30	3.01
July	1.20	2.03	2.69
August	1.17	2.27	2.98
September	1.62	2.31	3.19
October	1.84	2.42	2.99
November	1.64	2.26	2.80
December	1.74	2.42	3.12
January, 1846	1.47	2.27	2.90
July	1.52	2.26	2.94
January, 1847	2.13	2.62	3.03
July	1.53	2.24	2.77
January, 1848	2.07	2.68	3.20
July	1.41	2.24	2.80
January, 1849	2.17	2.56	2.91
July	1.60	2.23	2.67

WEEKLY LOWER QUARTILE, MEDIAN AND UPPER QUARTILE EARNINGS OF FEMALE COTTON MILLS OPERATIVES (continued)

Date	Lower Quartile	Median	Upper Quartile
January, 1850	$2.27	$2.69	$3.10
July	1.10	1.98	2.60
January, 1851	2.26	2.66	2.94
July	1.77	2.45	2.89
January, 1852	2.11	2.53	2.77
July	1.71	2.39	2.88
January, 1853	2.06	2.64	3.02
July	1.88	2.50	2.99
January, 1854	2.09	2.64	3.21
July	2.03	2.54	3.04
January, 1855	2.38	2.95	3.40
July	1.97	2.50	2.97
January, 1856	2.34	2.90	3.34
July	1.89	2.48	2.99
January, 1857	2.22	2.77	3.24
July	1.60	2.39	2.96
August	1.47	2.41	2.98
September	1.62	2.36	2.82
October	.86	1.24	1.49
November	1.17	1.37	1.51
December	1.14	1.38	1.60
January, 1858	1.13	1.40	1.63
February	1.29	1.52	1.71
March	1.42	2.11	2.68
April	....	....	....
May	1.66	2.46	2.72
June	1.87	2.52	2.74
July	1.75	2.39	2.70
August	1.64	2.47	2.71
September	1.62	2.45	2.72
October	1.30	2.24	2.61
November	1.63	2.37	2.67
December	1.65	2.34	2.68
January, 1859	1.65	2.45	2.74
July	1.72	2.42	2.84
January, 1860	2.17	2.69	3.20
July	1.95	2.60	3.08
January, 1861	2.01	2.69	3.18
July	1.26	1.73	1.94
January, 1862	1.24	1.53	1.72
July	1.02	1.65	2.25

PIECE RATES FOR SELECTED OPERATIONS AS COMPILED FROM PAYROLL 1 OF COMPANY "C", MAY, 1841-JANUARY, 1846

Date	Warp Spinning	Warping	Speeding	Weaving
May, 1841	4.2 Cts.	.... Cts.	2.5 Cts.	48 Cts.
June	4.2	....	2.5	48
July	4.2	....	2.5	48
August	4.2	12.5	2.5	48
September	4.2	12.5	2.5	48
October	4.2	12.5	2.25	48
November	4.1	12.5	2.25	48
December	4.	12.	2.125	48
January, 1842	4.	12.	2.1	48
February	3.8	12.	2.1	44
March	3.8	12.	2.1	44
April	3.8	12.	2.1	44
May	3.4	12.	1.8	38
June	3.4	11.75	1.75	38
July	3.1	11.75	1.75	38
August	2.9	10.5	...	34
September	2.9	10.5	...	34
October	2.9	10.5	...	34
November	2.9	10.5	1.7	36
December	2.8	10.5	1.7	36
January, 1843	2.8	10.5	1.7	36
February	2.75	10.5	1.7	33
March	2.75	10.5	1.7	33
April	2.6	10.5	1.7	33
May	2.5	10.	1.7	31
June	2.45	10.	1.7	31
July	2.45	10.	1.7	31
August	2.45	10.	1.7	31
September	2.45	10.	1.7	31
October	2.45	10.	1.7	31
November	2.45	10.	1.7	31
December	2.45	10.	1.7	31
January, 1844	2.45	10.	1.7	31
February	2.45	10.	1.7	31
March	2.45	10.	1.7	31
April	2.45	10.	1.	31
May	2.45	10.	1.	31
June	2.45	10.	1.	31
July	2.5	10.	1.	31
August	2.5	10.	1.	31
September	2.5	10.	1.	31
October	2.5	10.	1.	31
November	2.575	10.	1.7	31
December	2.575	10.	1.7	31
January, 1845	2.575	10.	1.7	31
February	2.575	10.	1.7	31
March	2.575	10.	1.7	31
April	2.575	10.	1.7	31
May	2.575	10.	1.6	31
June	2.575	10.	1.6	31
July	2.575	10.	1.6	31
August	2.6	10.	1.6	31
September	2.6	10.	1.6	31
October	2.65	10.	1.65	31
November	2.65	10.	1.65	31
December	2.65	10.	1.65	31
January, 1846	2.65	10.	1.65	31

BIBLIOGRAPHY

I. Unpublished Manuscript Material[1]

Ames Papers. Miscellaneous documents, account books, letters, reports, dividend book and other papers relating to the Ames Manufacturing Company. In the possession of Mrs. E. W. Hale, Chicopee.

Appleton Papers. These consist chiefly of letters received by Nathan Appleton, and are on deposit in the Library of the Massachusetts Historical Society, Boston. The Greeley and Webster letters printed in Chapter II have been used with the permission of Mr. W. S. Appleton.

Bagnall Papers. These papers consist of data intended to be used for a second volume of William Bagnall's *Textile Industries in the United States.* Baker Library, Harvard Graduate School of Business Administration.

Edward Chapin Diary, 1745-46. In the possession of Miss Ruth McKinstry, Chicopee.

Connecticut Valley Historical Society miscellaneous manuscripts.

Dwight Papers. These are the property of the present Dwight Manufacturing Corporation, and consist of the records of the Dwight Manufacturing Company, the Cabot Manufacturing Company and the Perkins Mills. They contain payrolls, tenements rolls, ledgers and journals, semi-annual statements, letter-books, and various miscellaneous items. Records covering the period 1836 to 1864 have been used. In order to disguise the exact source of the data, the companies have been designated by letters of the alphabet in the text. The records are on deposit in the Baker Library, Harvard Graduate School of Business Administration.

First Massachusetts Turnpike, Directors' Book, 1797-1810. Connecticut Valley Historical Society, Springfield.

Judd Manuscript, Vol. II of Northampton Series. Forbes Library, Northampton.

Massachusetts Joint Committee on Unemployment, Connecticut Valley Branch, *Report on Chicopee,* 1932. Forbes Library, Northampton.

Spence, V., *Industrial History of Chicopee.* M.A. Thesis, Clark University, 1930.

George S. Taylor Diary, 1843-1880. In the possession of Mrs. F. C. Rickert, Springfield.

[1] At two points in the text certain brief passages have not been documented. They are derived from sources indicated in this section of the bibliography.

II. NEWSPAPERS, BUSINESS DIRECTORIES AND ALMANACS

Adams, George, *The Massachusetts Register,* A State Record for the Year 1852. Boston.

Cabotville Chronicle and Chicopee Falls Advertiser, Nov. 15, Dec. 6, 1845.

Chicopee Telegraph, 1846-1853.

Chicopee Weekly Journal, 1853(?)-1862.

Hampden Post, Springfield, 1842-1844.

Hampshire Federalist, Springfield, 1812. (Title change to *Hampden Federalist* when Hampden County was divided off from Hampshire County in 1812.)

Hunt's Merchants' Magazine, Vol. 21 (1849) New York.

The Man, New York, 1834-35.

The Massachusetts State Record and Yearbook of General Information. 1847, 1849, Boston.

National Laborer, Philadelphia, Oct. 29, 1836.

New England Mercantile Union, *Business Directory* for 1849. Boston.

Newspaper Clippings, Chicopee Public Library and Connecticut Valley Historical Society.

Niles' Weekly Register, Baltimore, 1811-1849.

Olive Leaf and Factory Girls' Repository, Cabotville, 1843.

Springfield *Directories* (including Chicopee), 1845-1934.

Springfield Homestead, Jan. 27, 1927.

Springfield Republican, 1824-1930.

Voice of Industry, Lowell, 1845-1847.

Working Man's Advocate, New York, 1830, 1844-46.

III. GENERAL WORKS

Babbitt, G. H. T., *Chicopee Falls, Past and Present.* (Pamphlet)

Bacon, Edwin M., *The Connecticut River and the Valley of the Connecticut.* New York, 1906.

Biographical Review of Hampden County. Boston, 1896. 2 vols.

Bishop, J. L., *A History of American Manufactures from 1608 to 1860.* Philadelphia, 1864. 2 vols.

Bowen, Francis, "Memoir of Edmund Dwight," *American Journal of Education.* Vol. 4, Sept., 1857.

Burnham, C. G., "The City of Chicopee," *New England Magazine,* New Series, Vol. XVIII. May, 1898.

Chapin, Charles W., *Sketches of the Old Inhabitants and Other Citizens of Old Springfield.* Springfield, 1893.

Chevalier, Michel, *Lettres sur l'Amérique du Nord.* Paris, 1836. 2 vols.

Clark, Victor S., *History of Manufactures in the United States.* New York, 1929 ed. 3 vols.

Cole, A., "Wholesale Commodity Prices in the United States, 1843-1862," *Review of Economic Statistics,* Vol. XI, Feb., 1929.

Commons, John R. and associates, editors, *A Documentary History of American Industrial Society.* Cleveland, 1910. 10 vols.

Commons, John R., and associates, *History of Labor in the United States.* New York, 1918. 2 vols.

Condition of Labor, The. Boston, 1847. (Pamphlet)

Copeland, A. M., *History of Hampden County, Massachusetts.* Century Memorial Publishing Company, 1902. 3 vols.

Copeland, M. T., *The Cotton Manufacturing Industry of the United States.* Cambridge, Mass., 1912.

Cowley, Charles, *History of Lowell.* Boston, 1868.

Daniels, George W., *The Early English Cotton Industry.* Manchester, England, 1920.

Davis, J. S., *Essays in the Earlier History of American Corporations.* Cambridge, Mass., 1917. 2 vols.

Davis, W. T., *The New England States.* Boston, 1897. 4 vols.

Davis, W. T., *A Professional and Industrial History of Suffolk County, Massachusetts.* Boston, 1894. 3 vols.

Dewing, A. S., *Corporate Promotions and Reorganizations.* Cambridge, Mass., 1914.

Dictionary of American Biography.

Everts, Louis H., *History of the Connecticut Valley in Massachusetts.* Philadelphia, 1879. 2 vols.

Goodrich, Carter, and Davison, Sol, "The Wage-Earner in the Westward Movement," *Political Science Quarterly,* Vol. LI, March, 1936.

Green, Mason A., *Springfield, 1636-1886.* Springfield, 1886.

Hacker, L. M. and Kendrick, B. B., *The United States Since 1865.* New York, 1932.

Holland, J. G., *History of Western Massachusetts.* Springfield, 1855. 2 vols.

Johnson, L. L., *Chicopee Illustrated.* 1896.

Kirkland, E. C., *A History of American Economic Life.* New York, 1932.

Lawrence, William R., *Extracts from the Diary and Correspondence of the Late Amos Lawrence.* Boston, 1855.

Lumpkin, Katherine D., "Shutdowns in the Connecticut Valley," *Smith College Studies in History,* Vol. 19, Nos. 3-4. Northampton, 1934.

Martin, J. G., *Seventy-three Years' History of the Boston Stock Market.* Boston, 1871.

Mass., *Annual Reports of Railroad Corporations,* 1837-1850.

Mass., Bureau of Statistics of Labor, *Annual Reports,* 1869-1915.

Mass., *Census of Manufactures,* 1910-1934.

Mass., Decennial *Census,* 1855-1915.
Mass., *House Documents,* No. 4, 1842; No. 3, 1844; No. 50, 1845; No. 153, 1850.
Mass., *Private and Special Statutes,* 1810-1850.
Mass., Secretary of the Commonwealth, *Abstract of Attested Returns of Corporations* Organized in 1863 and 1864.
Mass., Secretary of the Commonwealth, *Statistical Information Relating to Certain Branches of Industry in Massachusetts* for 1855 and 1865.
Meader, J. W., *The Merrimack River.* Boston, 1869.
Moody's *Manual of Industrial Investments,* 1917, 1923.
Morison, S. E., *The Life and Letters of Harrison Gray Otis, Federalist, 1765-1848.* Boston, 1913. 2 vols.
Nelson, C. A., *Waltham, Past and Present.* Cambridge, Mass., 1882.
Palmer, C. S., *Annals of Chicopee Street.* Springfield, 1899.
Parrington, V. L., *Main Currents in American Thought,* Vol. II, "The Romantic Revolution in America." New York, 1927.
Perlman, Selig, *A History of Trade Unionism in the United States.* New York, 1922.
Perkins, D. L., "Reminiscences of Manchester," *Manchester Historic Association Collections,* Vol. I, 1896. Manchester, N. H.
Pound, Arthur, *The Turning Wheel.* Garden City, N. Y., 1934.
President's Research Committee on Social Trends, *Recent Social Trends in the United States.* New York, 1933. 2 vols.
Roe, J. W., *English and American Tool Builders.* New Haven, 1916.
Seltzer, Lawrence H., *A Financial History of the American Automobile Industry.* Boston, 1928.
Thorp, W. L. and Mitchell, W. C., *Business Annals.* New York, 1926.
Tryon, T. M., *Household Manufactures in the United States, 1640-1860.* Chicago, 1917.
U. S., Bureau of Corporations, *Report on the International Harvester Company.* 1913.
U. S., Bureau of Labor Statistics, *Bulletin* No. 499, "History of Wages in the United States from Colonial Times to 1928." 1929.
U. S., Seventh, Eighth, Ninth, Eleventh, Thirteenth, Fifteenth *Census,* 1850-1930.
U. S., 22nd Cong. 1st Sess., *House Executive Document* No. 308, "Documents Relative to the Manufactures in the United States," 1832.
U. S., 52nd Cong. 2nd Sess., *Senate Report* No. 1394, "Aldrich Report on Wholesale Prices, Wages and Transportation," Part II. 1893.

U. S., 61st Cong. 2nd Sess., *Senate Document* No. 645, "Report on the Condition of Woman and Child Wage Earners in the United States," Vol. IX, "History of Women in Industry in the United States. 1910.

U. S., Industrial Commission, *Report,* Vol. XIII. 1901.

Van Slyck, J. D., *Representatives of New England Manufacturers.* Boston, 1879.

Villard, O. G., *John Brown.* New York, 1910.

Ware, Caroline W., *The Early New England Cotton Manufacture.* Boston, 1931.

Ware, Norman, *The Industrial Worker, 1840-1860.* Boston, 1924.

Warren, G. F. and Pearson, F. A., *Prices.* New York, 1933.

Weber, Max, *The Protestant Ethic and the Spirit of Capitalism.* New York, 1930.

Weeden, William B., *Economic and Social History of New England, 1620-1789.* Cambridge, Mass., 1899. 2 vols.

Winsor, Justin, *Memorial History of Boston.* Boston, 1880, 1881. 4 vols.

Wright, C. D., *A Compendium of the Census of Massachusetts, 1875.* Boston, 1877.

INDEX